Me

Me

Stories of My Life

by KATHARINE HEPBURN

Alfred A. Knopf New York 1991

To Mother and Dad

Contents

Me

Prologue

I have a friend who keeps asking me why I am writing this book. Especially as I have said a thousand times: "No, that is personal. No, I won't talk about that." What made me change my mind? I wonder myself. Something changed me. I think—and I am not saying I know—I think that I've always thought of myself as an actor. Now in the last few years I've seen that creature whom I created sitting around saying, "Hey, what goes on, what are we going to do? We're wasting time. Let's get going!"

Shut up! I'm sick of you. I'm not going to hide behind you anymore. Who are you anyway? You're not me. You're "that great big beautiful doll." You're the lucky side of the coin. You were born at the right time. You looked right. You sounded right. You were lucky. You caught on and got rich. Good. I'm glad that you've had a good time. Now I'm going to take over.

What is that you're saying? Who am I?

Well, I'm me—I'm what is called the power behind the throne. I am your—your character. Isn't that what they call it? Your "Do this. Don't do that." Your fundamentals.

I run your ship. You're the ship. You're getting a bit long in the tooth and I may not be able to sell you as easily as I used to.

You have a right foot which doesn't work all that well. I mean it hurts. In 1982 you ran into that telephone pole. Stupid of you.

Making a fancy comment about that shipyard just at the southeast edge of Saybrook Point. Listen—so it hurts! But at least they didn't have to cut it off. Yes, of course it threw your whole body off balance—and now your back is painful too.

Gosh, what do you expect! You've just taken your body for granted. You're lucky you had a good one to begin with. Oh yes, those two shoulder operations—rotator cuffs—isn't that what they were called? Yes, of course the right hip is fake. When did that go bad? In 1973.

Oh, that was a while ago.

Well, you're lucky—that operation really worked. Oh hell, you're lucky! You can see! You can hear! You can bicycle! You can garden! Yes, kneeling down—but that's restful, isn't it? Kneeling down?

Anyway, here's where I come in—your character. I don't think that you ever realized how handy I've been for you. I've been there. I tell you what that means—I'm your backup when you make a decision which is poor—and what you become involved in doesn't work. Here I am to try to explain it away.

You know what I really am? I'm my *main* gift from my parents. And when I realized this, I also knew why I had suddenly become interested in writing this book. I wanted to discover the real reason back of all the fluff. That bit of fiber which can be developed in all of us—there it is—waiting to be used. That is what suddenly struck me. How did I make it work? How did I have brains enough to survive *The Lake*—and the early failure of my movie career—the box-office-poison period? And how did I develop such a handy head of common sense? That is what can really keep you afloat. You can say, "You had money enough to swing it." Yes, I had. But money alone doesn't do it. I wasn't going to starve but I could have been defeated.

It's finding out where you went wrong and correcting it.

For instance, *The Lake*. I let Jed Harris, the producer, push me around. I knew that I was being pushed around and I didn't talk back. I didn't say, "Look, I am the one who has to sell this and if you make me into a mush, I'll just be a mush." And I was a mush.

The tale of *The Lake* and my survival was extremely important to me. I learned responsibility to say, "Talk to me. I'm to blame."

And the movies. In the same sort of half-assed way I let myself say, "Yes—O.K.," instead of, "No—I don't like it."

To learn responsibility—each of us has to learn responsibility.

Here we are. Live up to your potential.

But what to do! Well, don't you see what I'm doing and why I'm doing it? I am writing my life story. I've been driven to it. What else can I do? I have to say that's probably why people write their life story.

So before you begin to read, I have to warn you that the book which follows does not follow a path. When I say story—I mean stories of my life. And when I say stories I'm afraid I mean flashes—this—that—no no the other thing.

It's a hell of a long time ago that I leaped down that stairway in *The Warrior's Husband* with a stag on my shoulders. I had no idea that someday in the future I would be wondering if I could walk down a stair without falling down the damned stair. What is this thing called "living"?

Now we come to ME.

I guess that I must try to realize that I have had the most extraordinary use of this body—this back—these legs, etc. I have subjected them to the toughest treatment and they have performed great feats. I really can't blame them for sort of stiffening up. They've given me great service. They are tired.

Let us rest, Kath, let us rest. We just want to take it easy. Give us a break.

Oh no, not a break! We've had a break—give us a rest!

WRITE A BOOK!

I

Parents

efore I tell you anything about myself, I would like to tell you, or at least identify for you, the world into which I was born. My background. I mean of course my mother—my father. My two parents.

Mother died when I was forty-odd.

Dad died when I was fifty-odd. Thus I had them as my . . . Well, they were always for over forty years—*there*. They were mine.

From where I stood:

Dad at the left of the fireplace.

Mother at the right of the fireplace.

Tea every day at five.

They were the world into which I was born.

My background.

My mother:

Katharine Martha Houghton was born February 2, 1878. She was the daughter of Caroline Garlinghouse and Alfred Augustus Houghton.

Alfred Houghton was the younger brother of Amory Houghton, who was the head of the Corning Glass Company. It started in Cambridge, Massachusetts, moved to Brooklyn and ended in Corning,

New York. Alfred's first wife had died leaving him a daughter, Mary. He then married Caroline Garlinghouse. They had three daughters—Katharine, Edith, Marion.

Alfred and his wife were happy. They were financially comfortable. Not rich. Not poor. He played the violin—she played the piano. They were interested in Robert Ingersoll, "the great agnostic," and went to all his lectures. They had abandoned the recognized church. Alfred was about twenty years older than Caroline. Apparently his relationship with his older brother Amory was complicated. Amory had fired him from the glassworks because he was always late. Then Alfred became the head of the Buffalo Scale Works. He was a moody fellow by nature and a victim of severe depressions. During one of these episodes, he was visiting Amory in Corning and he disappeared. He was found, dead of a self-inflicted gun wound in the head, on the railway tracks. No note—nothing.

So Caroline was left with her three daughters to bring up. Then it was discovered that Caroline had cancer of the stomach. She knew that she was doomed to die in fairly short order. Caroline dreaded leaving her girls to be brought up by any of their available relatives, whom she considered hopelessly reactionary. She wanted her daughters to go to college. She visited Bryn Mawr College with my mother. She made arrangements for Mother to go there and made arrangements for Edith and Marion to go to Miss Baldwin's boarding school, almost next door to the college.

By the time her mother died, Katharine was sixteen, Edith fourteen and Marion twelve. Katharine was filled with her mother's feeling about the future. She wanted to go to college, to Bryn Mawr. She wanted to lead her younger sisters in the right direction and was not about to let Uncle Amory boss her around. Uncle Amory, by the same token, was used to having his own way. He thought that girls should be girls and should go to finishing schools to learn to be ladies. These girls wanted an education—to be independent. Everything seemed at a standoff.

The girls wound up the winners only after Mother figured out the guardian step which really foiled Uncle Amory. Before that, the girls were sent to one relative after another to sort of "try out."

Caroline Garlinghouse Houghton,
maternal grandmother

Alfred Augustus Houghton,
maternal grandfather

Mother at Bryn Mawr

They would move in determined to be charming and sweet *BUT* wildly noisy. They would bang on the floor above the living room. They would scream and yell at each other. Everyone wanted to get rid of them.

Then Mother realized that she was old enough to appoint her own guardian. Uncle Amory was the one who managed her money but he was not her legal guardian. She threatened to appoint a man very unfriendly to Uncle Amory as their guardian, and forced his hand and got her way. She went to Bryn Mawr. The girls went to Baldwin and later they both went to Bryn Mawr.

Just to give you a little idea of the atmosphere that Mother was born into, I'm going to insert here a letter from this same Uncle Amory to Mother in 1904. It gives you a good idea of the Uncle Amory who controlled her purse strings.

Corning, N.Y., Feb. 4, 1904

Dear Katharine:

I have your letter of February 1st, and note that you have, during the past seven years, been borrowing money of Mary Towle, until now it amounts to a thousand dollars, besides what you have paid her back from your salary. Your income has always been ample, and you never ought to have borrowed any money, and Mary Towle did a great wrong in lending you any money. My opinion of you is the same as it always has been—that you are an extravagant, deceitful, dishonest, worthless person. You have squandered thousands of dollars and left your honest debts unpaid. But I do not think you are capable of comprehending the mistakes that you have made. Now that you are paying up Mary Towle, how would it do to pay the various other accounts that you owe? When you see Tom, please tell him I do not think he could do worse.

I enclose your draft for one thousand dollars, and have charged same to your account. I suppose you will endorse on the back of this draft—Pay to the order of Mary R. Towle, sign under it, Katharine M. Houghton, and then send the draft to Mary R. Towle.

disgusted
Your affectionate uncle
A. Houghton, Jr.

When you were a little girl and went into Buffalo and got trusted for some dry goods which you were not allowed to keep (they were returned) your father remarked "Kathie is a feather head." It is true. Kathie is a feather head; always has been, and doubtless always will be.

When Caroline Garlinghouse died, she was thirty-four years old. She must have been a very strong character. My mother talked a lot about her: her beauty, her strength of character—her determination that the daughters get an education and live lives independent of the very dominating Amory Houghton Corning Glass group. Her credo: Go to college! Get an education!

I can see Mother to this day as she described herself sitting next to her mother. Her mother was lovely-looking. And I felt the enormous effect she must have had on my mother, the eldest of the three girls. So my mother was that one who received the powerful philosophy of George Bernard Shaw:

> This is the true joy in life, the being used for a purpose recognized by yourself as a mighty one; the being thoroughly worn out before you are thrown on the scrap heap; the being a force of nature instead of a feverish selfish little clod of ailments and grievances complaining that the world will not devote itself to making you happy.

Don't give in.
Fight for your future.
Independence is the only solution.
Women are as good as men.
Onward!
You don't have too much money but you do have *independent spirits*. Knowledge! Education! Don't give in! Make your own trail.
Don't moan.
Don't complain.
Think positively.

My sister Peg said that once she was sitting crying because our sister Marion and a friend wouldn't let her play with them. "I don't blame them," said Mother. "You're a moaner." Peg learned her lesson. She began to make things fun.

"So-and-so doesn't like me."

"Well, if he had good taste he'd like you," said Mother. "If he has bad taste, why would you want to arrive with him?"

Once when she was at Bryn Mawr, Mother needed money. She could only find someone who needed help in trigonometry. She didn't know trig. So she got the books—called the girl and kept two lessons ahead of her for six weeks. The girl passed the exam and so did Mother.

My dad:
Dr. Thomas Norval Hepburn. He was born December 18, 1879. He was the son of Reverend Sewell Snowden Hepburn and Selina Lloyd Powell.

He was the youngest of their children. The others were Charles,

Selina Lloyd Powell Hepburn,
paternal grandmother

Reverend Sewell Snowden Hepburn,
paternal grandfather, with Kate

Lloyd, Sewell and Selina. They lived in Virginia and also had a farm near Chestertown, Maryland. It is still in the family. It's called "Delight." Dad's mother was a member of the very distinguished Powell family. As with other families in the South, they had been quite impoverished by the Civil War. Dad really loved his mother. They were very close and he developed a high regard for the female sex through her. She was his ideal—a fighter with the highest standards. She believed in education.

Grandfather was a minister in the Episcopal Church. He never made more than six hundred dollars a year.

On his mother's side, the Powells had come over early to Virginia. Dad went to Randolph-Macon College in Virginia and took a B.A. and an M.A. He went to Johns Hopkins in Baltimore to study medicine. He met Mother's sister Edith at Hopkins. They used to fence for exercise.

Mother and Dad met at Edith's apartment. When he met Mother, she was fascinated by him and took a teaching job there in order to snag him. She succeeded. They saw a lot of each other. Dad seemed to her to be very interested in her but he didn't propose. She began to think that he was just stringing her along. Finally, in desperation she said, "You know the great thing about our relationship is that whenever one of us marries it won't hurt our relationship at all."

Dad was indignant. "I don't know how you can say such a thing. If I don't marry you, I shall never marry anyone."

Mother said, "May I take this as a proposal?"

Dad said he'd been proposing to her for six months. She was too literal-minded. "Where's your common sense!"

Edith gave up the study of medicine and married Dr. Donald R. Hooker and lived in Baltimore.

Dad was offered several very good jobs in New York hospitals but he thought New York a poor place to live. Mother and Dad were married and moved to Hartford. They wanted to have a big family. They were both dedicated to the bettering of the position of men and of women.

At the beginning Mother and Dad lived opposite the Hartford Hospital, where Dad was an intern and then a resident. The residents

TOP: Mother and Dad on honeymoon

BOTTOM: House on Hudson Street

were supposed to sleep in the hospital at the end of a bell. Dad found a house just across from the hospital on Hudson Street. He strung up his own bell system. He was very fast on his feet, and as he was never late he was never found out.

Time passed and Mother was walking through the park one day. Tom, her first son, was walking along by her side, with me, Kathy, being wheeled. Well, thought Mother, here I am, these two adorable children, a handsome, brilliant husband looking forward to his brilliant career. But me, what of me, what of me? Is this all that I'm here for? There must be something. I have a Bachelor's degree, I have a Master's degree.

She went home sort of puzzled, and Daddy came rushing in and said, "Look here in the paper. A woman named Emmeline Pankhurst is speaking about women and the vote tonight, let's . . ." They went. Dad obviously had begun to realize that Mother was getting restless about her spot in the world. He found the solution. Mother became the head of the Connecticut Woman Suffrage Association.

Women
Their problems
The vote
Prostitution
The white-slave traffic
Teenage pregnancy
Venereal disease
Huge public meetings

They discovered many of the problems on Hartford's conscience:

"Did you know that there was a big house of prostitution right next to the police station?"

"Did you know that a child drowned in an open toilet at such and such an address?"

Mother had a booth at the Connecticut Fairgrounds, and we had a gas cylinder in the booth so that we could fill balloons. VOTES FOR WOMEN balloons, purple, white and green. I was about eight. I used to fill the balloons, tie a six-foot string onto them, go out into the street, pursue visitors to the Fair, follow them till they were willing to accept one of our balloons, whether they wanted one or not. In

MRS. CARLOS F. STODDARD,
President
New Haven Equal Franchise League

MRS. THOMAS N. HEPBURN,
President
Connecticut Woman Suffrage Association

MRS. M. TOSCAN BENNETT,
President
Hartford Equal Franchise League

VOTES FOR WOMEN

Joint HEARING before the Committee on Constitutional Amendments and the Committee on Woman Suffrage,
State Capitol, Hartford, Hall of the House of Representatives, March 3rd and 4th, at 2 P. M.

DUPLICATE OF SUFFRAGE HEARING
AT
HOTEL GARDE, HARTFORD
(dining room, second floor)

MARCH 3rd, at 2:15 P. M.

Members of the General Assembly and all others who are unable to secure seats
at the Hearing at the Capitol are invited to go immediately to Hotel Garde. As
soon as each speaker has finished at the Capitol she will go at once to the Hotel
Garde to speak.

MISS EMILY PIERSON
State Organizer
Connecticut Woman Suffrage Ass'n

Coffee and sandwiches will be served. Come and wait for your train.

MISS ROSE WINSLOW
of New York

TOP: Flyer for suffrage hearing

BOTTOM: Kate and Bennett sisters dressed for suffrage parade

what was a rather insistent voice I'd say, "Votes for Women—here, take it—Votes for Women," and they took it.

When the men were voting about something, the Suffragettes always had their own voting booth right next door. There was a large sign on it saying (one of Dad's gems): WOMEN, IDIOTS AND CRIMINALS VOTE HERE. Mother was one of their favorite debaters. She was quick-witted, lots of fun and proof for your eyes and ears that women were not fools, they deserved the vote.

Oh, I forgot to tell you. On the first day of "Made in Hartford Week," Mother had a photograph taken of the open toilet in the tenement in which a child had drowned. Took it to the *Courant* (the local paper) with a story. And, believe it or not, they published it without really studying it or the article. Naturally, it was yanked for the second edition.

Dad had a patient come to him to be sure that everything was O.K. and that he could safely marry. He was fine. Then months later he brought his wife in. She had serious gonorrheal peritonitis. She died. Dad discovered that the night before the wedding, at the bachelor party, they had all got drunk and gone to a whorehouse. The husband caught gonorrhea and gave it to his wife. This began Dad's fight to establish the New England Social Hygiene Association, which tried to educate the general public about venereal disease.

He went to Dr. Charles Eliot of Harvard. He wanted him to be president of the society. He rang the bell and asked the butler to give Dr. Eliot a paper he had written about the idea. Eliot came down and said that he had just received a letter from the President of the United States asking him to be Ambassador to the Court of St. James, but he thought Dad's proposition more important. So Eliot became the first president of the Social Hygiene Association of New England.

There was one very controversial meeting, at Parson's Theatre. It was in 1912. The purpose was to advertise the desperate evils of venereal disease and prostitution. The white-slave traffic. What to do? Mother had persuaded the then Mayor Edward Smith to chair the meeting. Distinguished speakers on venereal disease were to appear:

Dr. Robert M. William of Philadelphia—an authority on the disease.

Dr. Edward Janney.

Clifford Roe of Chicago and Baltimore for his work on prostitution.

Then too there were white-slavery investigators.

The very conservative papers—the Hartford *Courant* and the Hartford *Times*—were downgrading the whole meeting. The Connecticut Equal Franchise League was advertising it wildly. The opposition was violent. The telephone at our house, 133 Hawthorn Street, never stopped ringing. The Mayor was trying and failing to get out of chairing the meeting. Dad's favorite quote, "The Truth Shall Make You Free," was on banners everywhere. Finally the night came. Dad drove the speakers to Parson's. On the trip the back tire came off his car. He didn't stop—he rode on the rim—he didn't dare stop. The ushers were women in nurses' uniforms or caps-and-gowns. The crowds inside and out were tremendous.

The meeting was a wild success and Mother and Dad were much praised for their efforts. January, 1912. It was an enormous departure to discuss these topics publicly. Socially it labeled Dad and Mother. They were snubbed by some and praised by others. The fight continued, and of course now we all know that they were right.

In 1917, Mother resigned from her presidency of the Connecticut Woman Suffrage Association and joined Alice Paul's National Women's Party, as its members were more aggressive. They won the vote in 1920.

Then came birth control.

Brought up in the midst of all this, Tom and I were used to being in parades and we were used to being well snubbed in the most subtle sense of the word. But then, of course, the snubs ended and we were praised and regarded as being the children of very forward-looking parents. So not only did *we* look up to our parents but also we soon realized that we were the product of two very remarkable ones.

They were indeed amazing, these two. The door of our house was always open. Come in. Well, tell us about it. Come with us—spend the night—stay to lunch. No no, there's plenty of room, always.

And I think, How I miss you two. I was so used to turning to you. It was heaven. Always to have you two to turn to in despair, in

Dad

Mother

joy. There you were: strong—funny. Two rocks. What you did for me—wow! What luck to be born out of love and to live in an atmosphere of warmth and interest.

I look at the rooms I live in—here at my house. The rugs Oriental. The furniture old pieces: English, French provincial. The fireplace usually blazing. The smell of the ashes. Vases full of flowers of the season. Now in July lots of yarrow (white, pink), Queen Anne's lace (white), butterfly weed (orange and red). Loosestrife—purple spikes. Heavenly vigorous. Besides at Fenwick, our summer house, all the garden flowers—the fields. Every Sunday when we were kids, we used to go flower hunting.

I remember the walks especially in Hartford. Dad would pile us all into the car. Tumbled together in the old Maxwell—no doors. Then that huge old Reo? Remember? It had little folding seats in the back, two extra besides the big backseat. Any grown-up sat in front. Rain or shine, off we'd go. To the reservoirs, the woods, the mountains.

I can remember poor Sinclair Lewis, who lived in Hartford when he was working on *Arrowsmith* (it must have been the early 1920s), trying to shinny up a tree. He just couldn't. Anything athletic was beyond him.

Oh, I have a wonderful story about Lewis.

He and Gracie, his wife, moved to Hartford to a house off Prospect Avenue. A side street. I've forgotten its name. And of course people went to call. One day Mother was at a party and Red Lewis came up to her.

"Why haven't you called on us?"

Mother looked at him—smiled.

"Go home now and I'll come to call."

Lewis went. Mother called.

When she got home, she told Dad that they were fascinating and that she had invited them to dinner Friday night. Then she added, "You know he's quite a drinker—I think we'll have to serve liquor —scotch."

It was Prohibition. Dad refused to buy scotch. Mother was desperate.

Suddenly, Dad said, "What's his number?"

Mother gave it to him.

Dad called him.

"Mr. Lewis, if you have to get drunk tomorrow night to stand our company, you'd better bring your own stuff."

The funny thing is he never had a drink, nothing at all, when he came to our house.

We were friends for years.

Oh, I meant to tell you. I was standing on my head the other day and I got to thinking how probably unusual it is for someone of my age to do this. I can go right up and I can stay up for a count of three or four minutes. My head is in my clasped hands and my elbows are what balance me. I have discovered that I am really almost standing on my forehead.

Then I began to think what in the world started me standing on my head. And then I got to thinking about Dad and all the tricks of this gymnastic nature which he taught us.

I could stand on my hands. I could walk on my hands. I could stand-bend *backwards* and touch the floor with my hands and then walk in this position hands and feet. I could turn handsprings. I could do a flying somersault off Dad's shoulders. Off a diving board I could do a one-and-a-half. I could do a half gainer. Dad once said that he would like to see me run off the board and go feet first with toes pointed, arms up, into the water. I tried it and I landed flat on my back and was knocked out cold. The important thing was to try. We could use our bodies as instruments. Get up. Get down. Get over.

It was very exciting to be able to do all these things. We had great fun and a real sense of accomplishment as small kids. Thank you, Dad.

Oh, Daddy—do you remember all those flowers in the woods—Talcott Mountains? Lady's slippers. Trillium (red, white). Mountain laurel, cowslip and columbine. Trailing arbutus. The person who found the first trailing arbutus got a prize. It was hard to come by. A lovely little bloom—covered by low-growing sort of dried leaves, very sweet-smelling bloom—pretty.

What can I say? The luck of having Dad and Mother. They really

Family portrait

loved each other. Dad with his red hair and his hot temper. Some say I'm like him. I hope so, I would be so proud. Mother with her real savvy of life. She adored him. She adored us. She was deep. She was witty. Some say I am like her. I hope so, I'd be so proud. They loved reading aloud—Shaw—Emerson—O'Neill. They took what life had to offer and they gobbled it up. Some send-off. A real set of values —and a sense of joy.

Dad and Mother had six children over a period of fifteen years:
Tom—1905
Kath—1907
Dick—1911
Bob—1913
Marion—1918
Peg—1920
We were a happy family.
We are a happy family.

Mother and Dad were perfect parents. They brought us up with a feeling of freedom. There were NO RULES. There were simply certain things which we did—and certain things which we didn't do because they would hurt others.

We were close and we are still close.

We were a big family. As children, we were Tom and me, Dick and Bob—then Marion and Peg. You can see that I was much older than my sisters. To them I was really another grown-up. They were eleven and thirteen years younger than I am—almost like my children.

Bob and Dick were closer—but they were boys. When I went to college, at seventeen, they were eleven and thirteen. So as children we really were not living as equals—it was my parents, and me and Tom, and then the children.

As children, they used to visit me in New York. I felt as though they were mine. I'd dress them up and take them to the theatre, to movies and museums and all the excitements. Mother used to tutor them when money became a bit scarce in the early thirties. She was a wonderful teacher and the girls adored it and her. I was a sort of rich aunt and we had great fun together. Visiting and adventures. I'm sure that this was why I never had children of my own.

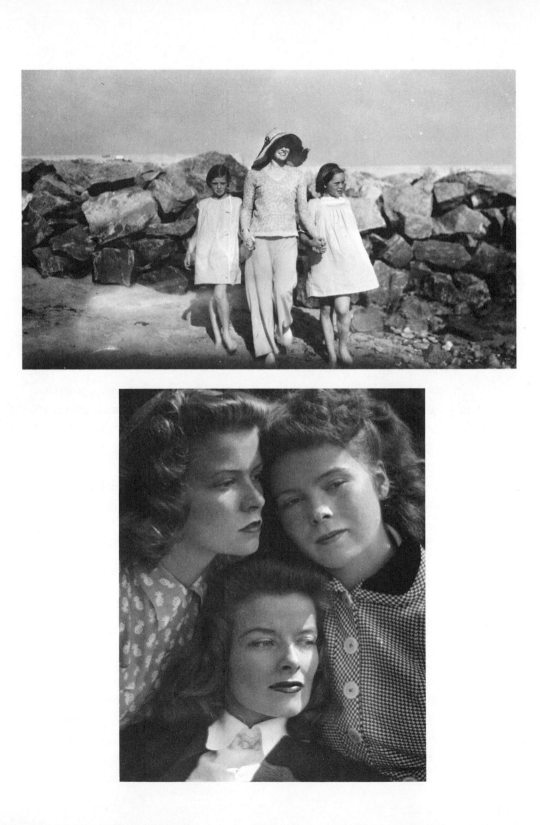

Kate with her sisters

The parents I knew were certainly not the parents Marion and Peg knew—and really Dick and Bob were not equals to me. They were kids. As I've said, I sort of had the experience of motherhood without the obligations.

As they grew into their teens and married, we remained very close. I was lucky—when my parents died, I still had my sisters and Peg's twins and Marion's three and, to a slightly lesser degree, my brothers Bob and Dick and their children. The family with us was strong and remains strong. Their problems are my problems and vice versa. We're sort of a "group" going through the world together. Isn't that wonderful? I feel so lucky. I feel cared for and I have always felt cared for.

Marion died very suddenly when she was about seventy. This was a real shock to all of us. We had felt that we would all just go on and on. I urged her husband, Ellsworth Grant, to quickly marry again. He and Marion had known each other all their lives and had married at twenty. He'd really never been alone. Then he found Virginia Tuttle. So he's O.K.

I cannot say anything in detail about my sisters and brothers. They are so much a part of me that I simply know that I could not have been me without them. They are my "box"—my protection. I miss Dad and Mother and Marion every day and every night of my life.

Hartford

o, I was born eighty-odd years ago, May 12, 1907, despite everything I may have said to the contrary. In Hartford, Connecticut—22 Hudson Street—then opposite the Hartford Hospital. The street doesn't exist anymore. The hospital grew over it. Dad had finished his internship and was no longer forced to live in the hospital itself.

Hartford is the capital of Connecticut. It is a charming city full of parks and hills and even elm trees—some lovely old houses—good skating and skiing in winter—hot in summer.

Very soon after my birth, we moved to 133 Hawthorn Street. It had a fireplace with "Listen to the Song of Life" scrolled across the top. It was a lovely early-Victorian house with three peaks—the center one bigger. Red brick painted with a black lace trim. It doesn't exist anymore either. It was next to the Arrow Electric Factory, east of us. Next to the corner of Forest, to the west of us, some people named Bennett built a house right on the corner. They had a cement tennis court and became close friends. We had the remains of a clay court at the south end of our property. Ours was a long and fairly wide piece of land with a stream along the factory side at the bottom of a sort of little woodland of trees—mostly hemlock and pine. At the front of the property the driveway was a big circle to the front door. The house was about seventy feet from the street. In the winter when there was a heavy snow, we'd enclose the circle in a high wall of snow, very thick. Terrible battles would ensue. It was like a feudal town.

The lawn was deep and ran back to the railroad track. Brownie Park was next to the track. Now it's all part of the highway. There was a lovely pond in Brownie Park. It was full of rats. I think rats can swim. We had a raft on it. A hedge of Paul's scarlet roses bordered the property on the west. To the east there was a gulch with a lot of trees so that we couldn't see the factory—a sort of woods full of daffodils and jack-in-the-pulpits and trillium. What a charming place! There was the railroad track—then Brownie Park—then a cedar hedge—then the remains of a tennis court—then another bit of wood—then the lawn—then the house.

To the east of the circle was a group of big trees. Some were cut down to make tables or chairs. We used to have tea there in the spring. It was pretty. It was fun.

People, friends in the neighborhood would drift in. Tea was a favorite gathering time.

There was a hemlock tree on the west side of the property. That was the tree I used to climb. The neighbors used to call Mother.

"Kit! Kathy is in the top of the hemlock!"

"Yes, I know. Don't scare her. She doesn't know that it's dangerous."

There was another tree, an elm, which played a big part in our lives. Just to the west of the driveway and about fifty feet in from the street. It had a tall trunk and went up straight without any branches. About sixty feet up there was a strong branch growing straight out almost parallel to the ground. To this branch Dad tied a swinging ladder. We would climb up this long wooden ladder to get to a trapeze on a pulley, which was all set to ride a rope which went from the elm to the very back of our long property. We'd get onto the trapeze sitting or hanging by our knees and ride down the rope, which of course started high up and went down to ground level. It was thrilling! Across the gravel path, down to our back door, across the back lawn and to the end.

It used to terrify people. Dad was a very good athlete. He wanted

TOP: 133 Hawthorn Street

BOTTOM: Tea on the tree stumps

us to be too—if we lived. Mother not being an athletic type would suffer as she saw her daughter riding the trapeze over the gravel walk hanging by her feet so high in the air. But she kept silent. She thought it looked fun.

On Sundays and holidays we'd walk in the woods. We'd climb. We'd swing trees, climb up as high as we could—then, holding on as tight as possible, we'd swing our legs out and bend the treetop over to the ground. Birches were best. They are very bendable. It was exciting.

It was great fun. Because of Dad we were the center of action. And because of Mother we were always able to provide cookies and ginger ale or sarsaparilla or birch beer. But the greatest gift she gave us was *freedom* to be noisy, to yell. No nags. Do it? Yes, do it! And tell me about it.

Dad, as I've said, had an old Maxwell car. The license was 3405. Well, here it is. That's me in the front seat. He used to come home early from the office in the afternoon, at four-thirty. He was determined to know his own kids. All the children in the neighborhood would be collected in our yard waiting for him. We all loved him.

We'd shout, "3405!" as he came into view—"3405!" Into the driveway he'd come. He'd change his clothes—have a cup of tea with Mother—then for the next hour we'd play baseball or prisoner's base. We'd play on our court or on the Bennetts' court.

Can you imagine that Dr. Thomas N. Hepburn, my father, used to drag us on sleds behind his car through the streets of Hartford, Connecticut, after a snowstorm—Hawthorn to Forest out Farmington to Woodland to Asylum to Elizabeth Park? Or straight out Woodland to Keney Park. A long rope played out off the backseat. All cars were open—at least I believe so. Anyone who wanted to could hook on. Anyone who could would stay on. Dad would try to sling us off speeding around every corner. He never got rid of me. Great fun.

I remember once it was my birthday and I thought, Well now, my birthday! I can choose prisoner's base. I liked it much better than baseball.

"Prisoner's base," I said.

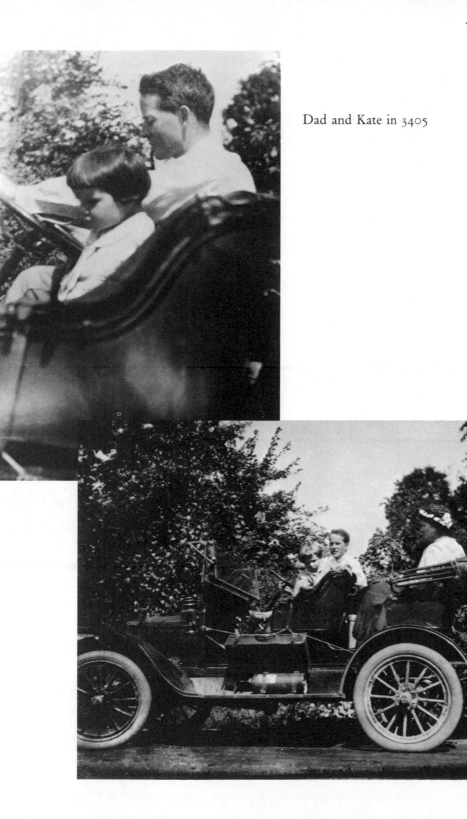

Dad and Kate in 3405

TOP: 133 Hawthorn in winter

BOTTOM: Kate and Tom

"Oh no, baseball!" they all cried.

"But, Dad—it's my birthday—certainly I have the right to—"

"You have the privilege of making everyone happy," said Dad. "It's your birthday."

We played baseball. Unfair!

Another incident, sort of similar. When we were much younger, about eight.

At birthday parties we used to have a pin-the-tail-on-the-donkey contest. We'd hang a piece of material with the donkey drawn out —a full-sized donkey. The guests would be blindfolded and given a tail to pin on the donkey.

On my birthday I did a bit of advance work. I knew where the donkey would be hung. I studied the rug edges which I could feel through my shoes—then nine steps—reach to the left—tail-high.

When at the party I pinned the tail almost exactly where it belonged, Mother cheerily said, "Well, that was excellent. You—"

"I won! I won!" I said.

"Oh no," said Mother. "You can't win anything. It's your party. You *give* the prizes."

Pretty dumb, I thought to myself. Life! Dumb!

Tom's and my first nurse was Lizzie Byles. She was married to Cecil Byles. She was very English and the whole setup was very very correct. Then when Mother got interested in suffrage and they opened the headquarters at 22 Pratt Street, Lizzie was asked down there. She could type. Goodbye, nurse.

I must say that during all this time we'd had a cook—Fanny Ciarrier—and her son Marcel, who was my age and who always lived with us. She was an Italian-French woman who was blind in one eye. She could cook anything and everything. If we needed a maid—a nurse—a whatever, Fanny would import them from Italy or France. She was an angel and was with us all our lives. And when Fanny died, Mother soon followed her.

Fanny's brother was a chef at the Hartford Club.

Dad and Mother had answered an ad to find her. She had had

Lizzie Byles, nurse   Fanny Ciarrier, cook, with Dick

herself listed as available for service—a want ad. Dad had a theory that if you want to hire help, go to their home to see how they live. So Dad and Mother went to meet her. In the middle of the meeting, the room was very stuffy. Fanny got up and opened a window. She's right, thought Dad, the air is stale. He hired her. Forever. Lucky us. She was sensitive.

I learned to ride a bike in Keney Park. I was three. It had been especially made at the Pope Manufacturing Company. Dad put me on and started me downhill. Terrified I was. Far in the distance was a little old man. He was slowly moving along at the bottom of the hill—the only figure in view. As if he were a magnet, I headed for him and I finally managed to bump him. But he'd seen kids on new bikes before. He was waiting for me.

Anyway, I learned quickly. It wasn't long before they would telephone Mother: "Your little girl Kathy has just been seen on her bike on Farmington past Sigourney heading downtown."

"Yes," said Mother. "Thank you."

I had a horse run away with me too in Keney Park. There was a family named Anninger. They used to rent horses at Troop B Armory on Farmington just past Quaker Lane. When I was in Oxford School—the girls' private school in Hartford—we had a riding class there. Sergeant Anninger used to put me on a pony named Leopard. He was speckled and I was speckled and I loved him dearly. So the years passed. I became famous and I went one day to Sergeant Anninger to rent a horse. He'd moved his stable to Keney Park. He apparently thought my riding had progressed along with my fortunes, so he put me on his special mount. Off we went—my sisters Marion and Peg and I—a wild ride tearing under branches over hills over streams. I am ashamed to say I "gripped leather." But I lived.

"Well, Kathy, how did you do?" . . . Dear Sergeant Anninger.

"I did fine. I'm here—ain't I?"

I went to West Middle School when I was a kid—four. A public school. Kindergarten and then on up to fifth grade. I walked east on Hawthorn, north on Laurel, across Farmington to Niles, a step right and there it was on my left. About a mile in all. I headed a group of kids who wanted Police Officer O'Malley to remain at the Farmington Avenue and Laurel Street crosswalk. They had decided to move him to a different location. He was fun. We petitioned and won. O'Malley stayed.

At the east end of Niles Street was Trinity Church. The daughter of the pastor was my great friend—Florence Miele. She was pretty— gorgeous curly brown hair—long. I was freckled—wore my hair like a boy's. In fact, with one brother Tom older and my two younger, Dick and Bob, being a girl was a torment. I'd always wanted to be a boy. Jimmy was my name, if you want to know.

Anyway, to wonder again as we do today about the unexplainable things kids do. We were in fifth grade. Our teacher was Miss Lynes.

Kate as "Jimmy"

She was thin and tall and severe-looking. But the opposite inside. I was good at arithmetic, which was her specialty. She liked me and I liked her. We'd indicated as much to each other.

One day at lunchtime Florence and I lied to our respective families as to where we were lunching and hid at the school. The teachers all used to have their lunch in a long thin room on the second or third floor—facing Niles. When we were sure the teachers were all eating, Florence (the minister's daughter) and I (the daughter of two very "state-of-humanity"-conscious parents) rushed out and at the top of our lungs and in vulgar tones screamed: "Old Lady Lynes! Old Lady Lynes!"

It brought shame to the school, shame to our parents and must really have puzzled Miss Lynes. Mother forced me to carry a potted geranium from Hawthorn Street to school and present it to Miss Lynes—an admission of my guilt and an indication of my sorrow. Miss Lynes put it on her desk. It was there humiliating me for weeks.

And there are so many geraniums in California—reminding me to remember: if you sin you pay.

Miss Lynes forgave me. We were friends for years.

Mother and Jo Bennett (Mrs. Toscan Bennett) were great friends and in the forefront of the fight for women's suffrage—for birth control—for recognition of blacks' rights—fighting prostitution. Jo Bennett's mother, Katharine Beach Day, was also a member of the group. She was wealthy—had a car and driver and was Old Hartford and very socially O.K. Another friend was Emily Pierson of Cromwell, Connecticut—daughter of the owner of Cromwell Gardens (a huge conglomeration of greenhouses—wholesale—beautiful roses). Emily had studied medicine and was Dr. Pierson. She practiced in Cromwell and was a dyed-in-the-wool reformer.

These were strong women, and not penniless, and socially in the right group, which meant a lot in those days.

Most of the husbands were of the same mind as the women. That was unusual.

Dad had the energy and brain but no money except what he earned. Toscan Bennett had money and local family connections.

Our house at teatime was a meeting ground. We kids were allowed in but we didn't do much talking—if any. We met Emmeline Pankhurst, Margaret Sanger, Rebecca West, Richard Bennett—and any number of distinguished doctors and professors.

Dad asked George Bernard Shaw to write the preface to *Damaged Goods*—a French play by Brieux about venereal disease. He had one hundred copies—or was it one thousand?—printed in English at his own expense, and sent them around with a note about the Social Hygiene Association. He asked them to return the price of the book if they were impressed by it. He had a 98-percent acceptance for his effort. Richard Bennett did the play on Broadway. He was the father of Constance and Joan.

I thought about this one day and sorted through some of Dad's letters to try to find his correspondence with Shaw. No luck. He had thrown it away. The important thing to him was that he had done

Fearless diver

Kate and Dick with Uncle Don Hooker and his son

it and that it had been presented to the world in a language which they could understand. Make the world a better place to live in for everyone—especially the underprivileged. Progress.

There were many people who violently disagreed with what Mother and Dad were aiming at. As I told you, we were snubbed by the reactionaries and became quite used to it. Whatever the opposition does, take it with a grain of salt. Smile. You don't hear or see bad things. Good morning. Thank you. How interesting. Oh, I guess she didn't hear me.

And gradually the majority joined our side. And Mother was right and Dad too of course. And naturally *we* were on the right side too. And it was all for the benefit of the helpless—the oppressed—the poor—of course! The things Mother and Dad fought for turned out in their favor.

We felt that our parents were the best two people in the world —that we were wildly lucky to be their children. And we still feel that way.

Often my sister Peg, who runs a farm, will look at me and say, "Can you imagine? Mother and Dad. Weren't we lucky?"

And my brother Bob, the doctor—he will just gloat about them. And Dick, who is a playwright.

We are all aware of our great good fortune. I think of the things I have enjoyed and have learned.

All the sports—golf, tennis, diving, swimming, running, jumping. Dad was responsible for building a good springboard and diving tower on the pier. Wrestling—mat work—gymnastics at Fenwick. He started the custom of contests—of track meets. Our family won so many firsts that they put a limit on the number of wins for one person.

I love diving. Hell—I love all sports. I was skinny and very strong and utterly fearless. There was a pier at Fenwick and a diving board on the pier. The height of the board from the water naturally varied with the tide. There was a railing on the pier about two and a half or three feet high. In order to get a better spring, I would stand on the top of the railing, jump off it to the end of the board and dive —either a jackknife, a swan dive, a one-and-a-half or a somersault.

Running off the end of the board, I would do a half gainer. Standing on the end of the board, a back flip or a back dive. It was fun.

All these complicated dives I did—big show-off ever. One day we had a contest. My great friend Ali Barbour, who—I tell you a lot about her in the chapter on Fenwick—well, she was no athlete—she did a prayer dive. It's just what it sounds. Kneel on the end of the board and fall off.

Well, as I said, we had a fancy diving contest. I assumed that I'd win. I did my half gainer. It's about as unsafe a dive as you can imagine. Run off the end of the board—throw one leg out up in the air—arch the back—let the other leg join the first leg—point the toes—and you dive back toward the board and twist your body into a front dive down into the water. I did it—brilliantly, I thought. Ali did her prayer dive—pathetic, I thought. Ali Barbour won it. Can you imagine? They said that my toes were not quite together and not pointed. Oh my golly. My toes. True disgrace. Beaten by a prayer dive. Can you imagine?

Golf became a sort of specialty with me and with Bob. We went to Fenwick in the summer where there was a private nine-hole course, and as very young kids we could play at any time. Dad was a Deadeye Dick putter. We began at five. When I was twelve or thirteen, Mother started me on lessons at the Hartford Golf Club from an Englishman named Jack Stait. Bob was a natural. We became really quite good. Mother, who had never had any athletic training, struggled with golf and with swimming and diving. She believed in teachers.

During that winter when we lived in Hartford, I decided to tutor instead of going to Oxford School. I wanted to be able to play golf every day. Well, actually I didn't want to be in any school. Too many girls. Too much curiosity. I'll tell you why.

My brother Tom, who was two and a half years older than I, had just died under strange circumstances. I adored him. I was fourteen years old.

Actually, Tom's death has remained unexplained. It was Easter-time. Kingswood—the boys' private school in Hartford—was on holiday. Tom and I were to go to New York to visit Aunt Mary Towle. She had a charming house on Charlton Street in the Village. She had been at Bryn Mawr College with Mother. They had become great

Kate and Tom

friends. Auntie was a lawyer. And the house next door on Charlton was occupied by Bertha Rembaugh. They had been partners. Bertha had become a judge. They were very nice and very successful. Mary Towle never married. We called her Auntie and she was generous and fun. When we visited her, she took us to plays and showed us the sights of the big city.

This visit we went to the theatre to see *A Connecticut Yankee in King Arthur's Court.*

When we got home from the theatre, I can't really tell you what we did. But as I later told the story, I said that Tom had looked at me and said, "You're my girl, aren't you? You're my favorite girl in the whole world." Why did I say this? Was it true? I mean, did Tom really say it? I don't know any longer.

At Auntie's, Tom used to sleep in a sort of studio attic at the top of the house. It was full of junk and trunks and had no ceiling—just roof and rafters. His bed was a cot next to the wall.

The facts were as follows. Next morning I went upstairs to wake him up. There he was—next to the bed—his knees bent—hanged by a torn piece of sheeting. It was tied to a rafter. He was dead. Strangled.

It made no sense.

In a state of numb shock I cut him down and laid him on the bed.

Tom was dead. He was just plain dead.

Yes. I touched him. Cold. He was dead.

What should I do? Whom should I tell? Auntie was too emotional—she would be frantic.

A doctor. Get a doctor.

I went downstairs and out the front door. I had seen a doctor sign on one of the houses across the street. I went to the door and rang the bell. It was about eight o'clock in the morning. The door was opened a crack by a woman peering out.

"Yes?"

"My brother's dead."

A moment's pause.

"What?" she said.

"My brother—he's dead."

"Then the doctor can't help him, can he?"

"No."

Bang.

She closed the door. She just closed the door.

I stood for a moment. No—yes, it's too late for the doctor. Yes, she is right. The doctor—too late for the doctor to help. Oh dear— poor Auntie. She'll . . .

I'd better go back.

Now what.

I rang the bell at Aunt Bertha's house. She answered. "Tom is dead," I said. Then I burst into tears. This was what I thought I should do. People die—you cry—but inside I was frozen.

Aunt Bertha took over. She told Auntie. They called Mother and Dad. Mother and Dad and Jo Bennett came to New York.

I just remember confusion then. We were on a boat crossing the Hudson with Tom's body, going to a crematorium in New Jersey. I can remember standing with Dad on the bow of the ferry. I looked across at Mother—standing with Jo Bennett—about twenty feet away. She was crying. My mother was crying. Oh dear. What can I do? I'd never seen my mother cry before. And I never saw her cry again. Never. She was stalwart.

She had had her share of serious problems. Her father's suicide. Her mother's death at thirty-four of cancer. She had been sixteen at the time. The responsibility of her two sisters as children twelve and fourteen. If she cried, she cried alone.

My father didn't cry either. He took what life had to offer.

I only saw him once—what shall I say?—thrown for a loop. It was one day in early 1951. Dad and I had gone to Fenwick. We had left Mother in Hartford to take her afternoon nap. We were getting back for tea at five. When we got home, we walked into the living room. No fire in the fireplace. Mother's chair was empty. No fire? We rushed upstairs and opened the bedroom door. Mother was there in bed—dead.

I looked at Dad.

"Oh no—no," he said. "I can't—she can't—"

"Go down, Daddy. Go down—don't look—"

Mother had had her nap every day. This was a must. She was

getting dressed for tea. She must have felt something queer. She went from her dressing room into the bedroom, got into bed and with her left hand was pulling the covers up—and bingo—dead.

I stood—my mother—dead—my darling mother—the only mother I'll ever have—gone.

I took her hand—still warm—unclasped her fingers from the sheet she had pulled up—and I kissed her and went down to Dad.

No goodbyes. Just gone.

After Tom's death, she went to the Cedar Hill Cemetery when we buried his ashes, but afterward she never mentioned him. She never said, "I'm going to the cemetery." Neither did Dad. They moved on into life.

At first the newspapers said Tom had committed suicide. There was no reason for this that anyone could see.

Then Dad made a statement that it was very possible that Tom was practicing hanging himself. Dad had told us about his trick of pretending to hang as a kid.

In football games or baseball, the teams that came from the North were very aware of the Southern attitude toward the Negro. And felt that the Virginians—Dad was a Virginian—were cruel and felt superior to the blacks. As a means of irritating these Northerners, the Virginians trained several blacks to pretend they were being hanged. Dad was an expert at this. It was holding his neck in a certain position—a trick—that prevented the noose from cutting off his wind.

Dangerous sport. Could it be that Tom was practicing this and using sheeting instead of rope—the noose was slippery and he could not control it? Dad felt this was a reasonable possibility. And how this must have tortured Dad, but we never talked about it.

None of the family or his close friends could imagine why he might do it deliberately.

Jimmy Soby, who went to Kingswood School with Tom, could think of no reason. Tom was tops in the school—a prefect—a great athlete—a fine student—a leader of boys. Why?

There seemed to be a sort of feeling at the time that he might have made a pass at his girl and maybe it didn't work out and maybe in despair he— Anyway, we'll never know.

I thought at first that it wasn't possible that he was practicing hanging. Now I wonder. Deep in my heart—I wonder.

It's amazing how Dad's and Mother's behavior left its mark. They simply did not believe in moaning about anything.

The important thing was that Tom was dead. In the first terrible shock Mother cried. Yes. But she never allowed the fact of his death to dominate the atmosphere. We were not a sad household.

My sister Peg had a son Tom, who was lost in the Vietnam War. He was missing at first, then pronounced dead. His twin sister was talking about him one day—he was so this, so that—to the other younger children. Peg heard her.

"Don't do that!" she said to her daughter.

"But—" she said.

"No buts," said Peg. "He's dead. We all love him but he's gone. Don't moan. It does no good."

She's right of course.

Anyway, this incident seemed to sort of separate me from the world as I'd known it.

I tried school but it was—well, I should say I was—I felt isolated. I knew something that the girls did not know: tragedy.

They were curious and I would not, did not, want to talk or to discuss it. The school year ended at the end of May and I never returned. In the fall I decided to tutor.

Luckily I was tall for my age and I was a good driver, and Mother used to let me take her car to go for my tutoring lessons. Physics, English, French and History. I could do it by bicycle but the car was better. As Dad had the Chief of Police as a patient, the cops were very careful not to see me. Actually, all went well until the day Mother and I went to look at Bryn Mawr. I had driven out to the Hartford Golf Club to get my clubs. I had heard a lot about the Merion Cricket Club, and since it was close to Bryn Mawr I thought I might try it.

As I was coming down Asylum Avenue—a big avenue—at a good clip east of Scarborough, an old man on my right (which fact gave him the right-of-way) shot out of a side street. In order to avoid him, I went over to the wrong side of Asylum. Instead of his turning sharp to avoid me, he too went to the wrong side and we collided. At the same time I knocked over the police telephone. Well, I had also caved in the side of his car. He wasn't hurt. I wasn't hurt. He wept and put his arms around me. I thought, Well, the thing to do is to weep. So I did.

The Chief of Police called Dad: "Hello, Hep, you've heard about Kath?"

"She collided with an old boy on Asylum. Caved in the side of his car. His fault yes, but she is in the wrong of course."

"Yes, quite completely. Oh, and Hep, she knocked down a police telephone. And I hate to say this, but the front of your old Reo is also quite badly . . ."

"Oh, I think five grand will probably cover everything quite well, Hep."

Mother and I were on the train to Bryn Mawr.

Happily!

My tutoring years were very pleasant. As I told you, I took daily golf lessons with Jack Stait. It looked as though I were going to develop into a pretty good player. I could hit it a mile. And I was quite accurate with irons. The only thing I just was lousy at was putting. Oh dear. I wonder now if even then my head and/or hands shook. Not so that you could see it but so that when tensed up I was sort of uneasy. Well, whatever it was, I just could not putt. Then— now—ever.

It had been a great relief to me not to have to go to school and not to have to associate with girls. My two really good friends, Ali Barbour and Timmy Robinson, had left Oxford to go to the Ethel Walker School in Simsbury. Being more or less alone didn't bother me. We had a seamstress—Mary Ryan—who used to come every Thursday. I used to talk to her. She was Irish and very nice. Then I also had a little theatre, which I had made out of a wooden box. It had a floor with lines cut in it every half inch—green—parallel to the front. I could stand the scenery and the actors in the cracks. I'd make up the stories.

I also had a curtain, which I could open and close.

I would give shows to my brothers Dick and Bob. They seemed to like it.

Dad used to take us to the movies every Saturday night. There were three theatres we could visit—the Strand, the Majestic, the Empire. The Empire ran Westerns and it was easy to park the car. Silent movies—Tom Mix—William S. Hart. My Western heroes. I adored movies. I still do. What a great medium! Leatrice Joy and Thomas Meighan in *Manslaughter*.

I have to tell the truth. There was a Poli's Theatre too, on Main Street. We never went there because there was vaudeville and Dad didn't care for it.

Oh, I remember one funny thing. Mother almost never came with us to the movies. She thought that movies were—silly. Didn't matter. I remember an incident at the Majestic. Because Dad was busy, Mother took us. It was a very sentimental movie but somehow it struck Mother as funny. She laughed quite loud—and she continued to laugh. The usher came down and asked her to leave. I was humiliated. Such a disgrace. You can see Mother just did not find movie stories palatable. She had a very highbrow brain. Curious that Fate gave her a movie-queen daughter.

They used to go to any good play which came to Parson's Theatre. If we wanted to go, they would get us matinée seats. Our visits were infrequent. I used to bribe Dick and Bob to go to the corner drug-store to buy me movie magazines. These I found fascinating. At the same time they'd buy themselves and me ice-cream sundaes covered with chocolate sauce and marshmallow and chocolate shot. They were called Chocolate Imperials. The money for these delights I earned in the winter by shoveling snow in our driveway and various side-walks in the neighborhood. Cutting lawns and leaf raking at other seasons.

The house at 133 Hawthorn, which Mother and Dad had occupied from early on, was to be torn down and the Arrow Electric was to extend its building to fill the 133 property.

Dad, with four children and another on the way, could not wait to find a place. He found 352 Laurel Street. Not anywhere near as nice as 133 but the best available at that time. He had altered 352 quite considerably and at quite an expense. We were ready to move when the Forest Street Association bought 133 as a historic building. They immediately called Mother. She called Dad and urged him to

201 Bloomfield Avenue

stay in 133. But Dad was adamant and refused. Said he'd leased 352
for two years and that was that. So we moved.

Mother had adored 133 Hawthorn. The house and property had
real charm and distinction. She had been heartbroken at the thought
of 352 Laurel. I thought Mother was right: 133 was unique and
beautiful; 352 was really nothing much. Poor Mother. She never forgot
it. And I remember thinking, When you have a choice like that, you
must be very careful not to just go down a road because you had
planned to. If you have a choice, be careful to be influenced only by
what is best in the long run. We weren't rich and Dad was thinking
of the wasted money.

We lived at 352 and we bought a piece of property at 201 Bloomfield Avenue, opposite Hartford University. There we began to plan
the perfect house.

Tom and I were born at 22 Hudson.

Dick and Bob were born at 133.

Marion and Peg at 352.

Now here I am in Hartford on one of those frequent visits. I've
driven up from New York. I've just passed Capitol and Laurel. There

is a huge highway system there now. They've been building it for some years. At that intersection there used to be a drugstore—Childs. Another of my crimes was to run up a charge account there. Hershey bars and licorice sticks. As my capacity was infinite, this finally had to be stopped. I can eat a pound of chocolates with joy—thanks to Childs Drugstore. Training *is* important.

Well, if you go up Laurel to Capitol and over the railroad bridge—corner of Laurel and Hawthorn (on our right)—there used to be Murphy's Grocery and Butcher Shop. The building is still there. Fig newtons—fly biscuits—and a poisonous concoction of chocolate and marshmallow on a vanilla cookie (so fine for the teeth and digestion that they stopped making it). Yes, Mr. Murphy, wherever you are, I remember you well. Those square tin boxes with the glass fronts so that you could see and taste, not the packaged stalies of today. And Mr. Murphy let us sample.

Well, we must leave Murphy's and turn left or west on Hawthorn to what used to be 133. First the factory, the Arrow Electric Company, then the edge of our front lawn is still there. The driveway.

Our house is gone—Victorian gothic—three gables, trimmed with black lace. The driveway—the trees—gracious, simple—the brook—the daffodils. Gone. Even the brook has been put into a pipe. Well, that's the style today—pipe things—can things—freeze things—computerize things. Have to be careful about that. You can't develop a mind full of beauty or tender imagination and independence of spirit tearing along in a box without a bit of space and air—number XY-133-609-00. Well, yes, there are indeed so many of us and we've got to make room.

Anyway, they saved the north end of Nook Farm. This includes the north end of Forest Street. Mark Twain's house and the Harriet Beecher Stowe house. My sister Marion was involved in this. What a great job has been done in restoring them! And although it is a generation before, it is the same atmosphere that I was brought up in. The matting-covered floors upstairs. The style of fireplace—the slate and marbleized mantels—the kitchen—the windows bayed to catch the sun. Cozy places to sit. It is full of ideas for living and enjoying. Go and see it. All the details. They've done it so carefully.

The carpets and lack of window curtains on the south side. Harriet Beecher Stowe's flower paintings. The furniture she painted. The garden: she grew tomatoes and geraniums side by side. Oh, *geraniums*!

As I told you, when I was a kid I drove all over Hartford to my various lessons. No license, of course. Well, I was turning off Asylum south onto Prospect. The corner of Elizabeth Park. I was stopped by a ditchdigger. We had waved at each other and smiled when I passed every morning—so I stopped the car and he came over and presented me with a big box of candy. I was thrilled. Off I went. And that night at dinner I told Dad and Mother about it. Dad was furious.

"You must give it back."

"Oh, but I've eaten half of—"

"You must give it back. You must not stop."

Well, I wasn't about to return a half-eaten box—I just changed my route.

Do you realize that in those days Asylum went only as far as Steele Road, then it was a path—through sort of bushes—trees—you know—really a dirt path? And as little girls we were warned about walking there because men would lurk and sometimes expose themselves—imagine!

"And what would you do?" I asked a friend who told me about how it happened to her. "What did you do?" I asked.

"What do you suppose I did? I looked. That was what he wanted, wasn't it?"

"Well, yes, I suppose it was," I answered.

And now I always smile as I drive out Asylum past Steele Road. Well, you laugh about it, but indeed—it was what he wanted.

Isn't it funny? Hartford is two places to me: it's what it was and it is what it is. I'll come back and find out all about that, but in the meantime I have a view, then I skip how many years and there's the present.

Connecticut. Aren't we lucky? We have wonderful wildflowers—parks—hills—lovely old houses. We have a pace that we like—sometimes slow—sometimes fast. Rivers—reservoirs—Long Island Sound. A wonderful climate—trees—gardens—snow—rain. And it's a good size—not huge—not small.

Dad in Greece, 1956

Mother

Well, it's home to me. I've been stuck in the snow. I've lost a house in a hurricane. I've tennised. I've golfed. It's been fun. I've lived there and I'll be buried there.

I was married to Luddy there on December 12, 1928. Grandfather Hepburn officiated. Marion and Ellsworth were married there—a big wedding. Peg and I were bridesmaids. Dad and Mother both died there. Mother in 1951—Dad in 1962. Santa (Dad's second wife, Madeline Santa Croce) was lonely in such a big house by herself. She moved into her sister's apartment.

Dad was really the last inhabitant of the Hartford house.

After Mother's death, he married Santa. She was one of his nurses. I had always felt that Dad married Santa because he didn't want any of his children to feel that they were responsible for him. It worked. Santa had always been in love with him, and she was thrilled with the idea. He gave her a wonderful life—full of adventure and study. They had fascinating trips to Greece and Egypt. I went with them twice. Frances Rich, my California friend, went with us once—it was fun. Then Dad got sick.

In 1960–61–62, Dad began to feel rotten. Santa took good care of him, and at a certain period when it got to be a bit too much for her, Phyllis, my secretary, whom you'll meet later, went to help.

I remember having a long conversation with my brother Bob on the telephone about Dad. I was on the West Coast with Spencer at this time, so that I was not really up on Dad's situation. Dad would never complain about how he felt. He simply *would not* say that he was suffering. Actually, Bob said that he must have been in a terrible state. They discovered that he had a burst gall bladder. It had been full of stones and of course his abdomen was full of stones and of bile too. Hard as a rock. He was gradually being poisoned. Bob said that the pain must have been really excruciating—not a word from Dad. He found moaning about one's health totally disgusting. He was operated on by Dr. Welles Standish. His blood pressure went down too far and it finally affected his ability to think and to talk. He had to then have a prostate operation. Bob did this operation. It wasn't customary to operate on a close relative but Bob thought that he could do it best. It was his specialty. So he did it. Bob said Dad at this time acted as though he were quietly studying his own demise—never a word of complaint. He just endured or he'd catch Bob's eye and would smile or wink at him.

I got back to Hartford for a little visit. Dad had moved down to the first floor, to the study, which luckily had a bathroom off it. He seemed happy, as always, but much weaker.

One morning Bob and I were eating breakfast in the dining room across the hall. We went in to see how Dad was and he seemed to be just quietly leaving this world. He smiled—he looked at us and he slowly stopped breathing. His chin fell. He closed his eyes—he was gone—just gone. Bob and I sat there. Such a remarkable man Dad had been. So strong. So definite. So tough and funny. He'll never be forgotten.

As Bob told the story, he would stop—really overcome with emotion. His memory was vivid—Dad's tolerance of pain was unbelievable.

Such a powerhouse coming to the end of the trail. He was eighty-odd. He wrote his own rules—and followed them to the smallest detail—"Row your own boat."

What wonderful examples our parents! Oh—we were so lucky.

Santa stayed for several years—and it was then that she decided to move in with her sister. The house was lonely and just too big for one woman. She told us what she wanted.

Bob didn't want to live there. Peg couldn't—I couldn't—Dick was in Fenwick.

So it was over—life at 201. Clean it up—move out—and give it to Hartford University.

The moving out was quite a job, a very very sad job for all of us—it was the end of our beginning.

Fenwick now

Fenwick

Now it's summer and we go to Fenwick. Fenwick is and always has been my other paradise. It is at the mouth of the Connecticut River about forty-five miles from Hartford. Dad discovered it in 1913. I was five and a half.

At that time Fenwick was composed of space—and about forty houses. They are big houses—shingle or plank. Three-storied. Slightly Victorian. Big porches. At that time terrible stony barnacled beaches—a pier—at the base of the pier a big sort of pavilion bathhouse (now gone).

There was a huge old hotel in the center at the present circle, which was between the original first tee and the ninth green of a very primitive nine-hole course.

At the northeast tip was a yacht club.

It is a peninsula which curls off Saybrook to the south. Then like the foot of a sock. Fenwick is virtually surrounded by water. It faces Long Island across Long Island Sound—on its south side. On its east side it looks across the Connecticut River at Lyme. On its west end it is attached to the end of Connecticut.

Originally it was Lynde Farm. On its southeast tip—the toe of the sock—it has a lovely old lighthouse built in about 1760. Later there was built an outer light, in 1860, which was connected to the shore by a breakwater. It gave a controllable end to the Connecticut River traffic.

Everyone knew everyone. They—that is, most of them—came from Washington Street in Hartford. They were Brainards and Brainerds and Davises and Bulkeleys and Buckleys and Goodwins. They were very nice—very Republican—very Aetna Life Insurance.

In 1917, by happy chance, the old hotel and the yacht club burned down in a severe west wind. (It was happy, but was it chance?) It handily removed the two drinking bars which brought a poor clientele to the community. As Fenwick was largely owned by the Aetna Life Insurance Company, this fire was accepted as a very sensible happening. They were insured by Aetna. Thus no one complained. And without bars the unfortunate element of weekend drinkers was removed.

For the kids it was heaven. As I told you, it had a nine-hole golf course which was private. Kids could play at any time. We got to be pretty good. There were two tennis courts. Now there are four—one is cement, the others clay. The golf course is no longer private. It has very good new greens and traps and it more than supports itself.

To me it *is*—well, as I said—paradise. I was and am nothing special here. I've been here since I was six. I had a drink last night with a man named Jack Davis with whom I won the three-legged race when we were about ten—over seventy years ago. Now Charlie Brainard and I are the oldest inhabitants. Life paints its pattern here as everywhere.

Fenwick was a great place for us. It was strictly a summer colony—deserted by the time in early September when school started.

As a kid, I lived the most thrilling life with my friend Alice Barbour. We were secret housebreakers. Never destructive, but could always manage to find a way *in*. One house we crawled in through an icebox opening. It was there that I stole a crocodile nutcracker. I took it home, had it in my bedroom and then felt so guilty that I returned it. No one ever caught us. I was the second-story man—Ali was the brain.

One thrilling episode was getting into the Newton Brainard house. It was a very high big house. I climbed up onto the roof over the third story. Ali could not get up that high. I was to drop in through a skylight, which they had carelessly left unlocked on the higher roof. Then I would open a second-story window and let Ali in. I took off

OVERLEAF: The old house

Estelle Rivoire with Bob, Dick and Kate

Family portrait

the skylight—there was total darkness below. Black. I dropped in. Luckily I landed in the third-floor hall next to what would have been a straight drop between circling stairways to the first floor. This was one most exciting act. Terrifying.

The funny thing was that our adventures were never found out until Ali had a flirtation with a fellow named Bob Post. He joined us on one of our ventures—our last one, as it turned out. We could not find an opening. "Let's smash in the door—the back door," said Bob. So we got a heavy six-foot log and banged in the back door. Naturally, it made a racket and the cook next door watched the whole thing.

When we got in, we found boxes of talcum powder with big feathered puffs and we tossed them around and the paneled walls got streaked with the powder. It was a real mess and, of course, we were caught and poor Dad had to pay for the damage—and we were disgraced. I no longer had any use for Bob Post.

Also with Ali Barbour we produced the play of the fairy tale "Beauty and the Beast." I was the Beast—Ali the Beauty. We did it on the porch of her house—with the audience sitting on the lawn between her house and the one next door. Everyone came and we made seventy-five dollars to buy a Victrola for the Navajo Indians. The Bishop of New Mexico had preached about them in chapel one Sunday. We were filled with noble thoughts.

We had great track races too at Fenwick—and diving contests and relay races and three-legged races. It was exciting. Well, of course it was. We were all very young.

Our house was at the east end of the main group. We had a lot of beachfront and a free view to the east.

Through the years, Dad had jetties built out into the water. These have brought us in a very nice sandy beach.

In the 1938 hurricane, which removed our house, the Brainard house was destroyed—a broken back. Morgan Brainard then bought the Prentice-Post house to the west of him, on slightly higher land —not as private but safer.

This is what is puzzling me at the moment. Now, you see, I have this house. Well, I don't really "have" this house. I should say— well, quite a group of us feel that we "have" the house. We drive in

Early acting efforts

Dad on the jetty

the drive—park our cars—go in the door—sit where we please. Well now, not really where we please . . . but . . . well, let me explain. There's a big kitchen. It was a kitchen and a pantry but my brother Dick didn't like the pantry, so he took the wall down, and now . . . Well, you can imagine. This surprised me quite a lot the first time I saw it.

Anyway, now there's this one big kitchen. It has two sinks—double. One big stove—two ovens, six burners. It was Luddy's stove. Luddy was my ex-husband.

Now Luddy's gone—he's dead and I'd always liked his stove. So we told his son or his daughter or both that we liked the stove because it was a six-burner and the right size for the space we had. My brother Dick went over and he couldn't find anyone in the house. So he just disconnected the stove and put it in his trailer and drove off. They must have been quite surprised when they came back.

So you see all the cooking is done in the big kitchen. Dick really, you might say, lives in the kitchen and you might also say that the kitchen looks it. Besides the two sinks, two sets of windows over the sinks—and between them the stove I've been telling you about. Above the stove a bunch of shelves for the thises and thats. This is one wall. The opposite wall has a big French clock about sixteen inches in diameter—handsome—old. A cuckoo clock. Various interesting pans and relics. Pretty against the white brick.

Then there's a big icebox upon a sixteen-inch tile platform—that's Dick's box. To the back and side of it, my smaller icebox on the same platform (in case of hurricanes). The iceboxes sort of take the place of the old pantry wall.

My end of the kitchen contains all the shelves for the china. Dick's part is, of course, bigger and has a round table in the middle of it with four chairs, and a Tiffany lamp hanging over it. It's the heart of Dick's empire. It's attractive. He has taste. His visitors gather here and much talk goes on. He cooks and serves. His son Tor and Tor's wife, Tess, cook and serve. And in the smaller end Phyllis and I cook and serve. Often we never meet the people who come in and sit and talk and spread out. Dick may be telling the plot of the latest play which he's seen at the O'Neill Center in Waterford. Or Tor giving

Phyllis, Kate and her nephew in the new kitchen

a lecture on the stock market. Sometimes the guests hold forth. It is definitely the hub of the house. Now—you see—we don't necessarily meet them but we hear them. The kitchen has no door and the pantry has no door.

The big old family dining room is next to the kitchen door. I mean, it's next door but there is no door. In the old days it was a swinging door. For some reason it irritated Dick, so he took the door off.

Phyllis and I feed our guests in the dining room or out on the porch, which is off the dining room. Of course we still hear the kitchen conversations going on. It's rather like a busy restaurant.

Then we all sleep in our old rooms:

I'm the east end, second floor.

Dick and Tor—top floor, east end and west end.

We're all here for better or for worse.

It's where I spend my free time.

You can see—it's a family house.

It's a bit odd but it seems to work.

Dick lives here.

I visit—long weekends.

Bryn Mawr

I went to Bryn Mawr College. I was in the class of 1928. My first year I lived in a suite—room and bedroom, ground floor, first door on the right. Pembroke West. There was also a Pembroke East, and between the two was a gateway and over it a huge dining room. My friends from Ethel Walker lived in another hall—Merion. Having not been in school for several years, I was really not at home or at ease with a lot of strange girls. I used to go to bed very early. Then I'd get up at four or four-thirty and I'd go down the hall to the bathroom and have solitude in the hot and cold showers and in the john. I used to eat fruit and cereal and milk for breakfast, so I could have that alone in my room and avoid too many girls. Actually, I finally avoided the dining room altogether. In the early part of the semester I had gone into the dining room and started for the Pem West table. I was dressed in a French blue flared skirt which buttoned up the front with big white buttons—and an Iceland blue-and-white sweater popular at the time. I certainly did not consider myself beautiful. I was just painfully self-conscious. To my horror, I heard a voice—a New York voice—from the vicinity of where I was supposed to sit: "Self-conscious Beauty!"

I nearly dropped dead. God knows I didn't consider myself a beauty. Oh dear. No. I continued into the room. I sat. I ate food. That year I never went back into that dining room.

I used to eat with my friends over in Merion, or I'd buy myself dinner at the College Inn. Dad gave me seventy-five dollars a month and food wasn't so expensive then.

I went to Europe for the first time with my friend Alice Palache the summer of our freshman year—1925. I had $500—she had $750. We were going to bicycle around England—but when we got off the boat and went to London on the train, we were horrified at the hills and small mountains, so we decided that we would buy a car and spend the night either in the car or on the ground or on a haystack to make up the expense. The agony of this for Palache was that she liked coffee in the morning. I didn't yet drink coffee—so I was fine with fruit and cold cereal and milk. What I missed most was the hot bath and the cold shower.

Sometimes we'd go in for a meal and go to "wash our hands," and if there was a tub I'd tear off my clothes and squat down in the tub and take a quick spray from the taps. I always traveled with a towel handy. It was fun. We went all over England, to Wales and to Scotland. When we got back to London, we sold the car for more than we'd paid for it, which was certainly lucky.

We then went to Paris—stayed at the Cayré Hotel on the Boulevard Raspail. There was a little restaurant across the street and we ate there most of the time. We had a table next to a long wall mirror and Palache had a fit because she said that I kept studying myself and my expression while we sat there.

We really went all over the city—which was of course thrilling —and went home penniless.

And my second year I roomed with a girl I'd gotten to know and so it wasn't so bad. Anyway, I'd gotten used to all the girls and I suppose they'd gotten used to me. I belonged to a particular group. Easier to function with protection of a few others. These have more or less remained my friends, especially the ones living in New York or Connecticut. My last three years at Bryn Mawr were nowhere near as traumatic. I wasn't a member of any club but I acted in several plays, which was fun—and fooled around with my pals and laughed a lot. One of my friends had a car (Lib Rhett). Oh, what a treat! We went everywhere.

I played the leading man in one play—*The Truth About Blayds,* by A. A. Milne. I played the juvenile. I had to wear a wig covering my long hair. And a pair of pants a bit tight in the seat. It was a modern play. I remember one frightful moment when we were giving a performance of it at the Colony Club in New York. Somehow or other I managed to put my hand in my pants pocket and then to sit down. After a bit I tried to get my hand out of the pocket. Impossible. I tried several times. I got a bit confused and kept yanking. This turned out to be a splendid laugh.

I also played Teresa in *The Cradle Song*, by Martínez Sierra.

In my last year I played Pandora in John Lyly's *The Woman in the Moon*. This was part of a big May Day production. It was done in the cloister of the library with the sun full on our faces. The play had not been done ever in this country, and a lot of very highbrow interest was shown.

I think I was chosen for the part by Samuel Arthur King. Dr. King gave a course in speech, which was a required course. It interested me a great deal. He had been hired by M. Carey Thomas, former head of Bryn Mawr, who was very conscious of American speech and its unfortunate production. Mother and Dad were also very voice-conscious and reminded us often that it was more attractive to make an attractive sound.

Pandora was a great part. She played in different moods under the influence of different planets. I was warlike under Mars. Loving under Venus, etc., etc. Funny, tearful, etc. My father said that all he could see in that performance were the soles of my dirty feet getting blacker and blacker. And my freckled face getting redder and redder.

When I was at Bryn Mawr, they didn't allow smoking except in the smoking room, first floor. I lived in Pembroke East at the time, on the second floor just outside the dining room which was the sort of bridge between Pembroke East and Pembroke West. This was my senior year—1927–28. I had just picked up my mail and was going through it. The door of my room was opened into the hall.

"Heavens—what is this?" A small package. I tore off the wrapping—a box of perfumed cigarettes.

"Oh, a good smell—I think I'll try one." I put one of the cigarettes in my mouth—lit it and puffed away.

"Oh, a bit weird. Well, that's that." Put it out—threw it away.

The Truth About Blayds

The Woman in the Moon

Self-conscious Beauty

Later that day a student-government officer said to me, "You were smoking in your room. Someone reported you. It's against the rules."

I looked and was dumbfounded. "Who reported me?"

"I can't tell you."

"Oh—I see. Yes—well . . ."

Now the truth of the matter was that I was not a smoker, so I didn't know any of the smoking regulations. Obviously, someone passing my door had seen me smoking that perfumed cigarette. It must have been someone who didn't like me—otherwise she would have yelled at me, "Hey, what are you *doing?*"

I couldn't say that I didn't smoke. It would put whoever it was in a very difficult position.

You can see by these letters that I was suspended for eight days. Never could tell anyone I didn't smoke. So—an eight-day holiday.

October 20, 1927

My dear Dr. Hepburn,

The copy of a letter to Miss Hepburn which I enclose will explain itself.

This particular regulation would be made by anyone who had charge of the college and its enforcement would always be imperative. I am sorry that after living in a community for three years your daughter did not feel responsible herself in such matters and that the community had to take it in hand.

Very sincerely yours,
(Signed) Marion Edwards Park

Dr. Thomas N. Hepburn

October 20th, 1927

My dear Miss Hepburn,

In view of your failure to keep the regulation which forbids a student to smoke in her college room, the Bryn Mawr Association of Self Government has asked me to notify you of your suspension from the college halls and from all college exercises from Sunday October 23rd at noon to the evening of Friday October 28th. Your absences from classes during the week will be regarded by the college as though they were unexcused cuts.

I am sorry that you have disregarded a restriction which has been established as a matter of common agreement among the students and which, dealing as it does with conditions in large buildings filled with casual people and inflammable things, must have the support of your own common sense if you give it thought.

I am sending a copy of this letter to your father in order that he may understand your return home at this time.

Sincerely yours,

(Signed) Marion Edwards Park

Miss Katharine Hepburn
Pembroke West

October 22, 1927

My dear President Park,

I am naturally much concerned that my daughter Katharine has been deprived for five days of her opportunity to work, as she has already had to miss several days because of the wedding of her best friend. It is perfectly possible that this additional handicap may endanger the successful completion of her year's work, necessary for her degree. While such a punishment may be deserved by the enormity of the crime committed, I, who am deeply interested in my daughter's successful work, naturally turn to an analysis of the crime. This crime is "smoking in her room at college".

I note that there is a regulation against students smoking in their rooms, "established by a common agreement among the students". In other words it is technically a regulation inspired by the reasoned conviction of a self governing body. I note in your personal letter that you say "This particular regulation would be made by anyone who had charge of the college". Such being the case, it is hardly a voluntary regulation of the self governing student body, except in a technical sense.

The reasons given for the regulation are "conditions in large buildings filled with casual people and inflamable things". In support of the validity of these reasons you appeal to "her common sense if she will give it thought."

I would suggest however, that in so far as you educate these girls and then appeal to their "common sense" and "thought", it would be well to see whether the reasons given for the rule against smoking in their rooms would stand the test of such an appeal. If they do not, the college, just so far, loss its educational authority.

In Katharine's experience both her parents smoke. They smoke in their rooms if they wish—and, funny as it may seem, Katharine rarely smokes, altho no home restrictions have been put on her.

Katharine has never been in a hotel or business office or even large hospital where smoking has been prohibited, altho they were filled with many more "casual people" and much more "inflamable" material.

I feel, therefore, that the appeal to her common sense and thought is ill advised.

The one and only appeal in this case should be that she must obey the rules—however irrational those rules may seem to her.

I shall take such a position with her. I shall emphasize the absurdity of endangering her degree and negativing all the money I have spent on her education by breaking a rule in order to indulge a passing whim. To such an extent can I back up your discipline. I can not back it up as a regulation having a spontaneous origin in the student body, or a regulation appealing to her "common sense" and "thought".

Very sincerely yours,
Thomas N. Hepburn

To President Marion Edwards Parks.

Before my senior year ended, I had made friends with a man named Jack Clarke, who lived in a house next door to the college campus. His best friend was Ludlow Ogden Smith.

Jack had several friends in the theatre and he happened to know Edwin Knopf, who ran a theatre company—a very good one, with big stars—in Baltimore. Mary Boland, Kenneth MacKenna, Eliot Cabot. I got him to give me a letter to Knopf, and one weekend Lib Rhett and I drove over to Baltimore. My mother's sister Edith Houghton Hooker lived there. I went to see Knopf and he said, "Well, write me a note when you finish college."

I finished college.

Dad always said if you want to get something, don't write. Don't telephone. Be there yourself. In person. Harder to turn down a living presence.

I thought, No—no note. I'll appear myself.

So I did. My aunt and her family had left Baltimore and gone to Maine for the summer, so I stayed at the Bryn Mawr Club. It, too,

Mary Boland

Edwin Knopf

was half closed, but they let me stay in their cheaper room, in a hall bedroom. On an air shaft. High ceilings, very dark and scary. Not too far from the theatre. I was too shy to go into a restaurant. I'd hardly ever been in a restaurant, in fact. And certainly not alone. My great friend Bob McKnight, who had a car (you see how wise I was in picking friends), had come with me. He was on his way to Rome to study sculpture. He'd won a Prix de Rome. He lived there with me. And we'd get food from a delicatessen. It was all very innocent. We were both wildly ambitious and thrilled with life and its possibilities. We weren't wasting our strength rolling around. It was all or nothing for *me me me*. With each of us. Don't get sidetracked. We protected each other.

I went to see Eddie Knopf. I found my way in from the front. I didn't even know there was such a thing as a stage door. I heard voices. It sounded like a rehearsal. I opened a door so that I could see the stage. It was a rehearsal. I crept in and sat in a back row like a mouse. An hour passed. I needed to go to the bathroom. Finally, I *had* to go to the bathroom. The whole theatre away from the stage area was black as pitch. I felt my way around the lobby—down a stairway into another lobby. And finally a john. Then I found my way out and went back to my spot. Another hour. Even a third. Then all of a sudden it was over. They were finishing. The lights in the auditorium came on.

Eddie Knopf saw me. He walked up the aisle. Stopped by me and said, "Oh—you—yes, report for rehearsal Monday—eleven o'clock."

And he was gone.

My God! I had a job! He gave me a job! He knew me! He gave me a job!

That Monday I walked into his office at ten-forty-five.

"I'm here for rehearsal."

"You're in the wrong place."

It was thus I learned about the stage door.

I went in. It was quite a large group. The play was to be *The Czarina*—Mary Boland, the Czarina. The parts were handed around. "Oh, mine is quite large—about ten pages."

There were a number of young girls besides myself but I had the biggest part.

We were all introduced to one another. Then we sat around a big table and read the play. Thrilling! My part was really very nice. Wasn't I lucky!

The rehearsals were many and long. It was announced that the costumes would be assigned in the morning at eleven. I thought: Well, get there early. I got there at ten. I was not the first to arrive. I was the last. Well, that was a big shock. I wasn't as clever as I thought. And of course I got the worst costume. Inches too short and not very becoming in the neck.

Then something very strange happened. One of the girls came up to me and said, "I was the first here. I want you to take my costume. It's the prettiest."

I was struck dumb. I'd hardly spoken to the girl. I looked at her. She had the dress on. It was lovely. I tried to talk.

"Oh, but I—but you—but oh no, I couldn't—"

She stopped me. "I'm going to be married," she said. "I'm not going to be an actor. And I think that you are going to be. I mean, I think you are going to be a big star. I want you to have it."

What could I say? Of course I said, "Oh yes yes. Thank you—I mean thank you very—I mean—oh, how lovely—I'm so relieved— it's so— But you—you are an angel—you are the soul of generosity. I can't believe that you— Oh, please— Oh, I'm thunderstruck—I — No, don't stop me—"

She stopped me: "Look, I'll take it off and you give me that and I'll give you this, and you'll be happy and I'll be happy."

We changed clothes. I turned and looked in the mirror. Oh, perfection. "Oh, I'm—" I turned back. She had gone.

Can you imagine anyone being that generous? Wasn't I lucky? Lucky. Do you think it will last? I got the best dress by far. And I don't even remember her name.

The play was about to open. I was totally ignorant of the ways of the theatre. I had no makeup and used no makeup except lipstick—Christy's No. 2, bright red-orange. Mary Boland told me what makeup to get. How to do eyes. I watched her make up. She was so generous. Gave me all sorts of bits and pieces.

They were all very nice to me, the stars of the company. The play opened. I got two very nice notices for my little part. I was known

Dear Frances

More customers!

First Miss Katherine Hepburn just graduated from Bryn Mawr — played two small parts here — her professional debut and wants to study. She really has talent and loads of personality and charm. Stands awfully and never sits in a chair if there's an inch of floor available! She'll be in to see you in a couple of weeks. We all think she is a bet.

With kind regards,
Kenneth MacKenna

Letter of introduction
from Kenneth MacKenna

a bit socially in Baltimore, as I told you. I hoped that that wasn't the reason I was noticed. But, for whatever reason, the *Printed Word* said I was "arresting." And I was given a part in the next week's show, *The Torch Bearers*. This was another play which Mary Boland had done. There was a part for me, not a very good one. And I knew that I was not very good in it. When I got nervous, my voice would shoot up into the top of my head. I didn't really know how to control this. I talked to Kenneth MacKenna. He suggested that when I left the company I should go to New York and study voice with a woman named Frances Robinson-Duff. Ina Claire was one of her pupils. Duff was very well known.

"She's the best voice teacher in New York City."

Well, why wait, I thought. I'll drop this and go to New York. I looked her up. Found out how much she charged.

My father had been disgusted and heartsick over the fact that I wanted to act. Thought it a silly profession closely allied to street-walking. That I had developed into a cheap show-off and that I was entering a shabby profession which was based on youth and looks. Definitely a foundation of sand for a silly life. He wasn't about to be the financial backer of such a project. My mother was all for it. Anything I wanted just so I didn't settle for the old routine of nurse-maid to the rising generation. She thought women should give life a whirl. See if they could swing it so that they could be more independent of the male sex. Dad was for this too. He just didn't care for the road I'd chosen.

But I'd saved up some allowance money and when I went to Baltimore I had over $250. A lot to me. But not enough for New York. And certainly not enough for Frances Robinson-Duff. So I wrote Dad a letter which I thought would sell him. The importance of training for the job I'd chosen. Would he back me? He had already sent me fifty dollars, which he said he had won on a golf match or a bridge game. Gambling money was not real money, so he was sending it on to me. After that, of course, I knew that with a small push he would be on my side. We were very close, Dad and Mother and I. None of us liked the separate ways. So, of course, he told me yes—he'd pay for Duff. And so I left Baltimore and away I went to New York City after the second week.

Aunt Betty Hepburn had an extra room in a brownstone in the East Sixties. She was the widow of Uncle Charles, Dad's brother.

Frances Robinson-Duff was an experience. A house on East Sixty-second—between Second and Third. She and her mother. Her mother had been an opera singer. She taught opera. Frances was tall—about five feet seven. She was stout—big stomach, medium bosom, corseted. Her office was the top floor. She sat and tried to teach me how to speak from my diaphragm. I would have to put my hand on her diaphragm and hold it there (my hand) as she pursed her lips to blow out a candle. It was a strange feeling. I had my hand on the top of a corset. It was somehow very embarrassing to me. Her bosom—her diaphragm—the top of that corset. I don't think that at that time I really got the notion of producing air from the diaphragm rather than straining the throat. Now I can call "HEY!" straight from the diaphragm. But my lack of success with really connecting my voice and volume to the diaphragm cost me great worries in my career. I lost my voice and would get very hoarse whenever I played a part which was fast and loud. It was an agony.

Too bad that I was not able to really understand all of Duff's candle-blowing, etc., in the beginning. I would have saved myself great agony. In a way, I can understand why I couldn't connect voice and diaphragm. I think that I was so excited by life and living and my future that I was simply wound up so tight I didn't—couldn't —relax.

Frances Robinson-Duff was really interested in me. She did her very best and she helped me to learn my way around in the theatre. And I had Mother and Dad backing me all the way—Mother on the telephone, Dad with his letters.

Dear Kath,

Can't let your 21st birthday go by without a wee bit of sentimental indulgence. You are now a free lance and your Dad has no control over you. Just think of that! Doesn't it make you shudder when you think of the past 21 years of servitude. Just for that I now shall order you around as successfully in the future as in the past.

First, don't take life or its happenings too seriously. Lift up the corners of that mouth that I gave you one moonlight night.

With Dad at Fenwick

Second, try to do one thing well—utilizing the experience of all preceding life and your own wit.

Third, never let yourself *hate* any person. It is the most devastating weapon of one's enemies.

Fourth, always remember that your Dad is liable to call you all sorts of names when he disapproves of your behavior, but don't take him too seriously, and always come to him—whatever your difficulty—he may be able to help you. Impossibly, he may not be as stupid as he looks.

Fifth, forget all the above and remember only that I would love to kiss you 21 times and give you a million dollars—

Your hopeless Dad

II

Luddy

So I was in the big city—New York—studying with Frances Robinson-Duff. I didn't know the city at all really. Neither would you. I had the use of a car in New York. You could park almost anywhere in those days. It was totally unlike New York today. There was no FDR Drive. No West Side Highway. No GW Bridge. The Holland Tunnel was just about ready. The Lincoln not yet existing.

Ferry to Staten Island
Ferry to New Jersey
Bridges to the Bronx
Bridges to Long Island
No tunnel to Long Island

In my area—the East Forties and, earlier, East Thirty-ninth Street—there were elevateds on Third Avenue and also on Second. I'm talking the late twenties and early thirties. Central Park was open to cars and I used to drive up there and park and spend the day. Very few people used the Park then. No running. There was no Pan Am Building ruining the view of the silhouette of Grand Central against the sky.

It's hard to remember when the bridges came in and the tunnels and the huge skyscrapers and the wildly crowded streets. My days were really spent hoping that the telephone would ring and offer me a job.

I was to live in an extra apartment which my aunt had. It was a room at the front—fourth floor—in a brownstone on Sixty-second. A minuscule bath . . . kitchen and bedroom. Aunt Betty Hepburn was out of town.

I didn't really know anyone well in the big city. Jack Clarke, of course . . . his two sisters Aggie and Louise. They were from Bryn Mawr—the town, not the college. Their friend Ludlow Ogden Smith. They had apartments on Thirty-ninth Street east of Third. They were all nice to me.

Then there was H. Phelps Putnam.

During my senior year at Bryn Mawr—actually, in late spring, 1928—I was invited to lunch at Helen Taft Manning's house. She was Dean of Bryn Mawr. Her husband was Fred Manning and he had a great friend, H. Phelps Putnam, who was also at this luncheon. Putnam was a poet. He was sort of medium-sized and had a very handsome head.

And he was fascinating. I took one look at him and I was stricken with whatever it is that strickens one at once and for no reason when one looks at a member of the opposite sex. He absolutely fascinated me. I flew up onto a pink cloud and I was literally sailing through those last weeks at college. I was living in a single room, second floor tower, Pembroke East, and I actually used to go out the window and climb down the vine to go for a midnight walk. I think I was the inspiration for this poem.

> . . . She was the living anarchy of love,
> She was the unexplained, the end of love,
> The one who occupies the dreamy self,
> The one appearance in the finite world
> Which is seen by us one time, and then despaired
> Beyond romantic comfort afterwards.
> She was my nourishment, my sister and my child,
> My lust, my liberty, my discipline,
> And she laid fair, awkward hands upon my head.
> She was discourteous as life and death
> And kindly as a dry white wine is kind
> On a blowzy summer day.

In praise or blame, my voice drowns in my blood,
I cannot speak, I could not speak before,
Although I knew love fattens on smooth words,
I could not speak at all.
For beyond space she was my quality,
She was the very mask of my desire . . .
    —"The Daughters of the Sun,"
    by Phelps Putnam

I arrived in New York. Phelpie was living on Fifty-fourth Street East on the river. In a tenement, a railroad flat belonging to Russell Davenport of *Time/Fortune*. Davenport was out of town. The railroad flat was charming. Davenport had a full bathroom, which he had installed, and a fine kitchen and the iron fire escape on the river side was great to sit out on and watch the boats go by. Great spot. Quiet, romantic. The Tracy boats were the dominant tugs. Being very practical, I soon realized that I would be much better off living in the tenement too. Handy. So one night I moved my belongings out of the Sixties and into the Fifties. I had no intention of living in sin with Phelpie. I just wanted living. Sin could wait. Living itself was a sort of ecstasy . . . the opportunities . . . the hopes. I was on my own in a high state of excitement. I did not need anything else.

Phelps knew everyone. I mean, you know, Robert Benchley, Tony's Speakeasy. Well, Places. You had to know Places, People. You had to be on the In. I've never been any good at that. I just seemed—still seem—to trot along my own trail—nose to the ground going my own way. One track leading there. Where "there" is I am not really sure ever.

Phelpie was vaguely married. Also, he had no money. And I didn't have much. And he was accustomed to the best in the way of food, drink and accommodations. I had a lot of common sense and I could clearly see that until and only if I could support him, it had better be a glorious friendship. And so it was.

I did not know at that time that my father had said to Phelps: "Look here . . . I hope you are aware that my daughter Kath has her eye on you. You are a fascinating fellow. Hence I cannot blame her. But you are married and you are considerably older than she is. Now

. . . she will make every effort to seduce you. I can only compare her to a young bull about to charge. So . . . you had better look out. Because if you lay hands on her, I shall shoot you."

Phelps, I think, was startled by this. He liked the company of women. But what he really liked was drink. And he certainly didn't want trouble. So he left me in the tenement and went to visit his friend Supreme Court Chief Justice Taft in Nova Scotia.

And I remained in my romantic daze—walking through the streets, ten feet above the ground.

Davenport came back to the tenement. So I got out. I moved into a big empty family apartment of a college friend of mine, Megs Merrill. At 925 Park Avenue. Her family were in Huntington, Long Island, for the summer. I was studying with Frances Robinson-Duff every day. And I had my first New York job.

I had met Luddy in about 1927, in my senior year—Ludlow Ogden Smith. You'll recollect he was the best friend of Jack Clarke, who lived in a house next to Bryn Mawr College. Jack's lawn connected with the Bryn Mawr lawn. He lived with his father and two sisters. His mother was in an insane asylum. When his father died, Jack was handling the money and caring for his two sisters. The two girls and Jack had decided never to marry and have children. They never did. He was tall and skinny and fascinating-looking. He was about thirty. So was Luddy—about thirty, I mean. I was twenty. Luddy was tall, medium weight and dark. He was an odd-looking man—dark hair, dark eyes far apart. He was foreign-looking. Pink cheeks. An odd nose, long with a hump in it. A long mouth, full-lipped. Well, I try to describe him but this description sounds ridiculous. He did not look ridiculous, I assure you. Well anyway, there's a picture of him, so you can make up your own mind.

Luddy and Jack were really good friends. They both had money. Not a great deal, but enough so that life was easy. In the country they had a sort of—well, if I say "hut" it sounds forlorn. It was a tiny house—white plaster, dark roof and dark trim. A big fireplace. A little porch. At the bottom of a hill, a meadow. They owned about twenty acres and no other houses were visible. It was about forty minutes away from the college. It was fun. And we'd go out there

TOP: Luddy's "hut"

BOTTOM: Picture taken by Luddy

for picnics. By "we" I mean a group of girls called "The Tenement," who lived in the Bryn Mawr buildings adjoining Jack's and who got to be friends with Jack and Luddy. My friend Alice Palache, whose father was head of the mineralogy department of Harvard. Lib Rhett—she had a car! Remember? Very handy. Adele Merrill. Occasionally, Alita Davis. She was rich and came from St. Louis and was the niece of the tennis Davis Cup Davises. We were all about eighteen, nineteen to twenty, and full of joy and innocence.

Jack and Luddy were looking for trouble. But as far as they got was taking naked pictures. Photographs of me lying on a big sofa which they had in the living room. I posed with total confidence, as I rather fancied myself. I can't remember who else did. I know Palache didn't. They gave me blowups of the pictures. I remember I put them in a straw basket with a straw cover. It had a strap around it. I had it for years. I can't remember when it disappeared. I know that I had it in New York when I first moved there. Then I remember it specifically when I moved into Megs Merrill's apartment at 925 Park Avenue that summer. Megs had married a man named Armitage Watkins called "Wee Willie" Watkins. It seems to me that Willie came to spend the night in the apartment. He opened the straw basket.

"Lots of naked pictures of you," he said.

"Yes," I said.

I think he would have liked me to continue the conversation.

I didn't.

And now I can't remember any more than that. I can't remember what happened to the pictures. Did I tear them up? What happened to the straw basket? I think I must have thought, If I don't look at them, they don't exist. Odd. Now I still think that if I don't look at something, it doesn't exist.

I never look at notices. So they don't exist. Or at movies that I have made. They don't exist. My past sins, so to speak.

But I was telling you about Luddy, because it was really his generosity which sent me on my way. He was the soul of sensitivity. Luddy came from Strafford, Pennsylvania, which was several stations beyond Bryn Mawr on the Main Line. He had gone to Grenoble, a college in France, was a fine musician and could pick up any language

With Luddy

in a few days—he could function wherever. He worked in Philadelphia, then had moved to New York and worked there.

After Phelps Putnam decided to take Dad's advice and move to Chief Justice Taft's house in Nova Scotia, I was left in Davenport's apartment on the East River. Then Davenport came home and I moved out and to 925 Park—the Merrill apartment.

As I mentioned, Jack Clarke and his sisters were then living in New York, with Luddy living nearby. I began to see them for dinner and movies and whatever. Luddy had a car and he used to drive me up to Fenwick for weekends. And soon we saw more and more and more of each other.

What did you say? Where did it happen? Oh yes, of course, *it* was in the Clarkes' apartment. They were all away, and well I guess that I knew that Luddy was in love with me. But you see my hitch was that I was in love with myself. I mean, you know. I wanted to be a big star and—what? I told you all that before? Oh yes, I did. Anyway, Luddy and I were alone in the apartment and there was the bed and there didn't seem to be any reason not to. Well—what I'm trying to say is that—that's what happened. I mean—we did it. I mean, I guess, that Luddy knew what he was doing—and I didn't object. So we did it. And that was the end of my virtue. He was my beau from then on. Listen, let me tell you—yes, he was my beau but—and that's the biggest *but* you've ever heard:

He was my friend!

Early Career

ell, my first job. The Knopf Stock Company had suddenly decided to try a New York production, with Kenneth MacKenna, of *The Big Pond*, a play which they had tried out with some success in Baltimore. They had sent for me to be the understudy to the leading lady. Naturally, I was thrilled. I learned the part and sat on the sidelines quite convinced that I would be far superior to the leading lady I was watching, Lucile Nikolas. She was a very competent actress who did not have the advantage of being very young and absolutely outrageous and full of a sort of wild confidence based on nothing but energy and ego. Of course I thought I was scared to death, but all I can say now, looking back, is that I was not scared enough. Open a door, I'd go through. Even if the room I was entering was on fire. One lunch hour, after the play had been in rehearsal a week, they asked me to stay and play a scene. Pushed by a sort of frenetic boiling-over, I must have read it very well. They fired the leading lady and took me. I didn't of course know what I was doing but I did it with great style. I took this change in my status as a matter of course. I was the leading lady. I had been in the theatre about four weeks. This was happening just as I had imagined it would . . . it should. I was arriving.

Then a whirlwind of memories. Bergdorf Goodman for the clothes . . . the shoes . . . lots of flattery . . . the trip to Great Neck for a

The Big Pond, with Kenneth MacKenna

Saturday-night performance. This was a very popular place to play a one-night stand. I drove out in my car. The dress rehearsal had been done in New York at the National Theatre, now the Nederlander, on Forty-first Street where we had been rehearsing. Photographs had been taken there. Mine were gorgeous, I thought.

I arrived at the Great Neck Theatre about six o'clock for the opening. Thought, Well, don't go in . . . too terrifying. Stay away as long as possible. I could make up in five minutes. My hair was never a problem. Pretend it's not happening. Get in about eight-ten. So I fiddled around—ate my dinner, which I'd brought with me— in a field. Took a run. Finally turned up at the theatre ten minutes after half hour, to the fury of everyone. But I got made up. Got dressed. Rushed on at my cue. Very quickly after my entrance I had to do an imitation of a Frenchman (Kenneth MacKenna) who was our guide. My mother and father and I were touring Europe, supposedly. I had a good French accent.

It brought down the house. They burst into applause. Naturally I thought, Well . . . that's that. I'm a star. Overconfidence flooded in. My voice went up. My tempo increased. And apparently—that is, apparently to everyone but myself—I became very difficult to understand. Too high . . . too fast. I wasn't MacKenna's leading lady—I was the star. He was *my* leading man.

The play over, I noticed that no one particularly bothered to come in and tell me I was remarkable. But as I'd never really been a big star of an opening night, I didn't know what to expect. So I thought they must have problems. It never occurred to me that I was the problem.

A man named Harlan Briggs was playing my father and I asked him if he would like a ride into town. Fine, he said. Off we went. The fact that no one had said anything bothered me enough to make me ask him if he thought anything was wrong. He must have been told by that time that I was to be replaced. But he didn't let on to me. I dropped him, went back to my Park Avenue apartment . . . went to sleep.

Next morning I was about to leave for rehearsal when Frances Robinson-Duff called and told me to come to her house before I went to work. I said, "I'll be late." She said, "They won't mind."

On my way to her I thought, They won't mind? What does that mean?

I got to her house. She sent for me. I climbed up to her studio. I went in and the minute I saw her long and very serious face it dawned. "I've been fired," I said.

"Yes," she said.

"Well . . ." At a loss for words: "I'm not crying . . . aren't you proud of me!"

"No," she said, "I'd be prouder if you were. That was the trouble with your performance last night. Too self-contained."

"Well . . . fired . . . oh dear, how embarrassing. They must feel dreadfully. Who's going to play my part?"

"The one who was . . . Lucile Nikolas."

"Oh yes, well, she must be very happy. That's nice. Now I think I'll just run down there to the National so that they can see that I'm not too upset. Oh dear . . . so embarrassing for them."

"Katharine . . . I think that it would be better if you did not go."

"Oh no . . . that wouldn't do at all. I won't be long. I'll just . . ."

And I was off. Down to the theatre I went. Burst in on them. Congratulated the leading lady. They offered me back my understudy job and I said no, I thought that that would be unwise. And thanked them all and left. What must they have thought?

Then I took the train to Hartford and told my family.

They decided that they would never again miss one of my opening nights. That that might be my only performance. We all laughed heartily. Ha-ha . . . Onward. Back to New York I went. The next day I received two calls. One from Arthur Hopkins . . . one from J. J. Shubert.

I went first to Shubert. He had seen my performance in *The Big Pond*.

"You were sweet, my dear. There were women . . . men . . . gentlemen . . . riffraff . . . whores . . . ladies and children in that audience on Saturday night. They liked you—all of them."

"Yes," I said, "everyone but the management."

"And they were fools to let you go. I'm offering you a five-year deal. Beginning at two hundred and fifty dollars and ending at fifteen hundred. Yearly options."

I thought quickly . . . Don't buy a pig in a poke.

"Well, that is very reassuring, Mr. Shubert, but I don't think that I would like to be tied up to anyone so that I couldn't do what I wanted to do when I wanted to do it. I'd rather be on my own. You might want me to do something that I didn't care for and then where would we be? But I am very grateful to you for your enthusiasm."

"Think it over. Don't be a fool, Katharine."

"Yes, I will, sir. I mean, thank you." And out I went. He couldn't believe it.

I walked through Shubert Alley and down Forty-fifth to Arthur Hopkins's office . . . found the stairway at the back of the orchestra in the Plymouth Theatre . . . walked up and came to his door. It was a small office . . . his secretary, Miss Hess, on the left, his own tiny office on the right. Miss Hess told me to go in. I heard her telephone him. So I went to the door and stood. He was at his desk facing me, reading a script. I stood for several minutes, it seemed. Finally, he looked up.

"Hello, dear. I saw you the other night." He smiled. "You were good. I'd like to have you work for me."

"Thank you, sir," I said. "I'd like to."

He looked back at his script. I stood. Minutes passed. Well, I thought, That's that. He'd like to have me work for him. So I'd better go. He seems to want to read. So I started to leave. His voice called me back.

"Don't you want to know what you're going to do?"

"Yes, sir. I'd like to very much."

He reached for a script at the end of his desk. "Read this . . . the part of Veronica."

"Thank you, sir."

"Yes . . . We go into rehearsals next week." He went back to his script. "Monday—eleven o'clock."

I left. I had a job. That's it, I thought. Arthur Hopkins was

Arthur Hopkins

entirely his own man. He was short, fat, round of body, round of head. His brown eyes were direct and bright and far, far apart. He was Welsh and he was a man of very few words. He said it simply. Thought it simply. Let it stand. A most amazing person. Nothing and no one influenced him. His record in the theatre is most distinguished. The Barrymores . . . *Richard III* . . . *Hamlet* . . . *Anna Christie* . . . *Holiday* . . . *Machinal*. He did it because he liked it.

He hadn't said anything to me about salary . . . about the part. Nothing. And as I stood there in his doorway, I thought, Well, the important thing is he wants me. He knows he's got me. So why waste time talking about it?

The play was *These Days*, by Katharine Clugston. My part was a schoolgirl. A nice part. She had one very good scene where she was questioned by the headmistress and answered her with "Yes, Miss

Van Alstyne . . ." "No, Miss Van Alstyne." Very cool. And giving away nothing about the girl she was being questioned about. This was the leading lady, played by Mildred McCoy. She had committed some sin. There was another girl, Mary Hall, who had a very good part in it, too. She was bright . . . and fat . . . and funny. Was from Yale.

We rehearsed in New York at the Plymouth Theatre. Hoppy had his own way of rehearsing. You sat around a big table and read the play. Over and over and over and over again. Until everyone knew it and felt that the play itself was thoroughly understood. Then in no time . . . on one's feet. The whole thing slid into place. This seemed to me then and now a very sensible way of doing. Jumping up immediately with a script in one's hand and wandering about before you know the part, I could never understand. I do it, but I learn the play first. I suppose I was exposed to Hoppy's method early on. And it made sense. So if I know the play before I rehearse, I'm in a better position to feel where I'd like to be to play a scene . . . and in a better position to argue with the director . . . having also studied the play very hard. So many actors say, "Oh, but I couldn't learn it until I know where I'm going." I never could see the sense in that. It's like saying you don't want to learn to walk until you know where you're going. Being one-track, I have to learn it. Then my instinct tells me sort of where to go. Or the director does. It doesn't really matter . . . standing . . . sitting . . . just so the audience hears it.

We opened *These Days* in New Haven, then Hartford. My hometown. Big excitement. Then New York, Thursday night. The New York opening was at the Cort Theatre on Forty-eighth Street. I dressed with Mary Hall. The reviews were withering. I was praised. Mary was too. Friday night everyone seemed a bit down. Not I, of course. I had been praised and that was the only part of the review which anyone with any sense would . . . certainly it was the only part that I read. To me it was a hit. I couldn't imagine what was wrong.

"Have you seen the board?"

"Too bad."

I didn't know what they were talking about. What board?

Just before my entrance, one of the stagehands patted my shoulder.

"Well, you don't need to worry. You'll get another job in no time."

"What do you mean?" said I, the truth beginning to dawn.

"We're closing Saturday."

"Oh, that," said I, pretending to of course know.

All the actors were piling into Hopkins's office to find out if he had another job for them. I thought, Well, he knows where I am—if he wants me he'll send for me.

And he did. Saturday night. Report Shubert Theatre, New Haven, Sunday noon to understudy Hope Williams.

Incidentally, he had paid me $125 a week for *These Days*. This was a very high salary for someone just starting out. Very generous. He paid me the same for *Holiday*. We never discussed it.

Years later he reminded me that in *These Days* he had told me to go out and buy my own costume. He wanted me to look real. I went to Mrs. Franklin's sweater shop in Philadelphia and ordered handmade a sweater suit . . . $175. It had been my ambition to own one in my Bryn Mawr days. Hoppy said when he saw the bill that it was $25 more than he had paid for all the leading lady's costumes, but that I was so pleased with my own purchase he didn't have the heart to chide me.

I fitted right into the understudy job. Hope Williams a big star—overnight. A charmer with a unique delivery. Great boyish looks. Also in the cast were Donald Ogden Stewart . . . his wife, Beatrice Stewart (he later married Ella Winter, widow of Lincoln Steffens), . . . and Babs Burden. They were all prominent New Yorkers by birth or by accomplishment or both. They were all very nice to me. I didn't get to really know any of them but they were sweet. It was a big New York hit.

After I'd been in *Holiday* as Hope's understudy for about two weeks, Luddy and I decided to get married. My grandfather was visiting in Hartford and I had a pretty dress—a Babani. It was crushed white velvet with antiqued gold embroidery sort of around the neck and a bit down the front and on the sleeves. So I told Arthur Hopkins that I was leaving the theatre, and we were married in the Hartford living room at 201 Bloomfield Avenue with all the families present and we went to Bermuda on our honeymoon. Luddy was always an angel of understanding—luckily for me. I said, "Oh yes—we'll live in Strafford, Pennsylvania," and we began looking for a house. Well, my enthusiasm lasted about two weeks. We moved back to New York and we centered ourselves in his New York apartment—146 East Thirty-ninth Street. And I went to Hopkins and asked for my old job. He said, "Yes, of course. I expected you." "Really," I said. "Oh yes." He smiled.

So it was December, 1928, I was married. I quit. I went to live in Pennsylvania. I came back to New York and got my job back. Poor Luddy. A proper wife for two weeks. Oh, Luddy! Look out.

I sat through every performance for about six months.

After about three months Arthur Hopkins came to understudy rehearsal. I had been trained by Jimmy Hagen, the stage manager. He later wrote a charming play, *One Sunday Afternoon*. Arthur sat through the rehearsal. I was acting away. I was secretly convinced that I was much better than Hope in some of the emotional scenes. When we were finished, Arthur came up onto the stage.

"Fine," he said, patting me. "Just don't ever be sorry for yourself."

A keen criticism of an overemotional youngster. Later on, in the fall when the play was preparing to go on the road (I had been in Europe for the summer), Jimmy Hagen called me at midnight.

"Do you still know the part, Kate?"

"Why?" I asked.

"Hope's sick. We're playing the Shubert Riviera Theatre on Upper Broadway. She doesn't think that she can play tomorrow's Saturday matinée and evening and then open Monday in Boston. Could you go on for her in the evening?"

"Well, yes . . . I should think . . ."

I got up, got the script and started to go through the lines. Actually, I still know the part. Things sink deep at that age. "Why, Julia. For shame, Julia. Is this a way to spend Sunday morning? Who's your partner—anyone I know?"

So I went on . . . in Hope's clothes. How, I'll never know. I was inches taller than she was. It was there and then that I found out how very good Hope was. And how I had to find my own personality in the part. Not imitate her. It was a baptism by fire. Places where she had got roars of laughter, I got nothing. But by the third act I had found my way a bit. The rest of the cast were as excited as I was and very helpful. Hope had asked me during the New York run if I would like her to stay home one night so that I could get a chance to play the part. I had had the sense to say no . . . no . . . no. Just stay well. I was right. It is a poor second-best, at best, to go on for someone.

Anyway, I lived through it . . . so did the cast. And so did the audience. I had only one disappointment. Hopkins did not come to see me play the part. Years later I asked him why he hadn't come. "Weren't you ever curious?"

"No," he said, "I'd seen you. I knew you were good."

But it didn't satisfy me . . . still doesn't. I wish he had come. Why do you suppose he didn't?

After *The Big Pond*—after I had been fired—my pictures went into New York and they were in a stand on the sidewalk outside the Bijou Theatre on Forty-fifth Street. A man named Henry Salsbury at Paramount saw them and he called me and asked if I would make a test. Well, I thought, that would be dumb. I'm not even an actor. I'm just a photograph. They would sign me for very little and I would have no control at all over what I did. I saw Mr. Salsbury and said just that. But I added, "If I ever do make a test for anyone, I will make one for you." I thought that was very gracious of me.

He took me in a big limousine to see the opening of a play with Jack Dempsey. Heavens, I thought, is this the big time? Don't keep company with strangers. Don't hobnob with the bosses—you lose your mystery. I had no agent. Some people had agents then, but they did not control the business as they do today. I used—well, I say used—once or twice I went to offices. I went and sat. At the end of the day a secretary would come up to me and say, "Why are you here?" The only incident of note was when I said to producer Al Woods's secretary, "I'm here to see about the girl in *A Farewell to Arms*." "Oh," she said, "that's been cast for a long time. But . . ." She had a warm heart. "Come on in and meet Mr. Woods anyway." So I did. He had a warm heart too. I asked him who was going to play the part. He said Elissa Landi. That was all there was to it. I was exhausted. Sit all day. All the poor things dressed up fit to kill. With no chance that I could see of ever getting there early enough to get a part.

Lest they think that I was making any effort, I used to get myself up in a sort of slouch costume. I had an old stocking cap . . . or no hat in a day of hats. And an old green tweed coat. I would pin the coat together with a safety pin. Throw a sweater over my shoulders; string my hair a bit . . . very casual for those days. I wanted to look as though it were really nothing to me if I got the part or didn't. I had a car and that gave me a sort of confidence. At least I could arrive cool. But actually I did not go out often to seek work. I was lucky. I was at the Empire Theatre one night and a perfect stranger came up to me and said, "I beg your pardon, but are you in the theatre?"

"I'd like to be."

"May I give you a letter to the Theatre Guild?"

"Thank you," I said. That was in 1929. The man was Maurice Wertheim, who was one of the backers of the Theatre Guild. And do you know who he was—I just found out—he was Barbara Tuchman's father. She was the author of such books as *The Guns of August* and *The Proud Tower*.

I presented my credentials to the Theatre Guild. The letter from Maurice Wertheim worked like magic. I met Terry Helburn (also of Bryn Mawr), Lawrence Langner, Philip Moeller. They were doing a play of Sam Behrman's, *Meteor*. Would I like to read for the ingénue . . . the Lunts are starring. Yes, I would. They gave me the script.

Years later I reminded Terry Helburn (she and Lawrence Langner ran the Guild) of the occasion. Terry said, "Oh yes! There was a list of girls or boys—Lawrence's, Wertheim's, mine. They *had* to be *used*."

Now I may not have been able to *keep* a part. But I could *get* any part. I just had a sort of knack. I could boil up out of nothing at a moment's notice . . . it didn't really matter whether I had read the script or not. I could arrest their attention. I could laugh . . . I could cry . . . I was fast. It used to fascinate me. I would think of nothing for days except that I was going to read for something. Or see someone. I would eat . . . exercise . . . sleep the moment. Then I would drive over in Luddy's car and I would be wound up tight, like a steel trap. And I would go to the bathroom forty times before I left. Then I would have to case the office for the bathroom before I went in. I was always very early. Then I went in. And I read. I was in a sort of coma of excitement. I was never easy with people. I suppose I was in an agony as to whether I was making a good impression. But the concentration was total. Not based on an intellectual conception of the part. Just based on the universal spark: spark the part . . . spark the person . . . spark the audience. Strike it. Light it. When all that energy became boxed, so to speak, and it couldn't get out, then I just didn't come off. I was always very aware of whether I was boxed or fluid. Take a bath . . . cold . . . hot . . . relax. How's the motor running? The intellectual part of studying came as a sort of framework. But the spark of life was the . . . is the spark of life.

Laurette Taylor's great story. She was doing *The Glass Menagerie*. Laurette always seemed to me—Spencer Tracy too, both Irish, both troubled ones—she seemed to me to sort of sketch and be the inside of the part, the outside of the part: just indicate dialing the phone —indicate anything which the audience had in its immediate experience—suggest it . . . let them get it . . . then get on with it . . . effortless, easy . . . then suffuse, illuminate the character. One could never see the wheels go around. It was always a happening. There was a framework indicated. But it was all magic. Spencer playing the flute as Judge Timberlane, lighting the cigarette with one hand, *Bad Day at Black Rock*, not heavily worked-over characterization . . . sketch it. They were my ideals.

I had first seen Laurette in *The Glass Menagerie* in Chicago. I was crossing the country with Terry Helburn. Theatre Guild. Flying. L.A. to N.Y., one stop, Chicago.

Terry said to me, "Kate, would you like to stop and see Laurette's *Glass Menagerie*—Tennessee Williams . . . ?"

"Yes, I would," I answered.

We got off in Chicago. I had heard wonderful stories about Laurette from George Cukor and I wasn't about to miss this opportunity of seeing Miss Taylor. We went to the Blackstone Hotel, then to the theatre and backstage before the play—early.

Laurette Taylor

There was Laurette. She was sitting at her dressing table, a nothing of a robe on, thin fine blondish-reddish hair in pin curls and just putting makeup on. Dipping into this—dipping into that. Those eyes—blond eyelashes and eyebrows, so far apart, so wide open— conveying a multitude of wild and moving and funny thoughts. Soft big mouth. Nose sort of verging on the clown. A vulnerable, sandy Irish-skinned, ruddy look.

George Cukor said once, about visiting old stars while they're making up, that they are surrounded by empty jars into which they dip their fingers. Rub the cheeks—pink; the lips red; the upper lids blue, violet. A line here, a line there, a powder puff, the lashes become black. All memory and magic.

She undid her hair. Sort of brushed it out. Poked it up. She was like Spence. They were both like baked potatoes: fundamental, basic, nothing fancy, rough in a way. And all the time talking and funny and like a clown—the top variety. This was her life. She could do it. She knew how in her bones. The minute she got to the little room, to the antechamber. A few strokes here—there. No agony of preparation—like the Method—no constipation. They were born able to show you—tell you—make you feel—arrest you—make you watch. It *was* the real life. The daily Monday Tuesday Wednesday Thursday Friday Saturday Sunday with which they were unable to cope. That's what tore them apart.

She was talking about what, I don't remember. Oh yes—Julie Haydon, who played the part of her daughter in *The Glass Menagerie*. And how at the curtain when they were taking their bows Julie had turned her back on the audience and knelt before Laurette (I really don't blame Julie). One would feel inclined. But Laurette thought that was the bunk.

LAURETTE

Don't do that, my dear—I'll give you a push. Send you sprawling.

Anyway, to get back to the point. Laurette's great story: Julie Haydon had been struggling with her part. Several months later I saw the play again, in New York. Julie seemed to be so very much better. I said so to Laurette. "Yes," she said. "She's having a good time doing it, too. That is very important."

She went on: "I remember when I did *Peg o' My Heart* the second time. After a five-year lapse. We opened in Philadelphia and the critics went on about how brilliant I was, how remarkably I had grown in the part. On and on. Going back to New York to open the play there, I said to my husband, Hartley Manners, 'Isn't it nice that they think I'm so great?' He smiled and said, 'Of course it is. But I like the way you used to do it. You remember? You had such a good time.' "

Laurette said she was furious with him. Wouldn't speak to him. Then got to thinking and realized what a subtle and brilliant remark it was. It became her key. If you are aware of the expert work and the effort, it is tiring to an audience. This is true, oddly, whether the play is comic or serious.

Anyway, I read *Meteor* in a state of great excitement. The next day I went back to read. Phil Moeller the director . . . the Lunts . . . Terry and Lawrence. And Cheryl Crawford. And of course, S. N. Behrman.

I did my bit. I got the job.

Then the same thing happened which always happens in the theatre. I got another call. The Shuberts. Would I come and read for the leading part in *Death Takes a Holiday*? The lead opposite Philip Merivale.

Well, yes, I would come . . . when was it to be done? Right away. Oh dear, I thought . . . what about *Meteor*? Well, try . . . pick the best. They sent me the script.

I read it and was swept off my feet. It seemed to me a wonderful part. Very romantic . . . a young girl going away with Death. And a leading lady . . . and Philip Merivale and James Dale. Lawrence Marston directing. I read for it and I got it.

So I decided that I must tell the Guild that I had a better offer. I did this. I felt a bit cheesy walking away from the Lunts and the Guild. But Grazia in *Death Takes a Holiday* seemed to me just a perfect offer and I couldn't resist it.

We went into rehearsal. From the start there seemed to be, well, problems. I had to scream. I used to go down into the john of the theatre and scream away . . . never did get that scream to work. The Merivales—Viva and Philip—were very friendly, also James Dale. They thought that I was very good in the part. We went to Washington—the National Theatre. Opened. I got one rave—"a new Maude Adams." One roast—"a new girl looking for all the world like a death's head, with a metallic voice."

Then we opened in Philadelphia. Again, one rave, one roast for me. I had not the vaguest suspicion that anything was dangerously wrong.

That Wednesday night the production man came back at half hour and said, "We are giving you the privilege of resigning from the cast."

"What?" I said, not understanding at all.

"Mr. Shubert is giving you the privilege of resigning from the cast."

"Oh yes, I see . . ." I replied, holding on to my senses. "Well, you tell Mr. Shubert that I have no intention of resigning from the cast. So if he wants to fire me, you go ahead and fire me. But shut that door now and get out. I have to give a performance tonight."

"Katharine, I had to tell you now, before the show. Otherwise we'd have to pay you an extra week's salary."

"Poor kid," I said. "Just get out."

Well . . . fired. I'd better let Mr. Merivale and Mrs. and Mr. Dale see that I'm still living. I went to their rooms. They were all weeping. Well, that dried me up. The show's started. They all had tears streaming down their faces whenever they looked at me. After the play, Merivale said, "You must come and have supper with Viva and me." I went and, lost for conversation, he read aloud a play he was writing about Napoleon. It was so long and dull that it almost killed me, and it exhausted me so that, fired or not, I slept like a log.

I called home. Told Dad and Mother what had happened. Mother had already seen it in Washington. So Dad came to Philadelphia. He thought the play a real bunch of junk. His comment was illuminating.

"Any young girl who was dumb enough to go off with Death has to be a psychopath. Your characterization is excellent. She is obviously crazy. You played an obvious psychopath."

Now, at least, I knew why I'd been fired. What I luckily didn't know was that Rose Hobart, who was to replace me, had been watching the show every night for my last ten days. That would have put me off a bit. To say the least.

Back in New York. *Meteor* had opened. I'd better get something . . . anything. Fast. Don't wallow about, being sorry for yourself. I

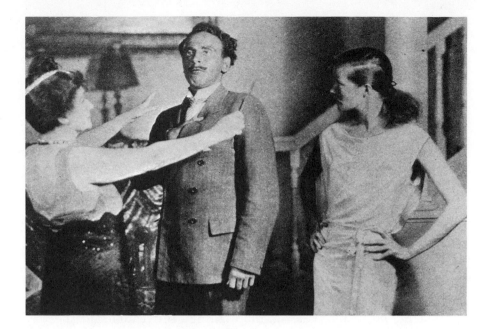

The Admirable Crichton

went to the Guild. Saw Cheryl Crawford. They had no understudy for Eunice Stoddard, who was playing the ingénue with Nazimova in *A Month in the Country*. I could do that. Minimum salary. "Fine," I said. "I'll do it." It was thrilling watching Nazimova every performance, and Henry Travers and Dudley Digges. Twenty-five dollars a week. Then Hortense Alden, who was playing the maid, was leaving for a better part. I said, "Fine, I'll take the part. How about a bit more money?"

"No . . . no more money. We can get plenty of people to do it for minimum. Will you do it or won't you—make up your mind."

"I'll do it anyway," I said—and I slunk away. Five bucks . . . why couldn't they give me *five bucks*? Well, someday . . . someday it will cost them. It did.

That was the spring of 1930. I seemed to be getting nowhere. That summer I went for two weeks to Europe with Eunice Stoddard. Then I went to Stockbridge to Alexander Kirkland & Strickland Company. To play whatever turned up. My friend Laura Harding went with me. We were both Frances Robinson-Duff pupils. She seemed very sophisticated to me. Laura had been to Stockbridge the year before. She had a car. Luddy was hard at work in New York but would come up as often as he could.

We boarded in an old New England house owned by a minister and his wife. Richard Hale lived there too. Geoffrey Kerr and June Walker were also in the company. And Phyllis Connard. The first play was to be *The Admirable Crichton*. Richard Hale playing Crichton. June Walker playing Tweeny. Geoffrey Kerr playing the son. And Phyllis Connard, Lady Mary. Her two sisters, Lady Agatha and Lady Catherine: Me, Agatha; Laura, Catherine.

From the start it seemed just plain wrong to me that I wasn't playing Lady Mary. I thought all my qualities more suitable to the part than Phyllis Connard's. Other leading ladies always seemed just too old and dull to me. I could only imagine myself in all the leading parts. This, no doubt, is a common failing. But Laura said she was absolutely horrified when I voiced this sentiment. She felt she was lucky to be there; I felt they were lucky to have me. The fact that I'd done practically nothing never occurred to me.

Laura had lots of beautiful jewelry. We covered ourselves with it.

That was a very lively time. We were both mad about Richard Hale. And he was mad about his own lady friend. George Coulouris was there, too. And we had wild deck-tennis matches.

The second week of *The Romantic Young Lady*, with me playing some sort of femme fatale, all in black, very slinky. I thought that I was wasting my time and wasn't going to get any decent parts, so I left. Laura was shocked. I was happy to get away. I spent the rest of the summer at Fenwick. Luddy and I had a great time.

A long pause in fall 1930. There were little hopes here and there but nothing real. I studied. Then in early 1930 came *Art and Mrs. Bottle*.

Kenneth MacGowan and Joseph Verner Reed were going to do this play by Benn Levy with Jane Cowl and Leon Quartermaine. And G. P. Huntley, Jr., and Noel Coward's friend Joyce Carey. Clifford Brooke directing. They had already done *Twelfth Night*. *Art and Mrs. Bottle* was to be the second play of a repertory season at the Maxine Elliott Theatre on Thirty-ninth Street off Sixth Avenue. They had an office very close to where Luddy and I lived on Thirty-ninth. They were at the corner of Lexington and Forty-first Street.

Art and Mrs. Bottle, with Jane Cowl

They sent for me. I went up to see them. I read for them and they seemed to like me. They had seen me in *These Days.* I was signed for the part. Any kind of English or WASP part I had a good chance for in those days. They didn't import so many English actors. And there weren't too many good accents available. I was to get $125. It was a very good ingénue part. I had little of the carrying chore of the play. That was all Jane Cowl's. My part just had several very good scenes. The perfect setup for an ingénue to run away with the evening.

We went into rehearsal. I wore old rags to rehearsal, as actors do today, but then unheard of. And I wore no makeup. Only very bright red lipstick.

Benn Levy thought me totally unattractive as to looks and personality and talent. "What does she do? Does she wash her face with yellow kitchen soap every morning?" Benn Levy was almost right. I did fancy a sort of polished look.

Jane Cowl took me aside. She said that she liked me very much but that Benn Levy was not accustomed to this type of American looks. And would I mind if she made me up to sort of soften my appearance, which she assured me she liked but he didn't.

So she made me up. But it didn't help. Levy still found me unattractive and they let me go. I thought, of course, that they were stupid, and would rue the day. Well, they did. And a week later they called me back. I said that they would have to pay me $150 instead of $125, as they had hurt my dignity. I was traveling on pretty safe ground because I knew that everyone liked me but Levy and they were running short of time. And they had tried all the available girls in town. They gave me the $150—a bit shocked by my Yankee trading.

We opened—I made a hit. As in *These Days*, I got very good notices. I have to add here that Jane Cowl was an angel to me. She seemed enormously pleased with my success and did everything she could to help me and put me forward. As always with the old and the new, I had been praised somewhat at her expense.

Noel Coward came to see the play and climbed up five flights to the dressing room I shared with Alfred de Liagre to tell me that I was good and to keep at it. I was in the process of discovering the enormous generosity and enthusiasm of people in the theatre. Often one heard of jealousy. I have never met it. I think that it is such an obvious and fertile field for jealousy that everyone with any sense starts early in the fight against it.

The season closed and I went for the second summer to Ivoryton, Connecticut. Lawrence Anhalt and Milton Stiefel ran a very good stock company there.

Ivoryton was where I really learned a lot. They gave me a job as a sort of half leading lady. I played when they couldn't get someone well known. I had done very little at that point in the theatre. But I was known in the neighborhood because of Dad and Mother. The company had a good reputation. It was only about fifteen miles from Fenwick.

That year Henry Hull—a big star at that time—had agreed to do several plays with them. Henry had a house in Lyme; that's across the Connecticut River from Old Saybrook and Fenwick, my home. I used to drive my car to Lyme, go north a bit, then east and arrive at Henry's property. I would park in an open field above a lake, then walk through a small woodland to Henry's house. We'd rehearse for several hours.

One day I did just this. But when I got finished and went to the field to get my car, it was gone. I was thunderstruck. Stolen. Obviously stolen. I went back to the house. Henry and Mrs. Hull came to the field. No car. Then I stood and I looked down at the lake. Oh dear, what is that? It's a square sort of flat tan . . . It's . . . oh my golly . . . it's my . . . It's my car. Look . . . My car . . . the top.

I rushed down the hill. Yes, my car—about twenty feet into the lake. My car with the top barely showing. We rushed back to the house and called the Lyme Garage. Asked them to come fast. Bring a tow truck and line, etc. They came. Dragged the car out.

"What now? What?" I asked.

"Wait about an hour. Then try it," they said. We waited. Then turned the key and tried it. It started!

Henry was willing to take me as his leading lady in *The Man Who Came Back* (a play which he had done in the past). The last scene in this play took place in an opium den. Henry's wife was concealed onstage in one of the cupboards with the script, just in case he lost his way. The last two lines of the play always fascinated me.

HENRY

I'm going back every inch of the way from this den to my father's home.

K.H.

But me. What of me?

HENRY

You, I'm going to take you with me.

With Ivoryton founder Milton Stiefel

We also did *The Cat and the Canary* and a play that had been a big hit in New York called *Let Us Be Gay* starring Francine Larrimore. A big star part for a sophisticated woman of about forty. How did I dare? I was so nervous that I woke up one morning and my upper lip was totally swollen. I looked idiotic. I burst into tears and called Dad.

"Ice," said Dad.

It worked.

"And calm down," he said.

I tried to.

Anyway, I played that part. Incredible nerve.

Some of the other programs from those two summers I still have. But I have no idea what the plays were about. Or what sort of parts I was playing. I learned a lot.

Thank you, Lawrence Anhalt and Milton Stiefel.

During this summer at Ivoryton, the Gilbert Miller office called. Philip Barry had written a play called *The Animal Kingdom*. Leslie Howard was to star in it. There were two principal women's parts: his wife, his mistress. Phil wanted me to play the mistress, Daisy Sage. I read the script. I was transported. Gilbert Miller was to produce it. It was a wonderful part. It was really Howard's two separate lives, so that the two segments were separately rehearsed. The play was to go into rehearsal in about four months. Of course I would wait, and I agreed on terms with the Miller office—but I had not actually signed the contract. Luddy and I went to Europe that year. The time passed quickly. This would absolutely make me a star.

The rehearsals started about November of 1931. I went dressed as neatly as possible and in high heels. This was my first mistake. It made me taller than Leslie Howard. I tried to shrink, and at the noon hour I rushed home and put on flat shoes—not so becoming, but the point was how did I make *him* look.

From the start I felt that there was something distasteful about me to Mr. Howard. Try as hard as I could to be subservient . . . sweet . . . feminine . . . anything which would tame down my too vivid personality. I struggled. Nothing worked. I remember one hideous moment when I said, "What would you like me to do here, Mr. Howard?" And he answered—it must have happened, I couldn't make it up: "I really don't give a damn what you do, my dear."

Well now . . . that didn't sound very friendly. And I couldn't imagine what to reply. So I just kept a-going. Maybe he felt irritable. It never occurred to me that he was just finding me something he didn't care for.

The next day we were to rehearse on "our" set. Somewhere across town west of Eighth. I had my car. It was still not the end of the first week of rehearsal. I asked Walter Abel, the man who was my friend in the play, if I could give him a lift. We arrived at the place and found that they had decided to rehearse the wife scenes, so we were dismissed for the day. I told Walter that I would drive him home. On our way uptown—up Eighth Avenue—I told him how terribly excited I was to have this opportunity; that I felt it would really get me going; that Phil had really written it for me. That . . .

"Oh," he said, "no . . . nothing matters that much in this business. It is really funny. Of course, it's a great part. But there will be others."

"Oh, not for me," I said. "This is it."

I dropped him. And as I was driving to the garage, a feeling came to me—was he trying to say something—why didn't we rehearse— was there something— Oh no . . .

I went home. As I went in the apartment door, my telephone was ringing. It was my brother Dick, at Harvard. He started to tell me about the great party they would give for my opening in Boston.

Foreboding. "No," I said, "bad luck. Don't plan anything." And at that very moment a knock on the door to the apartment.

"Telegram for you, Miss Hepburn," said Mr. Brice, the concierge.

"Just put it under the door, please, Mr. Brice."

I concluded my conversation with Dick. Went over. Casually opened the wire. It was from Gilbert Miller.

Pursuant to Clause I in your contract, you are hereby given notice of the termination thereof. /s/ Gilbert Miller

Heavens. Fired. Oh dear. Oh no. And I had waited months for the part. And it was perfect for me. Why? Just plain why? Oh no. Well, there must be some mistake. I'll call Phil Barry. I had his number. After endless tries, I got him. He was taking a shower. I said who I was and that it was very important. Phil came on the line.

"I've been fired."

"Yes, I know."

"But why . . . why should I be fired?"

"Well, to be brutally frank, you weren't very good."

"Oh . . . yes . . . I see . . . Oh dear . . . Yes . . . No . . . Thank you. Goodbye."

I hung up. That was a desperate moment. I'd been fired because I wasn't any good. But I was good, wasn't I? I was doing my best. The part was just my dish. What was wrong? And I hadn't been fresh. I'd just shut up. Of course I felt Howard didn't like me—I mean, I was too big or too small or . . . well . . . something he didn't like. And no money. Not a cent. And I had waited four months

Gilbert Miller

for the part. Not nice. No, not nice at all. Not fair. And everyone would know about it. And what can one say? Well . . . just have to say I was fired. Oh, that was a blow. Stopped me dead in my tracks. Better get another offer fast. I felt so unwanted. I wondered what it was about me that didn't work. I felt that I really could play that part. I was still studying with Frances Robinson-Duff. She hadn't belabored me. I had watched my p's and q's. Tried to be soft and sweet. Why in hell did they fire me? I wasn't bad in that part. Some things I've been fired out of I've understood. But that one—no. That was my part! Why . . .

Later, someone who knew the Millers said that the day they fired me, Gilbert's wife, Kitty Miller, had said, "You boys are stupid.

That girl is going to be a big star someday. You're just scared she'll run away with the show." I wonder if she did say it. Maybe yes. Maybe no. Anyway, it made me happy and I never knew Kitty Miller, but of course I've always admired her.

There I was. Fired again. And very badly thrown. Get busy—get busy.

The phone rang. Would I like to play with Laurette Taylor in *Alice Sit-by-the-Fire?* It was being produced by Bill Brady, Jr. They didn't have to ask me twice.

We started rehearsals. I had only a small part. We were sitting around reading the play. Bill, Jr., corrected my reading of something and Laurette said, "No no, Bill. Let us see what she has to offer first." I never had a chance to see whether she thought I had anything to offer. The night of the first day of rehearsal, I got a call from a man named Harry Moses for the Broadway production of *The Warrior's Husband.* I read the script. It was a wonderful part for me. I would give up *Alice Sit-by-the-Fire* if I got the part.

I got it. Then they decided Jean Dixon would be better. For about forty-eight hours I thought I'd lost both parts. Then they shifted back to me.

The Warrior's Husband

The Warrior's Husband was originally a one-act play written by Julian Thompson, head of McKesson & Robbins. It was a Greek fable about the love affair between Antiope and Theseus. It played at The Comedy Club, an amateur group housed in a charming little theatre on Thirty-sixth Street. Hope Williams played the lead. Antiope. Hope is a real product of New York's Four Hundred. The easy distinction, the independence, the integrity. A lovely New York accent. A forthright manner. Great good looks. A slim figure, a boy's haircut. And a walk. Her walk was an arms-swinging stride. It called for a horse, a prairie. It was stylish and original. She died just a bit ago. She was ninety-one.

Her first really professional appearance was a small part in *Paris Bound*, Philip Barry's play, with Madge Kennedy. Her first entrance was to walk across the stage from one side to the other and exit. She was dressed in a very frilly, airy bridesmaid's dress and wore a big hat. Enter one side. Exit the other. Straight walk. Arms swinging. By the time she got halfway across stage, the audience exploded. Hope saw nothing funny about it. Unaware of the ludicrous contrast of walk and dress. She continued. The audience burst into applause. Actually, just off on the far side of the stage, Arthur Hopkins, the producer, was waiting for her, arms extended.

"I thought so," said Hoppy.

"What?" replied Hope.

"You're a star."

And she was. And the half-boy, half-woman had been born. *Paris Bound* was followed by *Holiday*, also Philip Barry. Then *Rebound*. This was written for her by Donald Ogden Stewart. Another big hit. All produced by Arthur Hopkins. It was during the run of *Rebound* that Julian Thompson called her and said, "Would you be interested in a full-length play of *The Warrior's Husband?*" She was, and he wrote it. Hope loved the script. Hopkins seemed enthusiastic too.

Hope went away for the summer. When she got back, Hopkins had found a wonderful new play for her by Gretchen Damrosch. *The Passing Present*. Hope read it, was not enthusiastic. But felt that she must abide by Hopkins's decision. And *I* got Hope's Antiope.

Hoppy was wrong. The Damrosch play was a disaster—three weeks. And Hope was the loser.

Hope Williams obviously had a tremendous influence on my career. Vocally, walk-wise, I incorporated a lot of Hope into my so-called personality. It was in the air, that boy-woman. My arrival in the big city was well timed.

So *The Warrior's Husband* was up for grabs and it was bought by Harry Moses, who had money and also had a wife who was theatre-struck.

They knew that I had understudied Hope in *Holiday* and I had been quite noticeable, especially in Benn Levy's play with Jane Cowl, *Art and Mrs. Bottle*, and in *These Days*. So during the early part of the casting I was very much in the running for Antiope. Then suddenly—as I've told you—they decided that they should have a star. I was out; Jean Dixon was in. Several days passed. Another switch. And I was definitely Antiope. Irby Marshal was Hippolyta. Romney Brent her effeminate husband. Colin Keith-Johnston was Theseus. A man named Burk Symon was to direct. It was 1931, almost into 1932.

We opened cold at the Morosco Theatre in New York. My whole family came. They were taking no chances. I had an entrance down a narrow stairway which ran across the backdrop. It was about twenty

Kate as Antiope

Hope Williams

steps and steep. Then it swung around to the audience about four steps forward. There were lights on the upstage side of the stairs, making it look thrilling. I had a stag over my shoulder. A tight tunic made of metal links. Beautiful silver leather shin guards showing the legs to good advantage, and a silver shield and a high silver helmet, and a cape. A great costume. And I was very surefooted. So the fact that the stairs were only about three and a half feet wide with a high narrow step and had no railings did not bother me at all. And anyway, I didn't mind risking my life for fame.

I leapt down the stairs, three or more steps at a time . . . rounded the corner . . . one jump for the last four steps . . . threw the stag on the ground and landed on one knee, paying obeisance to Hippolyta, my sister, Queen of the Amazons. The audience, of course, burst into applause. They could hardly do anything else. I had all but asked for it. But I was unaware. I was just full of the joy of life and opportunity and a wild desire to be absolutely fascinating. At that point in my progress, I was sailing through the air anyway—down a stair—up a stair—no guardrails. Hell . . . no stair whatever . . . no matter— life—joy—youth.

And I was pretty new. And presented to advantage. And I made a hit. The play they quarreled with.

I had a maid (first time): she was tall and black and hefty and very dominating. I can't remember her name—"Lily" comes to me, but I'm not sure. And she knew her job. She got $75 a week. She got that from me. That's what she said she wanted. And that's what she got. I myself was getting $150. The show ran for about six months; then we were asked to take a cut. I was cut to $75. She wasn't cut-minded. She took the salary that I got as a star. What's money? Everyone wanted to test me for movies. Everyone wanted me in something. The agents wanted me. I was arriving.

In *The Warrior's Husband*, I began to feel for the first time like a real actress. My dressing room was on the stage level. It was a charming old theatre—the Morosco. Oddly enough, right next to the Bijou on Forty-fifth Street opposite Shubert Alley where *The Big Pond* had played with my photographs on the outside. Both these theatres have been demolished.

With Luddy

I didn't go out a great deal. Luddy and I still lived in the apartment at 146 East Thirty-ninth Street. It was a brownstone apartment house of five stories—apartments front and back. First we were on the second floor back. After a short time we moved to the whole top floor where we had double the space. It was charming. A long climb but we were young and didn't even think about it. An Englishman named Herbert Brice and his wife ran it. The house had a dumbwaiter shaft and you could have meals sent up from downstairs. The food was delicious. Really a wonderful way to live. We were lucky. Sometimes, Colin Keith-Johnston would come back for supper. No one else really. I never got very close to anyone in the theatre or movies. I suppose it was because I was a member of a big family and I always tried to get enough sleep. It sounds odd today when people say "What was he [or she] like?" and I have to answer I honestly don't know. But there it is.

Oh—one terrible thing happened there. I had been in all afternoon. It was cold. I'd been burning a fire. Luddy usually got home at about five-thirty. I went in to take a tub—I heard Luddy come in. "Hi—hi!"

All of a sudden I heard: "Kate! Kate! Come here!" His tone of voice made me leap out of the tub. I rushed in. Luddy was in flames—a trail of flames to the fireplace. The kerosene can in Luddy's hand burning and he couldn't drop it. I was stark naked. I belted Luddy in the stomach, knocked him down, grabbed a throw rug, smothered the fire on Luddy and knocked the kerosene can out of his poor hand—yelled, FIRE!

The house was entirely inhabited by men—one by one, they rushed in—and put out the fire on the floor, etc. I stood up. Luddy's fire was out—the front of his suit coat and pants was burned. He had apparently come in, put logs on the fire—he took the kerosene can and then threw some on the fire and the fire exploded. He jumped back and splashed the kerosene over his front and on the floor.

I was still stark naked and unaware, and telling everyone what to do, when a young man rushed in to help and was frozen in his tracks. I rushed into the bathroom, "Oh! Pardon me—"

Luddy was O.K. He had third-degree burns but was O.K.

Terrifying!

First Trip to Hollywood

It didn't look as though *The Warrior's Husband* would survive. It had opened in March. What next? Henry Hull had asked me to play opposite him in a week of stock at Ossining in late June, 1932. *The Bride the Sun Shines On*. I had said of course.

A man came to my dressing room and offered me $500 to play one performance in Philadelphia of *Electra*, with Blanche Yurka as Electra. Katherine Alexander would be one Greek chorus, I the other. Very highbrow the whole thing. Stokowski conducting the music— and $500! The production was to be given on Sunday in Philadelphia at the Academy of Music. My expensive maid, Lily, insisted on going with me. I didn't really want her but I didn't dare say no.

On the train going over I asked Katherine Alexander if she would like to share a room at the Bellevue-Stratford. She said fine. I didn't really know her—just how do you do. We went to the theatre to rehearse and to organize the makeup. It was to be done by Madame Daykarhanova and Akim Tamiroff—very stylized Greek. It seemed totally disorganized to me. I couldn't believe that it would actually happen. I went back to the hotel room. Katherine said she had to go out again. I offered to go with her. She said no, she would go alone. Later I learned that she too had been offered $500. And then when she got to the theatre she smelled a rat. So she went back and said that she would not go on unless they paid her first. So they did. I wasn't so clever. It never occurred to me that there might be no money.

So the play was done. Blanche Yurka spent a great deal of time on her knees on the floor and her hands got very dirty. Then she put them on her face, and as the performance went on she got blacker and blacker. Face—costume—everything. It finally ended. They said they'd send the money. I paid Lily. And the $500 for one performance remained a dream.

David Selznick and George Cukor were looking for a girl to play Sydney Fairfield in *A Bill of Divorcement*, by Clemence Dane. An agent in New York, Miriam Howell, who worked for Leland Hayward, the American Play Company, came to see me. Would I test for the part? I said I would like to very much. It was a wonderful part. And with John Barrymore. She showed me the test scene, and I said that I would prefer to use my own material from *Holiday*. They said O.K. I thought their scene not very good. And I also thought that seeing the same scene over and over again with different girls must be confusing to them and boring too. I asked Alan Campbell if he would do the test with me. I told him that he needn't bother to learn the scene, that he would be sitting in a wing-backed chair, back to the audience, and could read it. I had heard of people doing tests and the one who was supposed to be just assisting in the test got the job. I didn't want any of that. He said yes.

Alan Campbell was later married to Dorothy Parker. He was a good friend of mine—an actor—a sensitive and decent fellow. She was lucky to have him. So was I. He made no objections. Sat in the wing-backed chair and kept me cool.

A man named Eddie Senz made me up. I seemed to myself to be covered with junk—very white—very thick—and red red lips—lots on the eyes.

Miriam Howell was there and between us we arranged how the scene should be shot. It was material from *Holiday*: the scene where Linda Seton hears her father announce her sister's engagement to Johnny Case. Then a scene follows with her brother. She is listening—a glass in her hand. Very slowly she lowers the glass and sets it on the floor.

LINDA

What's it like to get drunk, Neddy?

NEDDY

It's—how drunk?

LINDA

Good and drunk.

I knew this scene backwards, as I had understudied it for six months. I was afraid that I would be very excited and I hadn't wanted to use material in which I could be easily thrown.

After doing the scene I then took off all the fancy makeup. And I put on the makeup which I used in the theatre. It felt more like me. And I did my hair straight back as I did in life. I was determined to have it be me by me. I saw the tests a few days later. I thought, Yes, that's not bad. I saw it ten years later. It was heartbreaking. So desperately anxious, and I looked idiotic in my own makeup and straight-back hair. I had thought that I was being very nonchalant.

I was as far from nonchalant as one could get. It was what I really was—a kid desperate to be in movies. It had a kind of truth behind the eyes. This test has disappeared.

Then I called Paramount and told Mr. Salsbury that I had done a test for RKO. Did he want me to do one for them? He said yes, would I do it with material from *The Warrior's Husband*? I did and it was not very good. But I had fulfilled my promise.

The test for Paramount is in the UCLA collection of memorabilia. It was poor material for a test. I just did it. There seemed, as I looked at it years later, no spark—no real life.

George Cukor, who was to direct *A Bill of Divorcement*, liked the way I put down the glass in my test on hearing the engagement announced. I was offered the part. Years later Larry Olivier told me that his first wife, Jill Esmond, had also tested for *A Bill of Divorcement*. They were wildly disappointed when I got it.

Then came the dealing with Selznick. He offered $500 a week, then $750, then $1,000, then $1,250 and finally $1,500, which was the figure I had set. He had offered $1,250 with a four-week guarantee.

I took $1,500 with a three-week guarantee. And I insisted on a theatre clause and an O.K. of material. Or at least that I should be consulted about the material. It was an awkward contract for them if I made a hit.

The Warrior's Husband closed. Before I left, I insisted on fulfilling my *Bride the Sun Shines On* date. We played a week in Ossining in a tiny theatre. Henry Hull told me at the end of the week that the man who ran it had absconded with the box-office receipts on Thursday. He had the remaining money in his hat, what there was left of it. He gave me my share. And I went down to the station at Harmon to take the Twentieth Century to Chicago, and the Super Chief to Los Angeles to seek my fortune. Laura Harding, my friend, decided that she would go too. It would be fun and, of course, it was great for me. So Laura was already on the train with all her junk—and all mine. Laura had two dogs with her—Jamie, a Scottie; and Twig, a Shelbourne terrier.

I have to explain Laura Barney Harding to you.

The first real friend I had in New York was Laura Harding. As I've said, I had met her at Francis Robinson-Duff's. She was studying voice too—and hoped to have a career in the theatre. She had come out in New York several years before this. Her father was J. Horace Harding, a financier. She lived with her parents at 955 Fifth Avenue. She had a sort of understudy job at the time and the summer before had gone to Stockbridge as a student. She was great fun and she liked people and got on well with actors.

James Cagney was at Stockbridge the first year that Laura was there. He told this story about how Laura gave a party for all the little people who had been there at Stockbridge in the summer. Five o'clock at 955 Fifth. He said that he and his wife walked across town to Fifth Avenue. Then found 955. He couldn't believe it. A huge stone house. It couldn't be—yes. It was 955—one of the "Houses of the Dead." His friends on the East Side had always called them the "Houses of the Dead" because when they went over to Central Park to play in the warm seasons, these houses on Fifth were always shuttered and dark.

Feeling like a mouse, he rang the bell. Park, the butler—six feet two, wearing formal attire—opened the door.

"How do you do, sir. If you'll just go up this stair—follow me, please . . ."

Cagney and his wife followed—past an El Greco—past another El Greco. They got to the second floor. They could hear voices talking.

"And who shall I say it is, sir?"

Cagney looked. Quietly pushed past Park. "Just another ham," said Cagney, passing Park and going toward the voices.

Laura told me a wonderful story about beginning to be known a bit in New York and beginning to go to the parties. Not being really one of the New York inner circle—her family was Philadelphia—she would sometimes be invited to the party but not to any dinner beforehand. On a particular night she had Sailor (her chauffeur) drive her to the party. They had a car with an uncovered front seat. There was a top you could put up in case of rain. She got out in a state of terror, hoping that she wouldn't look too pathetic going in alone. Told Sailor that she would probably be right out. It was then 10:30 p.m.

At 4:30 a.m. she came out. There was the car. Sailor sitting and asleep in the front seat. A light snow had fallen, covering his cap and the visor of his cap. He had been there all night. Waiting.

Laura and I saw a lot of each other. She knew all the sort of highbrow customs of the time and I learned the way. The Vuitton luggage—the clothes—where to shop—what to buy. I would get little jobs. She was understudying someone in a Guild play. She didn't take her career very seriously. It was just something to pass the time.

People in Hollywood gossiped about Laura and me, and I never knew it. We would eat lunch in the restaurant on the lot. As you walked into the restaurant, there was a barbershop on the left. In it a telephone.

One day Laura went in to telephone me. The person who answered kept saying, "Who is this?" Finally, Laura said, "Oh, tell her it's her husband!"

Mark Sandrich (director), having a haircut, heard this and was absolutely shocked. He told me years later he thought that he could have been the one who was responsible for the very strong rumor that we were lesbians.

Anyway, the rumor certainly started and even New York was

buzzing with it. Finally, after about two years, Laura went back to New York. She worked as an agent for Leland Hayward, who had become my beau.

We all had a very good time together. She's been a good friend for all my life.

So, as I said, when it came time for me to go to California for *A Bill of Divorcement*, Laura decided that she would go too.

I had not traveled much in the United States. I'd been to Europe several times. I'd been back and forth to Bryn Mawr. But to go West. We spent the day in Chicago, taking a room at the Blackstone Hotel and enjoying the wonderful museum—the Art Institute.

Billie Burke and Ziegfeld, very ill, were on the train. And their daughter, Pat. Billie was to play my mother in *A Bill of Divorcement*; I didn't know that at the time. Because of Ziegfeld's illness, he couldn't leave the train. Our car was to be switched across Chicago and tied onto the Super Chief. I remember catching one or two glimpses of their drawing room. It was hung with special slipcovers which covered the walls, the chairs—every object in the room. This seemed quite an extraordinary luxury to me. But it was really "the thing to do." Just as Louis Vuitton luggage was "the thing." There were any number of "must"s in those days, which were definite indications that you knew how to behave.

Laura Harding knew what all those things were. I learned them from her. The baby pillows and blanket to make the drawing room cozy. She had traveled across the country to Santa Barbara in a private car. This was way beyond anything that I knew about. I had come from a small town—well, Hartford—a medium-sized town. But sophisticated in the luxuries I certainly was not.

We left Chicago and had a very exciting trip wondering what it would be like to be in movies. We got off at every possible stop with the dogs and walked up and down the platform. We had dinner in the dining car, lunch and breakfast in our drawing room. I was looking out the window—the window was closed. (In those days there was no air-conditioning, so very often we'd open the windows. It was filthy, so we'd close them. Then it was sweltering and we'd open them again.) This particular day, the first out of Chicago, I was looking out the closed window:

Laura Harding

"Oh—look, Laura—the new moon!"

"No, no, not through glass, Kate. Bad luck!"

We rushed out of the drawing room through the train to the back platform, to see the moon over my left shoulder and not through glass. Opened the door to go out onto the platform.

Oh—something in my eye.

It was indeed something in my eye. Several things, in fact. Tiny pieces of steel rail. Three of them. They lodged in my left eye in the white part. Scratching the inside of my upper lid every time I blinked. They were there and would not move.

I had gone to Elizabeth Hawes—New York's highest-priced designer—to have an appropriate costume made to wear getting off the train in California. It was a sort of Quaker gray-blue silk grosgrain suit. The skirt was flared and very long. The coat was rather like a nineteenth-century riding coat with tails. The blouse was a turtleneck with a ruffle around the top of the turtle. And the hat. Oh!

Well, the hat was a sort of gray-blue straw dish upside down on my head. I had long hair, screwed up tight. Someone once said, "*à la concierge.*" The dishpan sat on top of this—a bit formal and more than a little eccentric.

But it had been very expensive, the whole costume, and I had great faith in it.

Gloves, bag, shoes—dark navy.

It was, I realize now, hardly an appropriate costume to arrive in, in Pasadena on July 4th with a temperature of ninety-odd. A sweatshirt and an old pair of white pants would have been more appropriate.

When we arrived in Pasadena (me in my costume), my left eye under my dishpan hat was bright red. And the other eye in sympathy was certainly pink. Agony. And sweating hot.

We were slowly coasting into Pasadena. Past my first oranges and grapefruits—lemons—the sun—no smog in those days. The beautiful scent of the orange blossoms. And the dry dry soil. My red red eyes. We were pulling into the station. Suddenly Laura said:

"Good God."

"Why—" I said.

"That's Leland Hayward."

"Yes, he's my agent."

"Head of the stag line," said Laura.

"What . . ."

"When I came out in New York. At the parties. Sleek—head of the stag line. What a scream."

Leland Hayward was standing there with a short, heavyset man. They were talking. I was told later what they were saying:

"Which one?"

"The one with the funny hat."

"You're kidding—we got fifteen hundred dollars for that . . ."

"She's an original."

"Very. What does she drink? Get a load of those eyes."

"Hello—right here. Hand the bags out the—fine."

"Well—this is Myron Selznick, your other agent."

"Laura Harding . . ."

"Well, yes—hello—long time—fancy meeting you here. Give me the stubs. Oh good, all together. There's the car—the gray Rolls. Jackson, those are the bags. We brought a station wagon. It will take the bags to the hotel."

"Look, I have something in my eye. Do you know a doctor who is . . ."

Leland continued: "Well, they certainly are anxious to meet you. We'll drive straight to RKO. Cukor is waiting to see you. And Selznick. They want to start as soon as the clothes and tests are done."

"There we are. Good. I'll sit in front."

And we were off. Conversation was stilted. Myron, in an effort to be superfriendly, said, "I hear you're a golfer."

"Yes."

"Yes, well, maybe we could have a game."

Good heavens, I thought, golf with him—?

And Myron was thinking, I hope to God she says no. But at least I've tried. What a—well, I've never seen anything like her. She looks like a cadaver. What will David say? Say, hell! What will he do?

"Oh yes, that's very kind of you but I don't think that I'll have much time for golf. And the sun seems pretty hot here and . . . Do either of you know an eye—"

"Well, if you do find time I would be more than happy to—"

"Yes, thank you—but . . ."

"I remember where we met. It was . . ."

And the conversation turned to New York—deb parties. And soon we drove onto the RKO lot.

George Cukor's office: small, a bit dark, ground floor.

Cukor was extraordinary: rococo, fat man, medium height, full of energy, quick, bright.

"Well, isn't this fine? Now let me see—yes—now—shall we . . ." Looking me over—summing me up—summing Laura up . . .

"We've got some sketches of the clothes you're to wear."

"Oh—yes?"

"Where are—let me—yes—here we . . ."

I took the sketches. There were three or four. I had sort of imagined what she would wear in a vague tweed-and-sweater sort of way. To maintain an instinctive sort of self-protection, I looked through without much change of expression—and very piss-elegant. "Yes—well, I'm not sure that these are the sorts of things that a well-bred English girl would wear."

George looked me in the eye with a glint in his.

"What do you think of what you have on?"

Oh—yes, I see—you're a dangerous opponent. What do I say now—nothing. I'd better . . .

"I think it's . . ." Then I laughed.

"Would you mind taking off that hat?"

I took it off.

My hair was hot and matted.

"Oh yes—is it very long? No—it's long enough to do up. Just. Lots of it. Very fine."

"Would you mind cutting it?"

"Well . . ."

"Call up Jo Ann and see if she can come down here."

"Who is Jo Ann?"

"She's the head hairdresser. Jo Ann St. Auger. Or better, we'll go up there."

A man appeared in the door—fiftyish and obviously Barrymore.

Politely: "Well, you're here."

He looked at me hard.

"Too many people here. Come out into the hall. I want to say something to you."

"Go ahead," from George.

TOP LEFT: Myron Selznick; TOP RIGHT: David Selznick;

BOTTOM: George Cukor, Oliver Messel and Kate

I stepped out into the hall with him. He smiled. He was very warm—very personal.

"That was a wonderful test. You will be a big star." Then he focused on my eyes and he reached into his pocket and took out a small bottle. He indicated his own eyes, and an understanding smile. Very intimate.

"I have that same trouble. Try this—two drops—each eye."

"Mr. Barrymore, I have something *in* the eye. It's been there for three—"

"Yes, my dear. I know—try it."

And he was gone.

I went back into the office.

"Do you by any happy chance happen to know an eye doc—"

"Now. Shall we go up to meet David—and then we'll cut your hair."

And George led the way.

And we went to meet Selznick, who was busy and just said fine —fine. And must have thought: Well, so that's what we got.

Then we went up to the far end of the lot where the hairdresser and makeup departments were.

Very speedily my hair was cut off, leaving enough to curl. The head of makeup wasn't there.

Back to Cukor's office. It was late. "Well, tomorrow then. At nine. We'll do a— I'll call you."

"Do you happen to know an eye doctor? I have something in my . . ."

And I was talking to no one. George and his entourage were gone. They had all disappeared.

The day was over. Laura and I walked out of the office. On the street outside there was a man standing.

"I beg your pardon. Do you happen to know an eye doctor? I have something in my eye."

"Oh dear, yes. So you have. Well, I am a doctor."

"You are—eye . . ."

"No, I'm a surgeon. I'm new here. From New York. But I have an office. It's . . ."

He took a slip out of his pocket.

"It's down Wilshire, I think."

"I don't—we don't know the city at all."

"Well, I have a car. I'm not sure I can find it. But let's try, shall we?"

"Thank you. Do you think you can get it out?"

"I can try. My name is Sam Hirschfeld."

"I'm Katharine Hepburn—Laura Harding."

So we got into his car and off we drove—found Wilshire—found his office. I lay down on his table. He put in some drops. And he fished. And very quickly he gave up and said, "We must have an eye man. I haven't the right instruments."

He began to call. I didn't know who he was. A doctor would have known who he was. Who in hell would he dig up?

Finally he found a woman doctor who was still in her office. Yes, she would see us. We went to downtown Los Angeles. He parked the car.

She took a look. Three steel filings embedded. I could hear them click against her knife. She got them out. Dug them out. Flick flick went the white of my eye, like celluloid. Then she put a patch over my eye. Gave me some pills.

"This may be very painful when the anesthetic wears off."

The good doctor drove us all the way to the Elysee Hotel in Hollywood. It was too late for room service. They sent out for two chicken-salad sandwiches. And we went to bed.

Next morning I went to the studio with a patch. Of course I couldn't make a proper test with makeup and hair and clothes.

A Bill of Divorcement, with David Manners

Early Films

A Bill of Divorcement

A Bill of Divorcement was to be my first picture. John Barrymore
was my father. Billie Burke was my mother and Elizabeth Patterson
my aunt and David Manners my beau; George Cukor was the director.

The first shot was at a party my mother was giving. In a long
white dress I floated down the stairs into the arms of David Manners.
After me came Laura Harding. She tripped and the scene had to be
done again. George was furious.

Oh dear, did I forget to tell you the story of our second day in
Hollywood? There was a man named Carlton Burke—prominent in
horsey circles—and a beau of Laura's. He had rented a house for us
—or at least put a hold on a very nice little house in Franklin Canyon.
We went to look at it. As a matter of fact, we met Carty Burke there.
He had a woman with him—a Mrs. Fairbanks. We liked the house.
It was not very grand but was pleasant and conveniently located.

The Mrs. Fairbanks invited us to dinner on Saturday night. I
refused, saying that I never went out to dinner. And coolly changed
the subject.

Actually I thought to myself, She doesn't look very interesting so
let's not start that.

When Carty and Mrs. Fairbanks left, Laura said to me in a rather
stinging voice, "Do you know who that was?"

"You mean Mrs. Fairbanks?"

"Yes. She's Mary Pickford."

"Oh my God!"

Well, luckily she called later and invited us again, and I—full of thrills and charm—said, "Oh, how lovely—yes, of course—how very nice of you to bother with us."

So we got all dressed up and went to Pickfair!

Can you imagine? Pickfair—our first week in movieland.

I sat next to Fairbanks, Laura next to Mary. Carty Burke was there. We saw a movie—it was great fun. The big time. She was charming.

We were never asked again. Did you hear me? Never.

So I learned my lesson. Just be careful what you say and to whom. You may not know whom you are speaking to.

After no time at all we started the picture.

I've told you how I met Cukor and Barrymore. We quickly had hair tests—makeup tests—and got the clothes together. The plan was to shoot all of Barrymore's scenes first and get him out of the picture—save the money—he was expensive.

We started, as I said, with that party sequence so that the whole set could be lit. Then we began with Barrymore's scenes. The first was his arrival at the house. He supposedly had left the asylum and come to his house.

I watched him. I was in the living room when he opened the door. He went to the mantelpiece over the fireplace. Was he looking for his pipes? He fiddled around. I was standing next to the camera watching his every move with tears running down my face as I realized that this was certainly my father. Actually, I was also thinking with surprise and wonder that this was indeed Barrymore—the great Barrymore—and that he was giving a very hammy performance. I was shocked.

When the scene was finished, Barrymore came over and looked hard at me; then he went to George and said that he would like to do it again. I think he could tell that this was to me my great moment and he didn't want to let me down.

We started again. He was shattering. So sad. So moving. Full of desperation. And always so simple.

A Bill of Divorcement, with John Barrymore

What an odd man. Full of charm—a wonderful actor—a generous spirit—a wild sort of general passion for the opposite sex but not caring a bit whether or not he succeeded. It was as if he were driving a strange car.

He asked me to come to his dressing room on the lot one day. I went. Knocked on the door. He said, "Come in." I did. And there he was, lying on his couch in—what shall I say?—comparative disarray. I must have looked totally blank. There was a pause. A quick shuffle of blankets.

"Oh. I am sorry. See you later."

I went. Oh my, how very strange.

Anyway, he was an angel after that one feeble whatever you want to call it. His main object after that seemed to be to be certain that I made a big hit. He held my face to the camera in our many scenes together. He was sweet—he was funny—and he could certainly act. I was very lucky to have had such a wonderful opportunity.

The funniest thing that happened on the picture was a breakfast scene with Billie Burke at the head of the table—me at the side and Elizabeth Patterson at the other end. I couldn't seem to get the scene the way George wanted it. We did it over twenty times. Being an amateur in the business, I didn't realize that every time we did it I had to eat another breakfast—so did the other two ladies. You may imagine twenty breakfasts. I kept wondering why Elizabeth Patterson seemed so rather unfriendly to me. Years later she told me.

It took about five weeks to shoot *A Bill of Divorcement*. Three with Barrymore—the remainder with the rest of us.

I finished *A Bill of Divorcement*. I went to Europe fast with Luddy. On the chance that they would call me and tell me that I was a hit, I went to Schiaparelli and got myself a costume to get off the boat in. It was a sort of brown-purple—an eggplant color. A three-quarter coat and a skirt and blouse, and a knitted hat of knit 2-purl 2. Very easy to wear. I heard in Vienna that I'd made a big hit, so I was prepared. That was my first French outfit.

They took the picture to Santa Barbara to preview and it was very well received. When we knew definitely that it was a hit, Luddy and I switched our tickets from steerage to first-class. Before that I always traveled on the lowest class, in the forward part of the boat, figuring that as I was always seasick I might as well throw up third-class rather than first.

I was indeed lucky to be in the film. It was a showy part.

Christopher Strong

Dorothy Arzner—popular woman director. She had done many pictures. Was very good. This picture was fun to do but no extraordinary happenings. A story of an aviatrix and her affair with a famous man. It seems odd now, a woman director, but it didn't seem strange to me then. Several of the best cutters in the business were women. Dorothy was very well known and had directed a number of hit

Christopher Strong

pictures. She wore pants. So did I. We had a good time working together. The script was a bit old-fashioned and it was not a really successful picture. Colin Clive played the man.

With Lowell Sherman

Morning Glory

I went into Pandro Berman's office, saw the script on his desk, picked it up and started to read it. Was fascinated. Called my friend Laura Harding. She came. She read it too. It was by Zoë Akins. Laura thought it fascinating. Went to Pandro and said I must do it. He said no. It was for Connie Bennett. I said No—ME. I won. It was directed by Lowell Sherman, who was in the original *What Price Hollywood?* as leading man opposite Connie Bennett. A brilliant picture. He was very good.

I had seen Ruth Gordon in a play called *A Church Mouse*. She gave a wonderful performance, and I could visualize *Morning Glory* played just in that key—monotone of voice and observing everything around her. "My name is Eva Lovelace—L-O-V-E-L-A-C-E . . ."—I added the lace—"Do you smoke? I do."

I was sitting at a counter having a coffee talking to Aubrey Smith.

It was a wonderful part.

My first Academy Award. I couldn't believe it! It was in the early years of awards, in 1933. I believe only five people voted on it. Doug Fairbanks, Jr., and Adolphe Menjou were in it too. Doug and I did the balcony scene from *Romeo and Juliet* in it—in costume. They cut it. When we shot the scene, Mary Pickford and Doug Sr. came to watch. That was pretty scary, you can bet. We made the picture in seventeen days.

Little Women

This was one of my favorites. George Cukor directing again. There were a number of scripts done on this. They were all mediocre. Actually bad. Then Sarah Mason and Victor Heerman were hired. They wrote a brilliant script, in my humble opinion. Simple and true and naïve but really believable. It was amazing the difference between this script and its predecessors. Mason and Heerman believed the book. So did I. The others didn't.

TOP: *Little Women*

BOTTOM: *Spitfire*

The girls. The whole situation. Joan Bennett played Amy. She was quite pregnant at the time. Frances Dee, Meg—and Beth, Jean Parker. Professor Bhaer, Paul Lukas—and Laurie was Douglass Montgomery. Marmee was Spring Byington.

The sets were lovely—Hobe Erwin, who was a very well-known decorator in New York. They were really copies of the original in Massachusetts. The house and Mr. Laurence's house were built in the San Fernando Valley. Henry Stephenson was Mr. Laurence. It was exciting.

We had a sound strike when we were shooting the long sequence, when Beth was dying and everyone was weeping—especially me. It was agony. We had to do it over and over again because of sound. Agony. I finally threw up and we had to try again the next day.

Tallulah Bankhead came to visit one day. She was a great friend of Cukor's. He sent her to see some of our rushes. She was thrilled and came back weeping away.

All very satisfactory.

This picture was heaven to do—George Cukor perfect. He really caught the atmosphere. It was to me my youth!

Spitfire

Was a Southern sort of mountain spirit. Shame on you, Kathy.
Then I went back to New York to do *The Lake*, a play.
And again shame on you, Kathy.
No good.

Manhattan house

The Return to New York

I'd got off to a flying start with *A Bill of Divorcement*, *Christopher Strong*, *Morning Glory*, *Little Women*, *Spitfire*. All in the space of one year. Actually, a year and a half. Seven months of 1932. Almost all of 1933. I'd even won an Academy Award. Then came *The Lake*.

I'll have to explain to you my next, shall we say, "step." I was sort of—well, full of myself, as you may imagine. All my success in California. And now back to New York. My position was—well—yes—secure. And my relationship with former friends was different —I had definitely made it to the first hilltop. I was someone to be reckoned with. Actually, other people put you in this position. They look up to you—and from your new spot you try to pretend that you are unaware of any change.

Back in New York I thought that we needed more room. Luddy and I found the house I'm now in. It was for rent furnished—$100 a month. So we moved in and moved in the little furniture we had, and finally in about 1937 I bought the house for $27,500. I was lucky. The Schuyler Smiths, who had owned the house, came and took their furniture, most of which had been gradually removed through the years.

I changed a wall to make a big guest room on the top floor. And I put a john in on the ground floor and then—oh yes—I made a fireplace in my bedroom. Its chimney was already there. And I painted the whole thing white and that's all that's ever been done. It's handy and comfortable—faces south and used to be full of sunshine. Now the skyscrapers on the street behind me cut out a lot of sun—too bad—but it's quiet and convenient and it's mine and I like it.

I can't really remember the Schuyler Smiths moving out. Anyway, they left only a silver card dish, which stands on a table by the front door, and a very pretty chair in the living room. I think they had forgotten what was theirs with the passage of time.

Luddy only tried to help me in my career. He never even mentioned the fact that with *Art and Mrs. Bottle* and *The Warrior's Husband* I was of necessity climbing a ladder which was going to take me away from him. He took care of me. I used his car. His apartment was charming. He had moved his business to New York just so that it would be convenient for me. He was working on a system of automatic payment of salaried employees. This he installed for big companies.

When I left Luddy and went to Hollywood on July 4, 1932, it turned out to be the beginning of the end of our marriage.

What the hell would I have done without Luddy—my protector? I would have been frightened away from this big city and I would have shriveled up and died. And Luddy—all he wanted was me, and of course all I wanted was to be a great big hit star in the movies.

Now as I write this, I am horrified at what an absolute pig I was. You can see that when I say about Luddy I spent his money, I broke his heart and my sister (Peg) took his blood. That is the truth.

It was when she was having the twins in Washington, D.C., and had what they call eclampsia and was swelling up with fluids. Yes, they got her to the hospital in time. She and her husband were living on a farm. She had swelled up so that she couldn't wear any of her own clothes—even shoes. But it had taken place so gradually that she'd just gotten used to it. She began to feel that something was happening and that the baby was thinking of arriving and her husband agreed, and they got out the telephone book but couldn't find a doctor who was willing to come to the house. So they started for the hospital. But the car had a flat tire. Well, they drove on the rim. They really didn't know where in Washington the hospital was. It was wartime,

1942, and it was also rush hour. Anyway, they got there and it turned out there were twins and she was in a bad way. So Luddy was in Washington on business. He'd heard she was in trouble. We were divorced but he really was part of the family. And well, he had the right blood type. So, "Yes of course. Take my blood," he said. So they did. That was O.K., but they spilled some on the floor. Then they stepped in it. It was all very hurried, as you can imagine. But that was too much for Luddy. He fainted. So that's how my sister took his blood. All that was quite a while ago.

Dear Luddy. He would always meet the train or the plane when I came back from Hollywood. He would drive me to Fenwick or Hartford. We were separated. Then we were divorced—in Yucatán, Mexico. I didn't think that the divorce was any good, but I thought it made our position clear.

Luddy took another apartment. He continued to do for me any and every possible kindness.

You couldn't be expected to believe this, but it was in early 1941 when I was going around with Spencer that Spencer said to me, "Why do you keep stringing Luddy along? Why don't you stop using him!"

Then I thought. I *finally* used what sense or sensitivity I had. I stopped using him.

In about six months he was married. He had two children—a boy and a girl. *Then* his wife died. (*Then* means twenty-five years later.)

Luddy began to be sick. Spence had died in 1967. I used to stop at Luddy's to see how he was. I finally began trying to do things for him. For a while he would come to Fenwick. Then he had inoperable cancer and he would be in and out of the hospital and slowly he faded away. I really struggled to give back to him some of the love and kindness and extreme selflessness which he had given to me.

Can you see how responsible he was for my beginning? Absolute generosity—no strings—give give give. Dear Luddy, thank you.

But oh dear, I've left out the most awful incident. Listen to this. I made him change his name from Ludlow Ogden Smith to S. Ogden Ludlow. I didn't want to be called Mrs. Smith. I thought it was melancholic. Kate Smith! And I'm not a singer.

I hope you realize that I am remembering all this now. I am

looking back and realizing what the truth was. The motives back of the action. I don't think that it was all as cold-blooded as it sounds. I hope not. But the truth has to be that I was a terrible pig. My aim was ME ME ME. All the way—up—down—all about.

Luddy, who was a relative of the inventor Thomas Edison, had a very scientific mind and was a sort of inventor himself. He had invented a record-changing Victrola but had not had it patented. Luddy wasn't satisfied with the way the records slid across each other—thought it might injure them. In the meantime a record changer came on the market. Luddy was odd. He didn't seem to mind. I was furious.

He loved music and we had loudspeakers all over this house. The quality of the sound was extraordinary. When his friends installed fancy music players in their apartments, they would always insist on Luddy coming over to check the quality of the sound. He had a remarkable ear.

Luddy could make anything work—my life—the car—the furnace—the this—the that. Carpenter—mechanic—plumber. It was great. But mostly—from the beginning—he was—what shall I say?—he was *there*. Whatever. He was always there. As no one. Well, how can I describe to you my relationship with Luddy? He really was close to me. He was like Mother and Dad. He was there. He was like breathing. My friend.

I could ask him anything. He would do anything. You just don't find people like that in life. Unconditional love.

The Lake

One of my—well, I started
to write "friends," but with Jed Harris one was never really sure. Jed
Harris was one of the most successful producers to reach Broadway
in the middle to late twenties. He had endless hits:

1926 *Broadway*
1927 *Coquette*
1927 *The Royal Family*
1928 *The Front Page*
1930 *Uncle Vanya*
1933 *The Green Bay Tree*

These were all *smash hits*. He made millions. Then he struck a lull,
until *Our Town* in 1938.

When I first got to New York—fall of 1928—he was flourishing.
Then I used to drive him around in my car as the thirties began, and
then I went to Hollywood in 1932. When I returned to New York
in 1933, *I* was a big hit and I had won the Academy Award for
Morning Glory.

As he became less successful, I became more so. Everything I did
seemed to work. I apparently thought that I would renew Jed's luck
if I did *The Lake* for him.

Well, here's what happened.

Although his career as a Broadway producer had tumbled, he was

still in his own attitude to himself and to me the King of the Roost. Modesty was a quality he did not deal in. He had a way of treating you as if you were an inferior creature. And of course I had known him when I was definitely on a lower rung of the ladder than he was. Now the situation was reversed, but neither Jed nor I could admit this. He was the genius and I was the lucky mutt. I got back to New York.

I called him to say hello.

"Oh—how are you?" he said. "I was about to call you. I have a play which you might enjoy doing. I'll send it to you."

What he sent was *The Lake*, by Dorothy Massingham.

My attitude toward the play was really cockeyed. I can't actually remember what I thought of it as a play—as an evening in the theatre. I think I was anxious to be a help to Jed. I hardly dare write this. I actually thought that if I did the play, it would get him back on his feet. I thought that his position must be very embarrassing to him and now that I was "important," I felt that as the little Mother of All the World, I could help him resume his proper status. How I could have been this dumb, I do not know. My relationship with Jed had indeed been curious.

I first knew him when I went into his office to get a job. His secretary at that time was Jimmy Schute, who was a friend of mine. Somehow Jed found out I had a car and I became useful to Jed as a sort of chauffeur. He never thought anything of me as an actor. He was a man of considerable reputation with the ladies despite his rather sinister looks. Laurence Olivier said he used Jed as his model for Richard III—a terrifying creature. Well, Jed certainly never gave any indication that he was interested in me. As far as I could see, I was just the girl with a car.

One day he said to me, "Why have you never invited me to Fenwick?"

"Heavens, Jed—you wouldn't like Fenwick!"

"How do you know?"

"I'll ask Mother."

So I asked Mother and she said, "Well—fine."

Now, every weekend that I was in the East I went to Fenwick—

Jed Harris

usually on Friday. And Luddy, my ex-husband, my dear friend, would come on Saturday. So on the Jed weekend I went with Jed on Friday. It was a pleasant weekend—golf, walking, swimming, talking. Luddy left on Sunday night. Jed and I were to leave on Monday.

Sunday night Mother came sauntering into my bedroom: "You know, I don't think that Jed knows that Luddy is your husband."

"Was," I said.

"Well," said Mother.

Next morning, Mother and Jed were having breakfast alone on the porch. We all ate at whatever time we pleased.

"What did you think of Kath's husband?" said Mother.

"Of her what?" answered Jed.

"Of Luddy?"

There was a rather long pause—then Jed changed the subject.

We—Jed and I—left about an hour later for New York. He didn't utter a word until we reached New Haven. Then he asked, "Why didn't you tell me that you were married?"

And I answered, "Why would I, Jed—I've no idea whether you are married. It never occurred to me. What difference would it make?"

Jed gave me a long long look from a land of thinking far far away from me: "I see," he said, and changed the topic. "What do you think of *The Lake*?"

"I don't really know. Do you think I could do a part like—"

"For God's sake, Kate—if I hadn't thought that you could— How much do you want a week?"

"Heavens, Jed, I haven't the least idea."

"How about five hundred a week?"

This was a meager offer. Stars' salaries were $1,000–$2,500 a week.

"Well, whatever . . ." I answered.

"O.K., it's a deal," finalized Jed.

So began *The Lake*.

Real disaster. Blanche Bates and Frances Starr—big stars. Colin Clive—star. And me—flash in the pan. Billed above them all. I had asked Jed not to star me. Or if he must, to star the older ladies before me. I asked this not because I was sweet and generous. I thought I was O.K. And I knew that I was riding high. Don't get me wrong. But I also knew that these two ladies were very much loved, and for me to be dumb enough to push them off first place would not make me very popular. (Who does she think she is?)

But Jed felt that I was the one selling the tickets and causing the excitement. And that I should be first. So there I was. Leading with my chin. A dumb step.

Rehearsals started at the Martin Beck. Forty-fifth Street. West of Broadway. Big. We weren't worried. We could fill it. Off by itself. We didn't care. We didn't need the spillover from the other theatres. Tony Miner directing. I was there doing my enthusiastic best. Which wasn't a very dependable best. I was in my mid-twenties. Had exaggeratedly been referred to as the new Duse—Bernhardt.

While I knew that all this adulation wasn't exactly deserved, still I did seem to have something. Just what it was I wasn't sure. And when it would happen I wasn't sure either. The acting, I mean. And this was indeed perilous. I could make them laugh. I could make them cry. But the atmosphere had to be perfect. O.K. in movies. Disaster on the stage.

Well. After the first week, Jed fired Tony. Helen Hayes, whom I barely knew, sent me a message saying, "Don't let Jed direct you. He will destroy your confidence." But I was young. I was unique. I can get on with anyone, I thought. I disregarded her advice.

Why he fired Tony Miner, I never knew. I suppose that he just wanted to direct it himself. Tony had given me confidence. The other actors gave me confidence. They were sweet to me. Of course, I know now that they must have been beginning to suspect what they were in for. From the very start, Jed seemed to be setting out to destroy my only commodity—my confidence. Or else he just didn't like what I could do. If I turned left, he said turn right. If I made a gesture with one hand, he said make it with the other. I sat. He said stand. It was undoing.

There was a piano on the stage. Keyboard facing the audience. I cannot play the piano. And I am so right-handed that my left is almost atrophied. It was a very important scene. Deeply emotional. He had me do it while playing the piano. Well, I felt an absolute fool. Felt and was.

"I can't follow the music with my hands—and it jogs me to be going down the keyboard with my hands and to hear the music from offstage going up. So I can't think, Jed, and the result is that I can't play the scene. I can only think: I can't play the piano. And certainly the audience can only think: She can't play the piano."

Jed just said, "Helen Hayes learned to play the piano for me."

Well, I thought, I couldn't learn to play the piano for God Almighty.

So I wept. Jed patted me. And we continued doing the same agonizing thing. And the cast was embarrassed.

Jed was far from a fool. And I wonder to this day what he thought he was accomplishing by tormenting and thus rendering useless a poor amateur kid who was trying—nay, struggling—to fill her own over-sized boots.

The Lake had been played in London by Marie Ney. Produced by Tyrone Guthrie. It was the story of a woman's last chance at marriage (she was in her late twenties). And on her own driveway—just after the wedding ceremony—the car in which the couple are driving skids and turns over into the lake, the bridegroom pinned under the car. And he drowns. Much drama. The true-blue bridegroom gone. The weak married man with whom she has been playing around is lurking.

Hence: "The calla lilies are in bloom again. Such a strange flower. I carried them on my wedding day. And now I place them here, in memory of someone who is dead."

Howard Greer of Hollywood was to do my clothes. Jeanie Barton was to do my hair—also of Hollywood. Cecelia, my maid in movies, would take care of me. They were all Hollywood-geared. The immediacy of the theatre, the cause and effect being almost simultaneous, was not within their experience. In Hollywood the actor is waited for. In the theatre nothing waits. The train leaves. So my staff was all on foreign ground. And they were all unhappy. And it was cold in the East.

I had a Lincoln town car and a driver, too. Charles Newhill. Charles had worked for me almost from the first moment that I hit New York. Part German. Part Italian. Some Irish. Moved early to the big city from Amsterdam, New York. Soft brown eyes and a kind

With Charles Newhill, driver

heart. He took care of me for forty-three years. When I was in California, he more or less ran my New York home and managed the sort of rooming house it was and is.

He got in early. And stayed late. Got my breakfast. Carried it up two flights. Time passed. Charles began to feel the years. The stairs got steeper and steeper. He struggled. Finally, I would pretend that I wanted to look at the morning paper. "Well, I'm down here. I might as well carry up the tray." Then, "Let me do it—I like the exercise." Then he'd begin to miss a few days. A sort of a cold. "Wouldn't want to give it to you." Then he didn't come anymore. I used to go to see him. Then he died. It was so sad. We were best friends. He helped me. I helped him. We had a good life together.

He was an angel. However big the flop. "Well, I don't know, Miss Hepburn. They just love you. That's all I can say. I just hear what they say. You're the greatest." All those heartwarming lies. They keep you going. Those liars who love you and protect you. For better or for worse. Till death do us part. How lucky I've been. Old Charles. He was known as "the Mayor" of my block.

Back to business.

We went to Washington to open. We were to be out only a week. I was to stay at the Hay-Adams. My room was 375–378.

I got to the desk with Laura Harding. We were checking in: "Leopold Stokowski is staying here too," someone said.

"Oh," I said. (Rather thrilled. I had met him once.) "Where—"

"Room 238."

"Oh, yes—I see—how interesting."

We started for the elevator. Got in. And who should get in with us but Leopold Stokowski.

"How are you?" he said.

"I'm doing a play," I said.

"Of course. I know," he said. "Perhaps we could have supper."

"Ah, yes. Fine," I said.

"Well, good," he said, "I'll call. What is the number of your room?"

"Room 238," I said.

There was a long pause and a smile. "That is the number of my room," said Stokowski.

"I mean 375."

"Yes—of course."

And he was gone.

We giggled, Laura and I. Thought it was a scream. And had supper with him one night on a yacht in the Potomac. John Hays Hammond's yacht.

So we opened in Washington. I was terrified. Bit by bit my confidence had left me. And confidence was all I had. Under perfect circumstances and conditions I could deliver a sort of naïve and forthright laugh and cry. But to force myself to concentrate in a state of terror was still beyond me. At the National Theatre in Washington, D.C.—sold out to the rafters—I really walked through the play in a daze. A few things hit. But mostly missed. I could actually feel the attention of the audience recede like the tide. I went through the motions but there was no heart in it—no joy. Trying but smothered.

When it was over, the audience went mad. American audiences are very kind. It hadn't been quite what they expected—this new young wonder. But maybe they were wrong. But—what the hell—she's young and all dressed up. Give her a hand.

Jed came back to my dressing room. Stood in the doorway. Kissed his hand to me and said, "Perfection—I can do no more."

"No more?" I asked, not understanding.

"No more rehearsals," he said. "We open in New York next week."

I was stunned.

"Couldn't we keep it out a bit until I know what I'm doing?"

"Not necessary," he said.

And he was gone.

Next morning came the reviews. They told me that they weren't bad at all. I don't read them. I just don't see the sense. Too late to help one way or the other. But, of course, I get the general feel: good—bad—great. In this instance, I thought that the critics were just being kind. Or perhaps they were reluctant to demolish the new wonder girl. My own judgment told me that I had failed to deliver. And I set about talking myself into disaster. I got worse and worse. And the New York tickets were selling like hotcakes.

On the pleasanter side, I received an invitation to tea with President Roosevelt. This, of course, was a command. I bought a hat. I had a dress. Charles and I had the car at the White House gate five minutes early. We waited. Watching the clock. With one minute to spare we drove in. The door of the car was opened by someone. I got out in a daze of excitement. The front door of the White House opened. There, as I remember it, and up about three steps, stood a man in a morning suit. I went forward with my hand out—better friendly than formal.

With Franklin Delano Roosevelt

"I am the usher," he said.

So I said, "Well," and, not altering my outstretched hand, "how do you do."

He smiled. I followed him to a small room—a very small room. Rather long for its width, it seems to me now. And I was told that President Roosevelt would be in in a few minutes.

He came in. I couldn't tell you for the life of me if he was or was not in a wheelchair. I think that he was on crutches and had an aide with him—who left the minute we were settled. No matter. There he was. That powerful and fascinating personality. Said he was sorry not to see me in the play. But that he had seen several of my movies. And that he wanted me to consider doing a movie of a short story of Kipling's—I can't remember the name—which had always been a favorite of his. Then he asked me about my mother. And her great friend Jo Bennett, whose daughter's husband had designed and built Warm Springs. A man named Tombs. I asked him how he could remember all those names.

"That's my job," he said, "and I concentrate on it. I meet someone and I say, 'You are Mr. Jones. That is your wife, Mrs. Jones.' I look at them. I absorb them. I remember them. And next time I say, 'Why, hello, Mr. Jones. How are you? And Mrs. Jones?' It makes a good impression."

Well, it certainly does. And I tried it out in Boston.

"You are Mr. Smith—and you are Mrs. Smith—" Think—concentrate—I keep forgetting to do that.

That visit was the only pleasant memory of the week in Washington. The President seemed to have all the time in the world. I got a bit nervous that I was staying too long.

"How will I know when to get out, Mr. President?"

"You don't need to worry at all about that, Kathy. You have to sit there until I go. Then after I go, you go."

What a charmer. Warm. Funny. He told about campaigning for Liberty Bonds in the First World War. And waxing so enthusiastic that he fell off the chair he was standing on and landed right in Marie Dressler's lap.

The whole visit was fun. Franklin Delano Roosevelt was a man of great charm and he had the gift of laughter. And a great gift it is. Lightens the load.

Back to *The Lake*. It was a slow walk to the gallows. We finished Washington. We went back to New York. I kept hoping that I would drop dead. But I didn't. We weren't rehearsing at all. Now, it could be that Jed felt that he had overdirected me. And that he was letting me find my way back. But by this time back to where? He—Jed—was invisible. Never appeared at all, as far as I was concerned. And as for finding my way back. Not a chance. The trail had grown over. Alone there was no way back. I was lost.

Inevitably they arrived: dress rehearsal—opening night. Luckily I was tough. My cue came. I walked on. And I walked through the whole opening night. It was perfectly awful. Like an automaton. My voice got higher and higher. I prayed. I prayed. I prayed. No use. I just went on and on and on. I hadn't died. I was there. Fully conscious of having given a totally nothing performance.

My family was, of course, out front. My much younger sisters. Noel Coward was sitting right in back of my sister Peg—a beautiful young girl. He was overheard to say: "Kate's sister looks the way Kate should have but didn't." Noel came backstage.

This time he said: "You mucked it up. But that happens to all of us. You'll get roasted. But keep at it. You'll find the way."

And indeed I was roasted. And became the irresistible butt of all the New York wits. Dorothy Parker summed it up:

"Go to the Martin Beck and see K.H. run the gamut-t-t of emotion from A to B."

Another: "She has a red carpet running from her dressing room to each entrance. And the carpet is screened in so that no one can see her. Who wants to?" Dorothy Parker was right.

The box office fell at the rate of twelve hundred dollars a week. We had had a very substantial advance for something like ten weeks. And it began to look as though we would run that length of time. No one with any sense was buying tickets. Those which had been sold could not be returned. The production, which had not been expensive, would pay off.

My main task now was to see whether I could learn to act under fire. And to learn how to be a star. I hadn't been either. I had lost my nerve. I had moaned. I had not passed the exam. I had not delivered the goods. And I had let everyone know that I was absolutely miserable and terrified. And that I didn't know what I was doing.

Well, as one goes through life one learns that if you don't paddle your own canoe, you don't move.

After the shock of the opening, we settled down to the gradual demise. People came out of curiosity or whatever in ever-diminishing numbers. I—very very slowly—was trying to pick up the pieces. I at least had the brains to know who was really at the bottom of the failure. *Me.* Jed had not done his best work, certainly. But my contribution had been a disgrace.

One night a woman came back to my dressing room. Very tall. Very fat.

The Lake, with Colin Clive

SELL-OUT

KATHERINE HEPBURN
whose Broadway show, "The Lake,"
which is to open the day after Christmas, is already sold out for the first
four weeks. Tickets for the following
four weeks will be on sale Monday

"I'm Susan Steele," she said. "I'm a singer. I think that I could help you."

"Well," I said, "if you could help me, I certainly need help. When do we start?"

"Now," she said.

We went back to my house. Talked about vocal troubles. Next day worked on the scenes which seemed to be causing the most trouble. And voice. Ever voice. And joy. You must not be a victim.

That night and every night, she came to the play. Bit by bit by bit, I pulled myself back from that cliff-hang of terror. And began to be able to take myself in hand. Regain my sense of being an actor. Not a terror-stricken mole. I began to enjoy it.

People came back and said, "Why, you're not so bad at all. You made me cry."

And slowly my confidence returned. It was thrilling. And thrilling is what we can do with ourselves if we really try. My dignity returned. I stopped making excuses. And I began to try to look at myself as the leader of a group. Not a poor little thing who was trying her best and had been mistreated.

It was fascinating. I worked on nothing else. Just be as good as you can be in that part. At it. Susan sat out there every night and every matinée. Then we went home and discussed where I held and where I didn't. We worked on voice. And relaxation. And it did improve. Jed never came back to the scene of the crime. As far as I know. The cast was all for me, even though I had indeed let them down by being bad when it counted. But they were all for me. Very kind—actors.

People came again who had seen it on the opening, and were pleased. And, of course, I was pleased.

I was learning to act.

I was learning to be a *star*.

About the third week Joe Glick, our company manager, came to my dressing room and said, "We're going to Chicago."

I couldn't believe my ears.

"What?"

"Jed is taking the play to Chicago."

"But they don't like it. They certainly don't like me. But they don't like Jed's work either. And we've paid off. Why?"

Joe shrugged. "Money."

"Oh."

Joe left my dressing room. He couldn't think of anything else to say. And neither could I.

I went home. What to do? I'd made a fool of myself in New York. But why broadcast it by touring?

Some kind soul sent me a clipping from the front page of a Chicago paper: "Chicago audiences are going to have the misfortune of having to look at Katharine Hepburn in *The Lake*."

I troubled about it for a week or so, then one night about 3 a.m. I called Jed at his house. I'd not seen hide or hair of him since the opening.

"Jed?"

"Yes."

"Kate."

"Oh."

A silence.

"I understand that you are planning to send us on the road. Chicago."

"Yes."

"But, Jed, why? I was roasted—but let's face it—so were you. Why send it out to—"

An interruption.

"My dear, the only interest I have in you is the money I can make out of you."

Plain talk, I thought.

"How much?"

"How much have you got?"

I reached for my bankbook, which I kept in the bookcase next to my bed.

"I have thirteen thousand six hundred and seventy-five dollars and seventy-five cents in the Chase National Bank."

"I'll take that."

"I'll send you a check in the morning."

And that was that. I sent him the check. And when the receipts dwindled to a nonprofit point, we closed.

I never saw Jed again until years after this. I went to the theatre one night.

"Hello, Kate."

"Who?"

"Jed Harris."

"Oh. Hello, Jed."

Several years later he went to Hollywood and asked Myron Selznick to help him get a job. Myron said, "You've asked the wrong person. I'm Kate Hepburn's agent."

"Oh," said Jed.

"She doesn't like you."

"Why?" said Jed.

"You took all her money to close *The Lake*."

"Why, I didn't know that she was upset about that."

"She was," said Myron.

"I'll send her a check."

Myron held out his hand.

"I'll take it," said Myron.

So I got it back. But I never cashed it. I tore it up. Sad money.

I'd learned a lot. I hoped. Next time around, no one was going to know that I was terrified. The hand on the tiller was going to be as firm as a rock—even if the ship was sinking—the Captain goes down with the ship. But he doesn't yowl about it. He just quietly does his best.

That's really all there was to it.

Oh me—there was one incident—years later. Leland Hayward, who had been my agent— Yes, that's right, he'd also been my beau—but years later Leland met Jed outside a theatre in Philadelphia.

Jed stopped him—looked him in the eye and said, "You know, Leland, I tried to destroy Katharine Hepburn."

Leland looked right back at him: "You failed, didn't you, Jed? Have a nice day."

And Leland walked on.

III

George Cukor

Nothing tonight, Johanna, I'm going to George's. You know. George Cukor—movie director."

He was my friend. I arrived in Hollywood only a few years after him. He had gone in 1929. I in 1932. He hired me for *A Bill of Divorcement*, the ingénue Sydney, Barrymore's daughter.

Right off, he had bought a house—a modest one-story house on Cordell Drive in the hills above Sunset. George was a success and his house grew. And it grew. And it grew. First the property from a lot to several acres. Then the house.

It was on the side of a hill. I mean, really, it was on the flat and the hill went up steeply in back of the house. The flat land grew wider to the south. This became a big garden. A Miss Yak planted trees, grass, flowers. A long swimming pool. A wide walk up to a sort of marble-pillared lookout. Near the pool was a fireplace in a vine-covered area. On sunny days, we'd eat there. And all this was enclosed by a high brick wall running along Cordell Drive.

On a lower level, a gardener's house and a grape arbor. Later, three small houses were built in this area—one was Spence's house.

By this time George's house was no longer a kitchen-dining-room, living-room, two-bed-one-bath affair. It had grown. And why not! *What Price Hollywood?* (the original *A Star Is Born*) with Constance

Bennett and Lowell Sherman, *Dinner at Eight*, *Little Women*, *David Copperfield*, etc.

The living room grew out to the south, a deep bay window looking onto a generous terrace, now a story above the garden level. The front entrance was through the brick wall and the stairway up to the terrace, which was really the main floor. This room was quite conventional —quite formal. I remember the arrival of three beautiful chairs from the Whitelaw Reid Castle in Purchase. There was an enchanting Renoir pastel of a lady with an umbrella over the fireplace. To the left a Grant Wood landscape. I had sent for it from the Walker Gallery in New York. George loved it, so he took it. In this room we had tea on formal occasions.

The old dining room lost its head and grew taller by about ten feet. It was dark and it sort of disappeared upward. Lit entirely by candles. You could hardly see. We all looked delicious. The china, linen, silver, glass (I mean crystal)—shining, exquisite, a delight. George himself picked it out for any and whatever occasion. He loved all his treasures. They represented his dream—a child's dream—that once-upon-a-time dream. It's come true—the prince—the princess. I'm riding a great white stallion.

The flowers in the center of the table were always too high. I used to sneak in before dinner and cut them down, if possible, so that we could see each other. I usually sat at the wrong end of the table. That's where I struck up a friendship with Irene Selznick. She, like me, was one of George's dependables. The food was great—the company the best. I was there at dinner once: dessert—a beautiful cake came in—seventy candles. Judy Garland quietly stood, and in her own particular hushed and heartbreaking voice she sang:

> "Happy birthday to you,
> Happy birthday to you,
> Happy birthday, dear Ethel,
> Happy . . ."

It was Ethel Barrymore's seventieth birthday. We all wept with joy and feeling and whatever it is. It was romantic. And all the shine. And that Selznick-Brice-Judy-Spencer-Peck-Walpole-Maugham atmosphere.

TOP: Cukor's house; BOTTOM: Ethel Barrymore's seventieth birthday, with Sam Colt, George Cukor, Constance Collier and Billie Burke

When I first began to go to George's—in fact, the first time—
he had cheesecake for dessert. I found it revolting but, of course, I
ate it. Swallow—swallow—don't breathe—swallow. "Oh, Kate, you
like that! Good! Come, Myrtle, give Miss Hepburn another piece."
"Oh no—no!" But they gave me the piece and I ate it. After that for
several years. Yes, years, whenever I dined: "We have your favorite."
Finally, I told him the truth.

No cottage now! To manage all this: a big pantry—a big
kitchen—eight burners—two iceboxes—a laundry—and the back
stairs leading up to three luxury maids' rooms and a bath. One of the
original bedrooms became an office. The other became a library. When
we were just folks, this is where we sat. He added a fireplace. He
had a great collection of books. On a table, casually, a signed photograph of Jack Kennedy and Jackie—of Maugham—of Spencer. Even
a little statuette of me as Cleopatra. Oh yes, I was there. I got moved
occasionally but that was O.K. I was family.

Now comes the big push. The house is expanding.

Strike the south wall to the library. We're adding a rather formal
but small hallway. Come in a new front door. Throw a coat or a hat
on a Victorian round mushroom seat or hang your coat in a cupboard
or have a drink—there's a tiny bar opposite.

But if you want a real thrill, turn right (south) and you are entering
the famous Oval Room. The leather walls, high ceiling, indirect
lighting separating wall from ceiling. Yes, that's a Braque. Yes, that's
a Matisse. The others, about five big paintings, the Braque above a
fireplace and inside the fireplace not a fire but a huge spike of crystal
quartz, a gift from George Hoyningen-Huene.

At the opposite end, a sofa built into a rounded glass window. It
was a huge sort of seat, very cushioned, very deep. In front of this,
as a table, the Corinthian crown of a pillar, table height, on top of
it a piece of marble for your drinks. Facing the windows and sofa
several chairs, two or three on either side of the Corinthian bit. Here
we had our drinks on great occasions. There we were all tumbled
together, the seat so deep you couldn't get out once you got in.
Stravinsky—Ethel Barrymore—Edith Sitwell—the Goldwyns—
Hugh Walpole—Somerset Maugham—Sir Osbert Sitwell—Groucho
Marx—Ina Claire—Gregory Peck—Fanny Brice—Judy Garland—

Natasha Paley—Larry Olivier—Vivien Leigh—Noel Willman—
Well, you name them—Gar Kanin—Ruth Gordon—anyone who
was.

I remember once getting onto that sofa and being penned in by
Stravinsky and Groucho Marx. I wanted to talk to Stravinsky about
the lyrebirds in Australia. Had he heard them?

"Shut up, Groucho." Well, he had tried to hear them, yes, he
had gone to Melbourne and gone to Sherbrooke Forest and listened
but . . .

"Shut up, Groucho." He had heard nothing. It was his kind of
sound. He had a symphony in mind. The birds were silent. For me
they sang and sang. What a waste! Poor Groucho, he wanted to talk
and I wanted to hear Stravinsky, who wanted to hear the lyrebirds,
and they chose not to sing. Life life!

Off we go again, still going south. The door straight ahead across
a little hall led into George's own quarters. Living room, sleeping
porch, white marble bathroom, and on the walls endless Garbos,
Ingrids, Viviens, Gladys Coopers, Grandma, Grandpa, Mother, Father (they were sweet, I knew them well), George as a baby, as a boy.
A Beaton portrait of Natasha Paley, one of me. All very cozy and
private it was.

To the left of the little hallway was the stairway down, covered
with letters, drawings, paintings. Even one of mine is there, "The
Chair." Down the stairs to the guest room—big bed—big
cupboard—lots of light—bowls of lovely soaps—boxes of candy—
baskets of fruit—the latest books—magazines—lovely sheets—
blankets—quilts—pillows—quiet—ring for breakfast. This was my
room whenever I came back to town. George would come down to
breakfast at six-thirty.

Oh well, it was all fun and posh and pretty and lovely and exciting.
It was a palace of tan leather and polished wood and high ceilings
and silver and gold and you know. And the conversation matched.
We laughed and we enjoyed life.

Thank you, George Cukor, dear friend, it was lovely. How we
miss you. No smog in your thinking. No drink, no pills. Just the
energy to make your dreams come true.

I've written about George Cukor's house and I've been thinking

I really should write something about George as a director. I made about—well:

A Bill of Divorcement, Little Women, Sylvia Scarlett, Holiday, The Philadelphia Story, Keeper of the Flame, Adam's Rib, Pat and Mike, The Corn Is Green, Love Among the Ruins.

His was an extraordinary career, and yet he is seldom listed with the so-called great directors: John Huston—George Stevens—John Ford—Willy Wyler—Billy Wilder—Hitchcock.

I think that I have finally figured out why. He was primarily an actor's director. He was primarily interested in making the actor shine. He saw the story through the eyes of the leading characters.

When I made *A Bill of Divorcement*, he set out to sell *me* to the audience: running down the stairs into the arms of David Manners—throwing myself on the floor—in Barrymore's arms. A sort of isn't-she-fascinating approach.

His own focus was the actors. He presented them.

John Ford's focus was the plot. I did *Mary of Scotland* with him. He really lost interest in it when he found out it was a weak story.

I think Huston's focus was the plot. That doesn't mean that these men did not have interest in the actors. It just means that they were more interested in themselves as directors. So when they had interviews, it was about the property rather than the actor—in short, about themselves and how they worked out the style in which they presented the story.

In George's interviews he would describe and focus on the brilliance of the actors' performances, and the interviewer would give the credit to the actor in his review. So we got the credit and George didn't. I wonder if I'm right. I think so.

When he talked to the press about any of his pictures, he discussed what interested him—the performances. So the writer then wrote about the actors. George had been trained in his Rochester Stock Company to try to sell his theatre in an era when performances were the thing—and when actors were really strong personalities.

As I've said, George Cukor gave me my first movie job—in 1932.

I've told you how I went to Hollywood with Laura Harding—and how I met George. He was really fat—about five feet eight inches

With Cukor

and over 220 pounds. He was very energetic, full of laughter and vitality. He summed me up very accurately for what I was: a lady, so-called—a sort of a snob—and totally insecure. I summed him up too. Very bright—sharp as a tack and a good sense of humor.

From the very beginning of our friendship, he began asking me to dinner and to his Sunday lunches. And of course, as Laura Harding was with me, he also asked her—so they became good friends too.

At this time a funny thing happened. Margaret Mitchell sent me the manuscript for *Gone With the Wind*. I read it and thought that it was fascinating. I gave it to Pandro Berman, producer and head of RKO, who gave it to his assistant to read. Joe Sistrom, the assistant, thought that it was a very unsympathetic part—bad for my career. In the meantime the manuscript was, of course, sent around. I went to David Selznick's house to pick up his brother Myron to drive him to Arrowhead for the weekend. David came to the door when I rang. He had the book of *Gone With the Wind* in his hands. I said, "Don't read it, David—just buy it."

Well, David read it and bought it and of course hired George as director—and George felt that I was not the right type for Scarlett, so they began to look for an unknown girl. After months of looking they came to me and asked if I would make a test. By this time I felt that they were being forced to take me because they *had* to start the picture at a certain date or they would lose the property. I also felt that I would really be a disappointing choice. And I knew that if I did a test they would sign me, but they would go on looking for an unknown and might find one and then just dump me.

The final arrangement was that the day before they had to start —the day before—I would agree to start work in the actual picture. I'd been dressed by Walter Plunkett many times, so I could become a part of everything very speedily. This was clever of me because then they found Vivien Leigh and certainly would have dumped me—and I would have been very unhappy. So George and I lived through that experience. Incidentally, George never told me why David fired him from *Gone With the Wind*—and I never asked.

Then on *Woman of the Year* with Spence and me—George Stevens directing—I had to explain to Cukor that this script had to be directed by a very macho director from the man's point of view and not the woman's.

I'm sure that George was very disappointed.

The only other episode which sort of threatened us was when I was fired from *Travels with My Aunt* and Maggie Smith was given the part. George Cukor wanted to quit as director because he felt that it was our property. I persuaded him that that would be senseless—that he should stay on as director. We might need the money. They had fired me because they felt that I was holding up the project. That was true—I was holding it up because I thought the script could be improved. Actually, I was right—and the movie was not a success.

Toward the end of George's life, whenever I was in California I used to see him every day. We had an old gang who used to eat dinner together. Frances Goldwyn, who had been his friend since the Rochester days when George was running his big stock company, was one of the group. Sam Goldwyn had died and I used to drive over and pick up Frances, and then at the end of the evening I'd drive her home. She was not too well at the time. George was very fond of her. He had been really influential in making her marry Sam. I often wondered if he had stepped out of the picture as a possible choice. Now George lies buried next to Frances in the Goldwyn plot.

George really liked me—and I really liked him. From the moment we met, we each had the capacity to give on certain issues which seemed important to the other. From the beginning to the day he died, we just got on.

George Cukor was really my best friend in California. We made many pictures together—always happily. Must have had the same set of standards. We both adored the business—we loved to work—we admired each other. He loved to entertain and I loved to be his guest. In the early days of our relationship he was very lavish; with the passage of time the group got smaller. He rented Spence one of the three houses on his property, and when Spence died I took over the rent for about ten years. It was as if George and I had been brought up together. Total comfort. The same liberal point of view—the same sense of right and wrong.

I miss him.

Leland

eland Hayward was a really charming human being. He was a big theatrical agent and partner of Myron Selznick in Hollywood. He was fun. He wasn't complicated. He was easygoing. Not too set in his ways. Loved the ladies and sailed from one island to another with joy and ease. I met him the day I arrived in Hollywood, but apparently he didn't strike me at that time, or vice versa—I mean me him.

Miriam Howell, as an agent, had first contacted me when I was in *The Warrior's Husband*. It was to do a test for *A Bill of Divorcement*. I got the part. I did the movie and then one after another. I was a big flash.

Just the kind of flash that fascinated Leland. It turned out to be mutual. And it wasn't long before we . . . Well, it wasn't long before we . . . Well, yes. There is a picture of him with me. It has been published many times as K.H. and Ludlow Ogden Smith. Actually, it is Leland and me. About 1933 or '34.

As you know, early in the thirties, Luddy and I agreed to separate. I felt that I was about to enter a new world, a world where Luddy would have no connection. I don't really know whether Luddy and I ever discussed it. I look back in horror at my behavior. At the time, I was looking forward to the future and not *our* future but definitely *my* future. I was obviously trying to climb to the top of the ladder.

The man in this photograph, often identified as
Ludlow Ogden Smith, is actually Leland Hayward.

Luddy did not complain. As I've said, he simply did everything he
could to help me follow my own road, and I was apparently totally
unaware of my piggishness.

Luddy and I had separated. I didn't care whether or not I had a
divorce, because I was certain that I would never marry again. But I
didn't want Luddy to be a "deceived husband." I knew that I would
have to go somewhere quickly to get a divorce. Laura Harding and I
went to Yucatán. And came right back.

I could see very quickly that I suited Leland perfectly. I liked to
eat at home and go to bed early. He liked to eat out and go to bed
late. So he had a drink when I had dinner and then off he'd go. Back
at midnight. Perfect friendship. We tumbled back happily into our
own ruts. It was an extremely easy relationship. He was my source
of the most luscious information about the world we seemed to be
living in. This took no effort on my part. All the gossip. Lovely. He

also had a room in the Beverly Hills Hotel and/or Beverly Wilshire Hotel.

Leland became friends with my mother. They got on. Well, that wasn't unusual because as you must have gathered by this time, everyone found my mother fascinating. And why not? She *was* fascinating. He liked Laura too, which was lucky.

We—Laura and I—had moved from a house in Franklin Canyon to a house in Coldwater Canyon. This one had a swimming pool and a tennis court. Quite a lot of property. With Leland about, the house was a bit crowded but fun. We always thought it was haunted. My brother Dick came out to visit us and said he felt that someone would come and stand at the foot of his bed and watch him. There were strange noises. It was an odd house built up the side of a hill, so that although the master bedroom was up the hill from the living room, it was also on the ground floor.

One very funny thing happened in that house. Laura had been sick and had gone to the hospital. There she had had a bit of a flirt with a very handsome young doctor. I came back from a location with *Spitfire* and we had the young doctor to dinner. We had artichokes— one of our favorite foods. Take off a leaf or petal and dip it in melted butter. The doctor found this a bit perplexing and finally managed to drip some butter on his chin.

We were discussing some very highfalutin topic and I couldn't keep my eyes off the butter on his chin. Finally I found myself saying, "Yes, I do of course believe in God—you have butter on your chin —but what I mean by God may not be what . . ."

He froze with horror. Wiped his chin. Left soon after dinner and we never saw him again.

By this time Leland and I were like an old married couple. He was lighthearted. He enjoyed living—eating—loving. We laughed. We did what we wanted to do when we wanted to do it. I played tennis and golfed with other people. He didn't like to do either. He enjoyed his agency business. Life was fun and easy. I was happy. I had a beau. I had a career. Leland wanted to marry me, but I really did not want to marry.

Then later in 1934, Laura and I moved into the Fred Niblo house on the top of Angelo Drive up above Benedict Canyon. Fred Niblo

had directed *Ben-Hur*—a silent picture—a big hit. This house later became the Jule Styne house and is now the Murdoch house. It was a great location, $1,000 a month then—a really luxurious house—pool—court.

There was only one other house on the top—the Frances Marion house. She had married Fred Thomson. She was a very successful writer of movie scripts. He became a big Western star. Then he suddenly died. The house was for sale. The house I was in was for sale too, for $25,000. I could have bought these two properties for a very small amount. Comprising about forty acres. I really could have owned that mountain. Dad, who managed my money, never came to Hollywood. But I doubt that he would have been interested in property. He was trying to build up a big income for me, so that I would have something to live on besides him when it all exploded. Having a screen-star daughter was something which did not inspire in him a sense of security.

My life was to me heavenly. Funny things would happen. I remember one day George Cukor and a friend came to call. They wanted to see the house. I turned on the lights in the living room and there in front of the fireplace was a big snake asleep.

"Oh dear," I said, "a rattler."

George and his friend raced out.

I opened the French doors to the outside so that the snake could escape, and I shut all the doors into the rest of the house. And the rattler, being a snake of very good sense, left and went back to his home in the woods below.

Another time, just after I'd rented the house, George Cukor and Garbo came to call. She'd been told about the house and wanted to see it. I showed it off. Went upstairs—showed her the bedroom. She walked over to my bed. There was a lump on the bed (obviously a hot-water bottle).

She looked at me, patted it and sighed. "Yes, I have one too. Vat is wrong vid us?"

One day I was taking a walk with my three dogs—Mica, a cocker

With Laura Harding, returning from Mexico

With Peter, Button and Mica

spaniel; Button, a French poodle; and Peter, a black cocker. We passed
Frances Marion's house. She was living there alone at this point.

She told me the following: "You can't imagine what has just
transpired here. Did a funny-looking old Dodge car pass you on your
way up?"

"Yes—a brown Dodge. An old man driving—fat woman next to
him."

"They're the ones! Well, I can hardly believe that this has happened. I was sitting on the little terrace outside the living room. I
heard the doorbell ring. I went to the front door. There stood that
lady (I use the word with reluctance) whom you saw sitting in the
front seat of that Dodge.

" 'How ya,' she said in a most unfortunate tone and quality of
voice. 'Is this place for sale?'

" 'Yes—it is,' I answered reluctantly.

" 'We seen the stables down that other road. Very good—lots of stables. I wanna see it.'

"She turned to the man in the Dodge: 'Ya wanna come, hon?'

" 'Naw—you look. I'll read the paper.'

" 'O.K.—les go,' she said to me. And I found myself showing her the house. From room to room we went. She hardly seemed to register anything.

" 'Ya, good.'

" 'Now what—where—you—we'll go out into the terrace.'

"I pointed: 'It's— Oh—well, this way—' And I led her to the kitchen.

" 'Ya—O.K.—that's enough. Where's the front—'

"I eagerly led her to the front door. Her husband still sitting in the front seat.

" 'Like it, honey?'

" 'Ya—pretty good.'

" 'How much?' the husband asked.

"Dumbfounded, I replied, 'It's six hundred and ninety-five thousand dollars.'

" 'Will you take a check?'

"They just bought this house. Those two people in that Dodge sedan. They just bought this house."

She showed me the check.

Apparently, these people had hit oil in Texas. They had a daughter who liked to ride. They had been down the road leading to the many stables which had been built for Fred Thomson's horses.

They lived in the house for two years. Never paid the taxes. Moved out. And then the house was sold for the taxes—about seventy thousand dollars. That's when I could have bought it. Stupid me.

Life with Leland had no problems. It was simply—how can I describe it to you? Nothing was a problem. There were solutions to everything. Joy was the constant mood. Everything was like a delightful surprise. He found life so easy. I don't remember any fights. We just enjoyed—enjoyed—enjoyed. Almost four years.

Then Leland had to go East. He had a client—Edna Ferber—and

Margaret Sullavan was opening in Edna Ferber's *Stage Door*. Edna had been a client of Leland's for a long time.

Oh, I can see it all. The play was a hit. Maggie was a hit. Everything was glorious. He found her fascinating. He must have her for a client. And the quickest way to succeed was to make her his. So he did. Joy was life. Life was joy. *Me*, faraway, became a sort of unreality.

She was there. He was there with her.

Oh, live in the moment!

They did.

And all of a sudden he found himself married to Maggie and starting a family, and I became a sort of dream. Years later he tried to explain it to me and he really couldn't—any more than I could explain my refusal to marry him.

Anyway, I got a wire saying that he and Maggie were married.

I was thunderstruck. What is this! No—not nice—not fair! I called Mother in Hartford. I was furious. Weeping. How could he? So wicked!

"But you didn't want him, Kath. Maybe he just wanted to get married. Poor man. You can't blame him. It's your fault. You must send them a wire. Don't be a poor sport. It's your fault."

Well, that wasn't a very comforting conversation. I sent them a wire but went right on weeping and moaning and complaining.

I must tell you that George Cukor said, "Kate, what's wrong with you? You could have married him if you wanted him. You didn't."

"Oh, stop saying that! What am I going to do?" And I went on moaning as long as anyone would listen. Of course Mother was right. I think that she told Leland to be happy, not to worry about me.

As there was nothing that I could do, I went my way too. I don't even think that I learned a lesson. They had three children. Soon they separated and he married Slim Hawks. Then he married Pamela Churchill.

Finally, when Leland was ill and dying, Pamela called me and said, "Leland is dying. He loved you more than he loved any of us. Will you go and see him? He's at . . . ."

I went. I'd seen him once or twice through the years—or maybe more than that. He was a funny fellow. I think that he found women really delicious. I was pleased that he seemed to like me. I think Pamela exaggerated his feeling for me. I think that as Leland looked back, he really was looking back at himself as a young man. We were both young and I had never married him, so he only had the experience of a thrilling love affair with me—no feeling of being locked in by a marriage.

Also I was not in the business of capturing anyone into a marriage. I just did not want to marry anyone. I liked the idea of being my own single self. Even when I was living with Spencer Tracy and he and I were together for twenty-seven years, we never really thought about or discussed marriage. He was married and I wasn't interested.

I think that psychologically Leland felt he and I could have gone on and on. I liked him and I did enjoy his company. Easy sailing. Fun. So few people are. Have you noticed? It was like eating ice-cream cones on a hot day. Delicious. And it's being young.

What can I say of Leland? He really danced his way through life. Do you know what I mean?

We met at a time when to each of us everything was joy and laughter and exciting and perfect. But we had such fun! Oh yes—Fun.

I was lucky to know him.

On tour in *Jane Eyre*, avoiding fans

Howard Hughes

I have to go back a bit now and tell you about what happened during *Sylvia Scarlett*. This picture we were shooting with George Cukor directing—Cary Grant the leading man and my father Edmund Gwenn. We shot a lot of it out beyond Trancas Beach in California. George and I used to alternate having gorgeous picnic lunches sent from home. Lunch for fifteen or twenty people. We'd have a great long table and Louis and Ranghild Prysing and Johanna Madsen, my help at home, would arrive from my house in the station wagon with: soup, hot or cold—salads—some hot main course—ice cream. It was fantastic.

One day an airplane circled overhead and circled and then landed on a dime in the field next to us—too close.

Who could that be? Who the hell would—?

Cary Grant piped up: "That's my friend Howard Hughes."

I was somewhat taken aback because I had heard it rumored that Hughes would like to meet me. And apparently this was how he'd figured it out. I gave Cary a black look and we all had lunch. I never looked at Howard. What a nerve!

The next step. I was playing golf with the pro at the Bel Air Country Club. We were on the seventh about to finish a nine-hole lesson. The noise of an airplane. Howard landed practically on top of us. Took his clubs out of the plane and finished the nine with us. He had to have a truck come in and practically take the plane apart to remove it from the course. I must say it gave me pause. I thought that he had a hell of a nerve and was very pushy. The Club was furious. Howard Hughes was nothing daunted. We finished the nine and I said, "Can I drop you somewhere?" He said yes and I drove him to the Beverly Hills Hotel.

The next time—about two months later—I saw in the paper that Howard was in Boston. I was playing *Jane Eyre*, a play by Helen Jerome, there. I was staying at the Ritz Hotel. We were playing at the Colonial Theatre. Howard moved into the same hotel.

I think that I must have been lonely, because Howard and I had supper with one another after the performance that first night. Thus proving that persistence pays. We had supper the next night too— so . . .

Howard Hughes was a curious fellow. He had guts and he had a really fine mind, but he was deaf—quite seriously deaf—and he was apparently incapable of saying, "Please speak up. I'm deaf." Thus if he was with more than one person, he was apt to miss most of the conversation. This was tragic. But he was absolutely incapable of changing. I had a good friend, Russell Davenport, who was also deaf. But he just said, "Speak up, please—I'm deaf." This is the real tragedy of any sort of personal defect. Just say it. Admit it. The person you say it to is not at all embarrassed. He or she just speaks up. He's just happy that he himself is not deaf. I think that this weakness went a long way toward ruining Howard's life and making him into an oddball.

He followed us on tour. We played Chicago. I stayed at the Ambassador Hotel. Howard took a suite there too. Yes—same floor. Yes—you're right of course—inevitable. The papers began to put us in headlines: HUGHES AND HEPBURN WILL MARRY TODAY. I couldn't move in that city without being followed. My apartment was on the ninth or tenth floor. One day I swung out onto the fire escape to climb down and not have to go through the lobby. I got down to the first floor and discovered one of those parallel ladders that you have to walk out on and your weight makes it go down. So I walked out on it but it didn't go down, and I had to climb back and then up the how many floors to get back into my room.

With Howard Hughes and his airplane

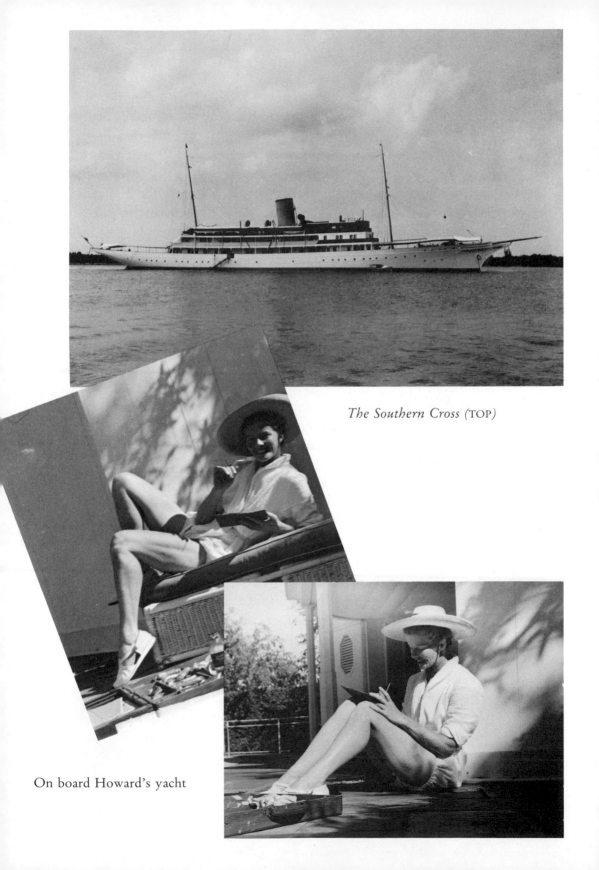

The Southern Cross (TOP)

On board Howard's yacht

Howard followed the tour—Detroit, Cleveland, Chicago. He conducted his life on the telephone because there he could hear. Finally the tour was over and we went back to California and moved into his house, which backed onto the Wilshire Country Club golf course. That was fun because we could just jump the fence and play golf. Howard had a woman named Beatrice Dowler working for him. She was a good cook. It was she who told me how when certain guests would come to dinner they would set the table with the cheap china and glassware and when the dinner was over she (Beatrice) would break the cheap china and glassware and throw it away.

I don't quite understand what this proved. I once said to Howard, "I think that if you picked your friends more carefully you wouldn't have to break so much china."

So we lived on Muirfield Road. My cook Ranghild and her husband, Louis Prysing, also took care of us. And my maid Johanna Madsen—and, of course, Beatrice.

Howard was a very good golfer. I was pretty good too. I had played a lot, as I've told you, but our attitudes to the game were quite different. I played for fun and for exercise. Howard played always to improve his game. He was slow—he'd take practice strokes. I finally used to be almost a hole ahead of him. I was busy admiring the sky—the flowers—the relaxation. He would be utterly disgusted with me.

"You could be a really fine golfer if you would only practice."

I used to think to myself, And you could be fun if you weren't so slow. So we drifted along. Misfits by tempo.

Howard had decided that he would fly around the world. He was an expert flier and knew everything there was to know about engines. He was going to fly out of Long Island. We had gone to New York and were living in my friend Laura Harding's apartment on Fifty-second Street. My house was surrounded by the press, who were aware that something exciting was going to happen.

We left Fifty-second Street early and were on the highway to the airstrip where he had his plane (ready to go). Charles Newhill, my driver, was at the wheel. We were in my Lincoln. He was an angel but he could be hot-tempered. All of a sudden we heard a police siren back of us.

I rolled down the window: "Charles, don't lose your cool. Take the ticket—take anything. He must not find out that H.H. is with us!"

Cool Charles!

Charles was cool. Took the ticket. And the cop never looked into the back of the car and we were on our way again.

The plan was for me to drop him at the airstrip and then to go back to the apartment. He would keep me posted.

Howard called and said that there was something wrong with the plane, which would have to be fixed. It would take about six hours or so. There were hordes of people surrounding the airport wanting to watch. The delay didn't bother H.H. at all. He was used to things not working and having to fix them. He finally left and broke the record. I got messages from various points. It was exciting.

We had a very pleasant life. Occasionally I would go East to see my family. I remember once I said goodbye to Howard. Left for the airport. Was sitting on the plane ready to leave. Luggage boarded.

A man in uniform came up to me and said, "You're not to go."

"What?" I said.

"You are not to go. Mr. Hughes says that you are not to go. The weather is bad."

Embarrassed, I got off the plane. Sending the rest of the passengers to their doom. Of course all was fine—nothing happened. It was a very peculiar experience.

I used to fly everywhere with Howard—across the country—here—there. Howard taught me to fly. I took off once under the Fifty-ninth Street Bridge. Sometimes I would just be lying in the plane in a sleeping bag. Once at Fenwick we flew to Newport to watch the boat races.

I thought I smelled smoke. "I smell smoke," I said.

"Well, what the hell do you think I've been smelling?"

We flew back to New London, Connecticut, and put out the fire. It certainly was always exciting.

When we used a seaplane, sometimes if it was hot we would stop in the middle of Long Island Sound and anchor the plane, take off our clothes, dive off a wing naked to cool off. It was fun.

Playing golf with Howard at Fenwick

Practicing for *Bringing Up Baby*

My family were not too sympathetic to Howard. In the first place, he was everlastingly on the telephone. And the telephone was in the dining room. And we were a big family and always had visitors. Long telephone conversations did not suit the atmosphere.

And Luddy was always there too. Especially on the golf course. And he was ever present with his movie camera. Howard couldn't stand this and objected.

Dad made his famous remark: "Howard, Luddy has been taking pictures of all of us for many years before you joined us and he will be taking them long after you've left. He is part of this family. Go ahead. Drive. You need a seven iron."

Howard in a fury drove—six feet from the pin. He was a good golfer. Sank a two. Not bad in a pinch. Cool.

During this period, my career had taken a real nosedive. It was then that the "box-office poison" label began to appear. The independent theatre owners were trying to get rid of Marlene Dietrich, Joan Crawford and me. It seems that they were forced to take our pictures if they got certain ones which they *really* wanted.

Actually, I felt sorry for them. I had made a string of very dull movies:

Break of Hearts
Sylvia Scarlett
A Woman Rebels
Quality Street.

On the good side:

Alice Adams, with Fred MacMurray
Stage Door, with Ginger Rogers
Bringing Up Baby, with Cary Grant
Holiday, with Cary Grant.

These last four were good pictures, but I had apparently become someone the independents avoided because of the four dull preceding. I did *Holiday* on a loan-out from RKO, who were anxious to get rid of me and had offered me *Mother Carey's Chickens*, which I had turned down. We made a deal: I would pay RKO $75,000 and they would let me do *Holiday* for Columbia. Harry Cohn (Columbia) had offered me $150,000.

At this point I became the leader of "Poison at the Box Office." The independent theatre owners put me at the top of the list. I had really slumped down down down. *Holiday* was completed.

So Harry Cohn was stuck with *Holiday* when all this bad publicity was coming out. Poor Harry. He thought of taking out another 24-sheet saying, "What's wrong with Katharine Hepburn?" I advised him not to: "Look out! They might tell you."

Then I decided that I'd better go back East and do a play or something else.

Paramount had sent me a script for which they offered me a salary of $10,000. A cut from $150,000. I called them. Thanked them very much. Told them it was the only offer I'd had. That I was sorry but I did not like the script.

Howard was very upset with this. He was really anxious for me to take that Paramount offer. I thought it would be a terrible mistake. He was very conscious of what he thought people were saying about him. He felt that I was embarrassed by my failure, but somehow I wasn't. Well, obviously it mattered but not enough to govern my actions.

I thought H.H. was wrong. And he thought I was wrong.

Howard and I were indeed a strange pair. I don't think—what should I say?—I think that reluctantly he found me a very appropriate companion. And I think that I found him extremely appropriate too. He was sort of the top of the available men—and I of the women. We were a colorful pair. It seemed logical for us to be together, but it seems to me now that we were too similar. He came from the right street, so to speak. And so did I. We'd been brought up in ease. We each had a wild desire to be famous. I think that this was a dominant character failing. People who want to be famous are really loners. Or they should be.

Certainly I felt that I was madly in love with him. And I think he felt the same way about me. But when it came right down to "What do we do now?"—I went East and he stayed West. We'd been together about three years. Ambition beat love, or was it *like*?

I advised all my help to stay with H.H. "You'll have a much better life than with me." So they did—they stayed with H.H. It was the end of 1937, the beginning of '38.

Holiday, with Cary Grant

It seemed to me that I was in a very odd situation. Certainly I had done some very boring pictures. But then, I had done four really good pictures, and they had just not done well. They had done O.K. but not as well as they deserved. That's really why I felt that I should get a breath of fresh air. A real change of atmosphere.

Again, as I look back, I have to realize that I took what I considered a good business step and did not let my personal life dominate my actions.

I did not want to marry Howard. I liked him. He was bright and he was interesting and his life was interesting, but obviously I was obsessed by my own failure and I wondered whether I could put it right.

I went to Fenwick, which was in full flower. It was June and the weather was heavenly and the golf-tennis-swimming-sailing were ever available. The family were all there and it was fun. Lots of talk talk. Lots of exercise. The people there were not really aware of my peculiar predicament so it was never discussed.

Dad certainly knew that there was no cash coming in. But as he had thought that a career in theatre and movies was a very chancy occupation, this sudden lull did not surprise him.

One day the telephone rang and it was Philip Barry in Maine: "I have an idea. I want to talk to you."

"Fine," I said. "I'm in Fenwick. Come down any time . . . Good . . . Tomorrow will be fine . . . Yes, about teatime. Good."

He arrived. As I said, people came often to tea and finally Phil said, "Can't we go somewhere? I want to talk to you, alone."

We went out to the pier and sat. Phil said that he had two plots: one, a father and daughter; the second, *The Philadelphia Story*. The latter sounded the better one to me.

Phil left, and in a few weeks he sent me a draft of the first act.

I read it. I was thrilled. It was almost exactly as it was when we did it.

I called Howard and told him that I had a thrilling new project. Howard said, "Buy the film rights before you open." And he bought the movie rights to *The Philadelphia Story* for me, which insured my success later.

I think we really liked each other, but somehow—

The next day God sent the hurricane of 1938. The house at Fenwick disappeared. Howard had a pilot fly in with bottled water —and I knew that Howard and I had become friends and not lovers. Love had turned to water. Pure water. But water.

Howard and I just seemed to suit each other. I admired his nerve and his stamina. He seemed to admire me. He could hear me with my sharp voice. I was happy with him because, like me, he was a "stay-at-home." I look back at our relationship and I think that we were both cool customers. He could do anything he wanted. And when I decided to move East, I think he thought, Well, I don't want to move East. I'll find someone who will stay West. I always thought it was lucky that we never married—two people who are used to having their own way should stay separate.

He was always a good friend. His doctor, Lawrence Chaffin, was my doctor too. He felt, as I do, that Howard's deafness finally did him in. Howard had had a serious airplane accident, which caused him unbearable pain. For the pain he was given morphine—and Howard finally found this blank road more comfortable than the endless life struggle. One cannot blame him, but it was very sad. He was a remarkable man.

With Red Hammond after the storm

Hurricane

ell—that hurricane of '38.

The hurricane of '38 was a real adventure. As I said, we were at Fenwick. It was a very curious happening. That morning—late September—most of the residents had gone back to Hartford and their houses were more or less closed. I swim all winter, so the season is never closed to me. In fact, we always enjoyed it most when it was sort of empty.

I remember going for my swim at about 8 a.m. It was a very fine atmosphere. The tide was low—almost on the change. The air clear—a light breeze. The color of everything very definite. I went back in—had breakfast. Went outside. A steady wind was blowing now, but it was very pleasant.

I decided to play golf. Jack ("Red") Hammond had come for a weekend in July, and here it was late September and he was still with us. We had a good time together and he was a good golfer and a pretty good tennis player and so was I. So we had fun.

Oh, there's a great story I must tell you about Red's father, Judge Hammond. He was at the theatre alone in Boston. When the curtain went up, the woman sitting in front of him was obviously not intending to remove her hat.

Finally he tapped her on the shoulder and said, "I beg your pardon but would you remove your hat? I can't . . ."

She indicated by a rude hand gesture that he should desist.

What to do? What to do?

Ah, yes.

He took his own hat and put it on. A folding top hat. Immediately the people in back of him whispered: "Take off that hat! Take off that hat!"

The woman in front of the Judge immediately took off her hat. The Judge then happily removed his. I think he must have been a very smart judge, don't you?

Now to continue the hurricane of '38.

Out we went to play golf. Red and I. By then I noticed that the wind had become, well, really quite strong. On the par three ninth, I made a very good drive, high, and it looked as if it had dropped right on the green. When we got there, we didn't see the ball. Where was it? I was sure— Oh my golly—look! In the hole—I got a hole in one. Can you imagine! That meant thirty-one on the nine holes. Certainly it was my record. We went home delighted. Let's take a swim. The tide was half in by now and the waves were beginning to be waves. "You know," I said to Jack, "that wind is really quite strong. I can lean against it and it holds me up."

We jumped the waves— Wow! What fun. We had a time holding ourselves upright. The water was lovely and we stayed in quite a while. When we got out and dressed, we realized that the atmosphere was really strong and getting stronger. The sand was beginning to blow. It stung as it hit us.

Gosh, I thought, my new car's paint job will be hurt. I think I'll have my chauffeur take it to Saybrook and put it in a garage.

Charles left with the Lincoln. He went by way of Cornfield Point, but the wind by then was wild and Charles, who had been shell-shocked in World War I, got scared and went into a house and stayed for the duration.

After that second swim we began to realize that we were in for something special.

Mother was there. Fanny, the cook, was there. Dick, my brother—Jack Hammond—me. The man came over from Frank Burton's to fix the screens on the porch. They had begun to blow like a lady's petticoat. He was hammering them down. All of a sudden the

car which he had come in from Saybrook was flying through the air. It had been picked up by the wind and landed in the lagoon. An ordinary-sized car—just lifted up by the wind. WHAT GOES ON!

Then there was a rip and a crash and the big laundry wing fell off the back of the house. By this time the wind seemed to have doubled its strength and the tide had risen up over the bulkhead and was rushing across the lawn. The house, which was a big old wooden house built in about 1870, was shaking like a leaf. Windows were being blown out or sucked in. Two of the chimneys had blown down. The house had been built on brick piles about three and a half feet high. Mother was convinced that since Dad had just had those brick piles checked, the house would be as firm as a rock. Dick finally persuaded her that it was time to leave. We decided to drop out the dining-room window on the west, cross a field and get to higher land. We found a rope and one by one—Mother, Fanny, me, Red—dropped out the window onto Dick, who was standing in water about a foot and a half deep. Dick leading, we all held on to a rope and crossed the field. The current in the water was quite strong. The wind was violent. We passed the Brainard house, on the north side, and finally got out of the water and onto higher land. Looking back at the house

(this was about fifteen minutes after we left it), we saw the house slowly turn around, sail off to the northeast and start down the brook which fed the swamp-lagoon. It just sailed away—easy as pie—and soon there was nothing at all left on the spot where the house had stood for over sixty years. Our house—ours for twenty-five years— all our possessions—just gone. LOOK—WE LIVE THERE! HEY—WHAT IS HAPPENING!

We forced open the door of a house (the Riversea Inn) on high land so Mother and Fanny could get out of the wind. Then we went to check any houses which were still occupied to be sure that they did not have fires of any sort burning either in the stove or in the fireplace. These we put out, much to the fury of the cook in charge. But the danger of fire in such a wind in a totally wooden colony was real.

Slowly the storm calmed, the tide went down, the water receded, the wind calmed. Darkness fell. We all slept at the Riversea.

Morning. Red and I awoke at dawn and went forth. Somehow I felt that our house would certainly have come to its senses and gone back to its right location.

I was wrong. There was nothing on our property. We passed the Brainard property. That house had been dislodged and, as I said earlier, its back was broken. Then our property. Flat as a pancake. No standing structure. Just a bathtub at a cockeyed angle and a toilet. The house and all its other bathrooms gone—just plain gone.

Luckily we had moved my Lincoln, as I told you, and we had moved our two other cars to higher land when we began to realize that things were a bit dangerous. We got into one of the cars and drove by a circuitous route to the Saybrook Telephone Company to call Dad in Hartford. We got through. Dad's first words were "Your Mother is O.K.?"

"Yes, Daddy, she's fine. We're all fine. The house is totally gone."

"I suppose you didn't have brains enough to throw in a match before it disappeared. I'm insured for fire."

We went back to our property. Strange feeling. Where was everything? The silver. What about all that silver in the dining room in that heavy sideboard? And Mother's tea service. Those heavy things would have fallen as the house fell.

We began to dig. And, believe it or not, we actually dug up eighty-five pieces of flat silver and the entire tea service.

Then we got some blocks and began to design our present house—built on the same location. We made one mistake. We raised the property only three feet. We should have raised it eleven.

I trust the last act is not a duplicate of the first.

The old house traveled about a third of a mile down the stream and stuck on a stone bridge about a hundred yards from the opening into the river. The top floor was dry as a bone. Dick's papers lay by the typewriter ready to be worked on.

My brother Dick said that after he got everyone up to higher land, he went to the old Moore cottage, forced a window, went up to the top floor and, looking down across the lagoon, watched as our house slowly turned to the right, bending slightly forward—the seafront of the house had turned from south to north—and quietly sailed off down the swamp—down the stream so quietly and in such a dignified manner it seemed to be taking its afternoon stroll.

L. B. Mayer

L. B. Mayer and I were friends. He was the head of Metro-Goldwyn-Mayer. I liked him and he liked me. I sold him quite a number of properties. He gave me a lot of freedom and I gave him a lot of respect. L.B. had a sense of romance about the movie business and the studio system. I must say I did too. It was a glorious time to be in the business.

L. B. Mayer was an amazing man. He knew more without any formal education than most. He had a sense of smell for the business. He was a real entrepreneur in the old-fashioned sense. He understood that an artist was something sacred. He understood that Judy Garland had something that he didn't entirely comprehend. Now, there are terrible stories about what happened to Judy Garland there.

When Judy began to fall apart, Mayer came to me. He said, "Do you know Judy Garland?"

I said, "Vaguely. Not really at all."

He said, "She is in a terribly bad way. She has made us millions of dollars. We should be able to help her. Do you feel that you could do anything? Would you be willing to go and talk to her and see her?"

I think that he thought I could help her. I think also that he selected me because he felt I liked him.

My beginning with Mayer started, as I told you, when my career was apparently coming to an end and I was offered a cut of about 90 percent in salary. I read the Paramount script and I said, "Thank you very much, but I really don't like the script. I am grateful for the offer, though, because I haven't had any offers at all."

I went back East. Phil Barry wrote *The Philadelphia Story*. Hughes bought the movie rights for me. Nobody knew it for nine months. All the obvious ladies wanted to buy it. I said to Harold Freedman, "Don't tell anyone that I own it." He was one of the few men in the world who could keep his trap shut. He was a literary agent.

Finally, people began to realize that I had some sort of control over it. I met Mayer one night. Norma Shearer was with him.

He said, "I would like to talk to you."

I said, "Fine."

He said, "Can I come and see you?"

I said, "No, Mr. Mayer, I'll come and see you."

So I went over to the office and he said that he would like to buy it.

He said, "Do you want to do it?"

I said, "Yes, I do."

He said, "Well, we'd like to have you do it."

He talked to me so shrewdly. He would talk to one person one way and another person another way. But he talked to me and smelled me out shrewdly. He said things that would really charm me.

I finally said, "You know, Mr. Mayer, you are charming me. I know that you are deliberately charming me, and still I am charmed. That's a real artist."

He then asked me what I wanted for it, and I told him. I told him that I wouldn't be making any profit. I said, "What interests me is who I play with, because people say that I am poison at the box office. I want it cast."

He said, "Who do you want?"

I said, "Give me Tracy and Gable."

He said, "I don't think they'll do it."

I said, "I presumed that they probably wouldn't, but ask them."

He said, "Yes, I will ask them."

He did and they said that they wouldn't do it. Then he said, "I can give you Jimmy Stewart, because we have control over him." Then he added, "I'll give you a hundred and fifty thousand dollars to get anyone else you want or can get. You get them. You can name the director."

I said, "I would like George Cukor to direct it."

He said, "Fine."

Then we got Cary Grant for the $150,000 for three weeks' work. He said that he would do it and that he wanted first billing over me. "O.K.," I said, "that's easy." He gave his salary to the Red Cross. We had him for three or four weeks. He had his choice of part and Jimmy Stewart played the other part. Incidentally, Jimmy won the Academy Award.

L. B. Mayer was a shrewd man with enormous understanding of an artist. He was not stupid, not crude. He was a very sensible fellow, and extremely honest. In all my dealings with Mayer, I can say that he was the most honest person I ever dealt with in my life.

So we continued our history together. Then there was *Woman of the Year*. I sent the material to Joe Mankiewicz, who had produced *The Philadelphia Story*. I said, "Read this in twenty-four hours and if you are interested I'll fly out there." The original idea of *Woman of the Year* was Garson Kanin's. His brother Mike Kanin and Ring Lardner, Jr., then joined him. Garson was in the Army at the time.

It was a seventy-eight-page treatment. It was a treatment with some individual scenes, but wasn't entirely complete. It had no names of the writers on it. I said, "I want Spencer Tracy or I won't sell it to the studio."

Mankiewicz called back and said that he thought it was great. He felt it was a wonderful part for Spencer, as indeed it was. I didn't know Spencer then.

I flew out and I went in to talk to Mayer. He said, "How much do you want for it?" I told him. He said, "Who wrote it?"

I said, "Mr. Mayer, I can't tell you." I added, "I want such and such for the author, and I want such and such for me. It's even stephen. Two amounts. Each $125,000."

He said, "We'd give you more than that, but I want to know who the writers are."

TOP LEFT: Philip Barry; TOP RIGHT: Garson Kanin;

BOTTOM: Joe Mankiewicz

I said, "Mr. Mayer, I cannot tell you who the writers are, and there is no way that you are going to find out. There is no possible way."

He said, "I don't like to do business that way."

I felt that he was going to turn me down, so I said, "Besides, it's not for sale. I simply wanted to know how interested you were. It's a great part for Spencer. If you are interested in seeing the script when it's done, then fine. The script will be for sale." I pulled back because I knew what happens when a big man says no. You couldn't ask too much and you couldn't ask too little. You had to figure out what you thought he'd pay and ask for it and get it.

I did not know at that time what troubles they were having with *The Yearling*. They were shooting it in Florida with Spencer. There were terrible photographic troubles with bugs. Bugs on the lenses. They had to call it off and Spencer, who was one of their big stars, was idle. Had I known that, I would have asked three times as much. But I thought I was being terribly clever at the time. I probably would have been better off if I had known a little more about the business. Anyway, we finished the script and I sent it to them. Spencer read it. Thought it was great. I had said that George Stevens would have to be the director of that one. I never saw Mayer again on it. He sent me to one of the other big men, and I knew then that they were going to say yes. From then on I never budged.

I made my deal with them myself, and Mayer said that he was satisfied. I said that I was satisfied. Then I said, "May I have your lawyer go over my contract, because I know that you won't cheat me?" From then on, their lawyer always used to go over my contract. That is the way I did business with Metro. And they didn't cheat me.

We had a kind of arrangement where I would usually bring things to them first. I think it was a three-year arrangement or something like that. This was after *Woman of the Year*. Then I brought them *Without Love*. I brought them a lot of material. But I always arranged the deal with Mayer. Luckily, Garson Kanin was a good friend and he was full of ideas for Spencer Tracy and me.

Now, when I made the speech on censorship, it was supposedly to introduce Henry Wallace, who was running for President against Harry Truman. But I was really making a speech against censorship. The times were very troubled. It was 1947 and the House Committee on Un-American Activities was flourishing. People were losing their jobs. Edward G. Robinson was supposed to make that speech, and I thought, Well, here I am. He's Jewish and very left of center, so he would certainly be suspect by that committee. My ancestors were "on the *Mayflower*." There's nothing that they can tack onto me. I've never been a member of any organization of any kind in my whole life. I'll make the speech. The headlines against me and the articles against me were vicious, absolutely vicious. To none of it did I reply, and the studio asked me to write a statement declaring my political status. I wrote something that would have fired anyone. The truth . . . that we've had freedom of speech for years—then, now and always. It's ours. It was never discussed again.

Mayer sent for me and he said, "Katharine, why did you make that speech?"

I said, "Mr. Mayer, I thought that somebody should make the speech and I thought that somebody should be me. I think the situation is idiotic and out of hand. People are being crucified who can't afford it, and I can afford it."

I had just finished a picture at Metro, where I was the big star. The picture was *Song of Love*, and they were going to try to sell it. The American Legion, etc. were violently against me.

I said, "Mr. Mayer, I do not blame you at all for being upset. You have got to sell the picture with me in it, and you are going to run into trouble. I agree with you; as I am under contract to you, I put you in an enormously embarrassing situation by making the speech. Had I asked you if I could make the speech, you would have said no.

"Now let's face it. I would have done it anyway. That would have put me in a very embarrassing situation. Anyway, I made it. On the other hand, I think you have a perfect right not to pay me a weekly salary from here on in, because I don't know how you can cast me in anything."

He said, "That's not what we're discussing."

I said, "Mr. Mayer, maybe we should be discussing that, because I have done something which an employee of a large institution has no right to do. If you presume to take a weekly salary from someone, maybe you haven't got a right to go out and walk naked down the street."

He kept saying, "We are not discussing that."

Finally, I just left the office. He had blown me up to a certain degree. He refused to take any kind of action on it, and that was it.

Of course, he was dissatisfied. He was a Republican and not on my side of the fence at all. The way those organizations were run was certainly not on the liberal side. They took total responsibility for the people at the studio. I always said that I liked to work for Metro because they knew how to get you across Chicago. That was the truth. They handled the whole thing with class. They paid less money, but they didn't force you to do something that you didn't want to do. There was never any argument about that. He never tried to use force or say, "I'll take your money away." They did not force their people. It was a paternalistic organization in the best and worst sense of the word. I have to say that Mayer never forced me to do anything that I didn't want to do.

I remember that they had a preview of *Woman of the Year*. They had accepted for an ending the last eighth of the picture, which I, alas, had suggested. I met Mayer on the lot the next day.

He said, "The preview was brilliant. We're absolutely thrilled. I'm proud of you."

I said, "The end stank."

He said, "What do you mean?"

I said, "I'm in the position to say this, Mr. Mayer, because I suggested the idea for the end. It's no good. The picture just nosedived."

He said, "How much do you think it would cost to fix it?"

I said, "It would cost about a hundred and fifty thousand dollars."

"Well, fix it," he said.

I said, "Mr. Mayer, are you saying fix it? Are we standing on the corner of the lot and you are just saying, 'Go ahead, it's all right with me, you can spend more money on the picture'?"

He said, "Yes."

So you can't quarrel with that. I am sure the people who had bad relationships with him will tell you exactly the opposite story. I can only say what my experience with him was. Some of the experiences cost him a lot of money. It wasn't all happy days in Dixie. We weren't great social friends. I always called him "Mr. Mayer." I was a great friend of Irene's, but that began a little bit after I went to Metro. It wasn't based upon the fact that I was his daughter's friend. He respected me and I respected him enormously.

Of course, some unfortunate things happened there. For example, there was the whole Judy Garland incident. How much of it can you say that he was responsible for? How much can you say the business is responsible for? Certainly, Judy isn't the only person who has fallen apart in the business. Since the new free era, they have fallen apart even more. It is a business that is fraught with troubled people.

I think Mayer understood the torment of Judy Garland. Of Robert Walker, who was married to Jennifer Jones. Mayer understood Robert Walker. He had trouble with the drink. This isn't a voluntary thing, and it damn well isn't a thing that people can just stop. You might be able to stop it. I might be able to stop it, but maybe others can't. It isn't always that easy. I think that he tried to understand situations. He tried to give people as much help as he could.

I went and talked with Judy. I certainly couldn't have done anything. If you are going to help anybody who is in trouble, this is not a two-hour-a-day job. It is a twenty-four-hour-a-day job. You won't do anything else if you decide that you are going to resurrect and rearrange a human being.

I think Judy was an enormously complicated creature. By the time all this began to catch up with her, she was twenty-odd years old or thirty. By that time she had worked hard. She had lived a lifetime. She was spent. In a way, for tormented creatures work is the easiest thing that they do. It's the living that is difficult. I think that Mayer understood this. You can say, "Why didn't he do something earlier?" Could he have prevented it? I don't know. I really don't know. I don't think that work ever really destroyed anybody. I think that lack of work destroys them a hell of a lot more. And bad habits cripple you.

With L. B. Mayer at the Santa Anita race track

Mayer was romantic and he had a passionate interest in people who could do things. He also had the nerve to take a chance and hire them. He trusted his own judgment. He didn't turn to anyone to ask, "What do you think?" He just took the flyer. He was a brilliant businessman. He was a great gambler, and he loved the business. He just loved the business. People would laugh at him and ridicule him for certain things, but he loved the business.

I think Mayer, Goldwyn and Sol Hurok were romantics. And Hal Wallis and other earlies. I think they were brilliant businessmen. But they were chasing the dream. They could hear it. They could catch it. They could see beauty and it fascinated them. It's the fairy tale, isn't it? These early producers were romantics.

Oh hell. We read fairy tales for years, don't we? Are they throwing all of that out? If you don't dream up your parents, your brothers and sisters, your friends, and the person that you love—if you can't dream them up, if you just see them in total four-letter-word reality, then God help you. You've got to dream up everything. I believe in miracles. I believe that here we are and we can be in severe physical trouble. But if our spirits aren't in severe physical trouble, then we can rise up out of it. That's what we've got that the animals really haven't got.

I think Mayer had that. You can say that it was idiotic. The literature that is done in a certain period in a way belongs to that period. It was the end of a posh era. Are things better now? I wonder.

I am sure that Mayer had his vices. He was a tough man if he disliked you. He happened to like me and I liked him. He knew it and I knew it. We disagreed on quite a number of things. So what? I was quite anxious to do *Mourning Becomes Electra* with Garbo and with George Cukor directing. We didn't get anywhere with Mayer. He listened to the whole thing. He heard it told by Mrs. Frank, his storyteller. It was customary for the heads of the companies at that time to have someone tell them the stories which were sent to the studios for possible pictures. I thought this was idiotic until I heard Mrs. Frank do it. I used to laugh at the idea of her telling the stories. I was wrong. She was brilliant. I was absolutely riveted and fascinated when she told *Mourning Becomes Electra*. Mayer had the courage of his own convictions. I liked that. He'd go along whether you agreed or disagreed with it. With a lot of people, you get turned down or you get accepted, but you don't know why. Do you know what I mean? When you went to Mayer, you got an answer, or you got some money, or you got what you went after or you didn't get it. You didn't have to go to five thousand people to do it either. He wasn't afraid to make up his own mind. If you thought you needed another two million dollars to do something, then he'd pay it. He was a real gambler.

You see, I didn't know him terribly well personally. But his life was his work. When the work ceased, he really sort of died. He had worked all of his life. He didn't know anything else. What was Mr. Mayer? I don't get this nine-to-five business. It absolutely baffles me. My mother always used to say to me, "Don't forsake those duties which keep you out of the nuthouse." How right she was.

I thought Metro was like a marvelous school from which you never graduated. That's what it seemed like to me. It was a marvelous school. I didn't feel that it was a prison at all. It was like a Chekhov play. It was so comfortable. We were underpaid, but we were very well protected. If you got into trouble, you called Howard Strickling, head of publicity. Your problems were taken care of. It was a wonderful sensation.

I was fond of Mayer. Let me say this. Churchill had personal charm. Roosevelt had personal charm. Mrs. Roosevelt had personal charm. Now, there are certain people who have big jobs who have not got that obvious kind of personal charm. Personal charm is a great help. You can sit there and be an awful ass, but if you have personal charm you can really put it over on the general public. Maybe Mayer did not have great personal charm. I think that Nixon had a terrible time with personal charm. Ronald Reagan, on the other hand, stands there with his eyes wide apart. He smiles and he has a face that is "familiar" to the American public. Spencer's face was really familiar to the public. It was Irish and solid and strong. He was a man. He was the American man with an Irish background. It represented MAN in capital letters. That is a very interesting thing. He was a familiar.

Yes. Me, for instance. I am a familiar. I have become a familiar. I am very aware of that now. I'm like the Statue of Liberty to a lot of people. When you've been around so long, people identify their whole lives with you. They identify particularly their moments of hope and confidence. It's rather the style now to romanticize certain of the older actors. All of this is a question of charisma, isn't it? It's a curious sort of thing. Churchill had that for me, as do certain other people and places. No matter what you want to say, you just can't toss the parental figure. You can spit on it all you like, but eventually it has to come back. It's the strong thing to us, because it affected us very early on. It's something that you cling to.

I don't think that the studio ever set up any image. I think the actors themselves always created the image.

It's bunk to say that you can play every part. Well, you can play every part, but you can't play every part brilliantly. You are better in some things than you are in others. I don't think the studios did that. I think they would see what the person indicated, but they couldn't create it. They didn't create Judy, for instance. There she was and she indicated the roles for which she would be best suited.

Show Mayer someone and he could say, "My God, yes." Sometimes Mayer was wrong, but very often he was right. Mayer had the nerve to say, "I like that." He was not afraid to be wrong. That is a terrible disease. He really wasn't afraid to be wrong. He would make up his mind alone.

I think Mayer would have loved to have been a most witty, charming and fascinating creature. I don't think he was particularly. I think that he was a fundamentally modest man. He always tried to make himself look nice. He had a nice office. But I don't think he ever thought that he was any great shakes socially. He certainly wasn't particularly witty. He was fun. His stories were great. He fascinated me. He didn't have to be all that thrilling to me. As romantic as he was about the image of other people, I suppose that he was romantic about the image of himself. I didn't know him well enough to know that. But I would assume that that is true. I found him enormously satisfactory.

Mayer was very nice to me. He would have let me direct anything, produce anything or do anything that I wanted to do on the lot.

I'm a one-track Charlie. I was an actress at that time. You see, although Mayer was very conservative politically, he wasn't at all that way as far as the business was concerned.

He was wild— He was a romantic. He *believed*.

Movies

hen I tested for the movies, it was immediately a warm experience—exciting but not scary. Why this is so I do not know. I just find this medium sympathetic—friendly. It must be that there is no audience—and no critics—in the immediate situation. And the camera never talks back to you. It was fun.

I've made forty-three pictures. Naturally I'm adorable in all of them—but I don't want to kill any of you, and some of them have a dangerous virus called boredom. When I left Hollywood, I expected that I would remember most of the pictures and the people who were in them. Well, the fact is, I don't—I'm trying to, but I can't. Why you remember certain things is curious—usually there's a story or something special which brings them to mind.

So here are some which I seem to remember.

Alice Adams

George Stevens was the director of many distinguished pictures, including *A Place in the Sun* and *Giant*.

I first met him when an assistant director, Eddie Killy, who had worked with me many times, suggested him as a possible director for *Alice Adams*. George was then shooting—I can't remember—a very low budget picture and Eddie Killy was working with him and thought he was very talented. He had done a number of Wheeler and Woolsey comedies and I felt that *Alice Adams* could benefit by being directed by someone with a good sense of humor. Otherwise it might be a bit heavy sledding.

I was shooting *Break of Hearts* with Charles Boyer at the time. I told Eddie that I would like to meet Stevens, and one night after work I was sitting in the front seat of my car flirting unsuccessfully with Charles Boyer when I looked up and there was a face looking in the window.

"Yes?" I said.

"I'm George Stevens."

"Oh yes—well, go to Pandro Berman's office and I'll meet you there in ten minutes."

Can you imagine?

So, slightly embarrassed, I turned to Boyer, excused myself and left.

I went up to Berman's office and there he was.

We talked. I had the feeling that he was fascinated by the *book*. I had somehow decided that the well-known directors who were interested in the job were mainly interested in working with me rather than being fascinated by the subject matter.

Anyway, George Stevens was signed for the picture.

Alice Adams was a study of a desperate social climb by a girl without enough money or family position to make it to the top. She was in a race she couldn't win.

Then Stevens came one Sunday to my house with Berman for a story conference and George did not utter a word.

"Well, Pandro," I said after he had left, "I think we've made a big mistake. I don't think he knew what we were talking about."

George told me later that at that time he had not read the book and that his great dream had been to work with me. Actually, he was so busy finishing the movie he was shooting that he wasn't able to read ours until after the first meeting with Pandro and me. No wonder I thought him a bit dumb.

He was a curious man, Stevens—a really brilliant director. Especially of comedies. He had learned all the great routines working

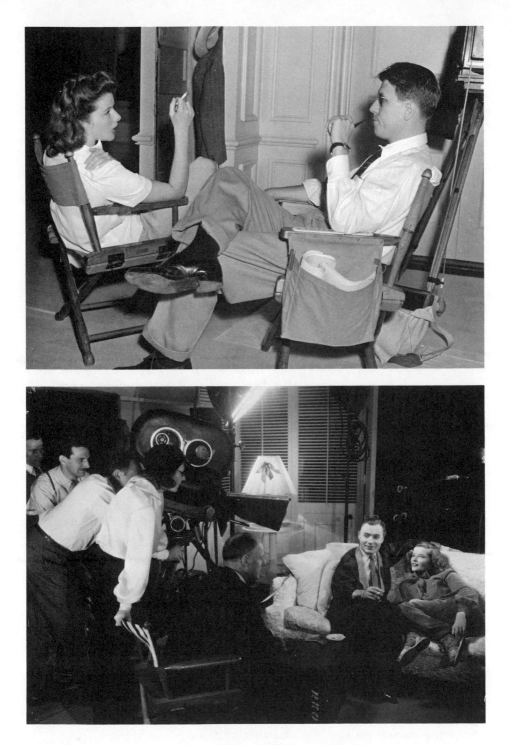

TOP: *Alice Adams*, with George Stevens

BOTTOM: *Break of Hearts*, with Charles Boyer

with or watching the great comics. To make people laugh—what a joy that is!

We had several meetings on the script. Stevens was an odd duck. Didn't talk much. Listened. Answered yes or no. Obviously, Pandro and I were doing all the talking. I must say that I felt we'd picked a rather peculiar director.

Finally he began to cast. Frankie Albertson as the brother. (I thought at the time that he was a bit common compared to me. I didn't dare say so, luckily, as he turned out to be great.) Fred Stone was the father. Ann Shoemaker the mother. Hattie McDaniel the maid.

We started to shoot. I had bought all the clothes for an insignificant amount of money. The only one which cost anything was from Hattie Carnegie—the party dress. I made it tacky-looking by putting little black bows on it and in my hair.

We started the picture. It coasted along very politely until the scene in my bedroom after the dance where I had suffered terrible humiliation as a wallflower. According to the novel (which was my Bible), I got back to the house—crept upstairs—tapped on my parents' bedroom door, "I'm back." Then I got to my bedroom, closed the door, threw myself on the bed and wept and wept.

Stevens came up to me and said, "I think it would be more interesting if you slowly went to the window, looked out in a big close-up. It is raining and slowly the tears well up in your eyes as you see the rain, and begin to run down your cheeks, and so on."

I thought this was an excellent idea. But cold water, which had leaked in as the window had not been built for a rain shot, touched my hands. And the cold on my fingers and arms shocked me and dried up my tears.

What to do?

I couldn't get the scene and I couldn't tell George why, because I knew there was no way that he could stop the rain seeping in.

Finally, after four or five tries, I went up to George and rather rudely said, "You know the trouble is I was all set to do the scene throwing myself on the bed and that's the—"

George, in a sudden sort of quiet rage, said, "Do you wish to do the—"

His sudden rage and violence freed me, and I said, "Roll them."
And I did it perfectly—frozen fingers and all. I was thrilled.
"That was O.K., wasn't it?"

George said, "Yes—fine," but he was still furious. I explained the problem weeks later. He told me that he had damn near walked off the picture.

George and I remained good friends. I did only two other pictures with Stevens: *Quality Street*, no good, and *Woman of the Year*, my first with Spencer Tracy—big hit.

I learned a lot from him. Often I would check certain "routines" with him.

Once, Spencer had to get into bed with me in a sleepwalking scene in *Without Love*.

"Oh no," said George. "If a man gets into bed and a woman is in the bed, that is serious, dangerous. You must get out of the bed —say, to get a hot-water bottle. You go into the bathroom and Spence sleepwalks and gets into the empty bed. Right off, the audience is laughing. Katharine comes back and gets into the bed."

Oh—oh—oh.

Stevens was an expert in these matters. I always regretted it when he turned his talents to *Giant* and *A Place in the Sun*, in spite of the fact that these pictures were very successful. But to make people laugh—

He would often come for the evening when he visited New York. I remember one night. We had been sitting in front of the fire, George drinking a little more than was good for him. I was occasionally throwing a log on the fire. All of a sudden I heard a roaring in the chimney.

I jumped up—very businesslike: "George, the chimney is on fire. I'll call the firehouse. You go down into the kitchen, get a saucepan, fill it with water, come back upstairs and put out the fire in the fireplace. I'm going up on the roof to take care of any sparks from flames coming out the chimney."

I rushed upstairs. When I came back after all the excitement was over, George told me the following:

He said he went downstairs into the kitchen, found a saucepan, filled it with water and there was a banging on the front door. He opened it, still holding the saucepan. Six huge men—all over six feet—rushed in (George was about five feet eight).

"Where's the fire?" they asked.

"In the fireplace," answered George.

Well, of course it was—but it sounded sort of silly. They pushed George out of the way and ran up the stairs. George followed them with his saucepan.

"Where's Katharine?" asked the firemen.

"On the roof."

They all rushed up the stairs. I must say that when they arrived on the roof, I thought they looked so huge. I said, "Be careful, you might fall through."

At this, one of them jumped up and down.

"Oh, please! No."

When they had gone (the fire was out, of course) and I went back to the living room and George was still holding his saucepan, I told him about the man jumping up and down on the roof.

He smiled: "If he had gone through, he would have landed right in my saucepan, wouldn't he?"

He was fun, George.

Sylvia Scarlett

Sylvia Scarlett—a real disaster—with Cary Grant. Our first picture together. It was a strange experience. Compton Mackenzie wrote the book. As we shot the picture, I began to wonder what Cukor was thinking. It just did not seem to me to work—just not funny.

I had my head shaved and for three-quarters of the picture played a boy. Brian Aherne was in it, and Teddy Gwenn played my father. Cary Grant's performance in this picture was magic. He was his true self—a real cockney—slightly plump and full of beans. His energy was incredible, his laughter full and unguarded. Teddy Gwenn and I were his stooges. It was a great setup, which didn't quite work. And the relationship with Brian Aherne was dull. Not Brian's fault.

George Cukor directed. That was the picture we previewed and

Sylvia Scarlett

then Pandro Berman, the producer, came back to Cukor's house after the preview, which had been a disaster. George and I said, "Don't worry, Pandro, we'll do another one for you for nothing."

Pandro gave us a black look: "Don't bother, please!"

Mary of Scotland

After *Break of Hearts* came *Mary of Scotland*. John Ford directed this one. The producer, I think, was still Pandro Berman, but it could have been Cliff Reid, who usually did Ford's pictures because Ford liked someone who did not talk back to him. In this case it was Berman.

I never cared for Mary. I thought she was a bit of an ass. I would have preferred to do a script on Elizabeth. Fredric March played James Hepburn (Earl of Bothwell). His wife, Florence Eldridge, played Elizabeth. The script was not very interesting. I never quite understood why Jack Ford was willing to direct it. Obviously, he was an extremely interesting man. We became friends, and from time to time during his life we met. I would go sailing on his boat, *The Araner*.

Jack Ford was certainly one of our most distinguished directors.

He was working at RKO when I went out to California for *A Bill of Divorcement* in 1932. At the studio, which was small, one got to at least say hello to almost everyone. And everyone looked up to Ford. His record was extraordinary. He had a gang of very macho men who always were in his pictures if there were possible parts. John Wayne was one of his buddies. Jack discovered him.

They were a group of six or seven men (including Ward Bond), each well over six feet. They all used to go on trips on Jack's *Araner* (a sailboat about 125 feet, as I remember), and they'd sail down the coast of California and Mexico and just get drunk. Then they'd come back, sober up and he'd do another picture and use any of them that he possibly could. He did *The Grapes of Wrath* with Hank Fonda. Then he used John Wayne in *Stagecoach*. *The Informer* with McLaglen. Ford and I became friends early on. I found him fascinating but impossible. He was definitely the skipper of his own life and you had better not disagree with him too often. Actually, his "gang," so to speak, was all male—but some of the time he would tolerate me. Claire Trevor and Maureen O'Hara were his favorite leading ladies. I'm sure that they never disagreed with him. Maureen was very pretty. He did pictures which called mainly for men, and the ladies were a decoration if at all.

One day Cliff Reid came to me and said that they had to have Ford do some work on one of his pictures and that Ford was on a bender at his house in the Hollywood Hills and wouldn't cooperate. Could I help?

"Well, my golly, Cliff, what can I do?"

"Get him—sober him up!"

"Well—why me?"

Mary of Scotland

Cliff said he'd tried and could do nothing.

So I went over to Ford's house, and somehow I got him into my car and I drove him to the RKO lot where I had a nice big dressing room. And I got him into my room. And somehow I persuaded him to drink a lethal dose of whiskey and castor oil.

I have never seen anyone so sick. It was terrifying. I thought he was going to die. And he thought he was going to die. Then he fell asleep and I thought he was dead.

Finally, after about two hours he woke up. I took him to the Hollywood Athletic Club and they pulled him together. He fixed the picture. Wow! I'll never forget it. I really nearly killed him.

I remember that one day Ford left the set and said to me, "You direct this scene." I said O.K., but will Freddie work with me? Freddie March said he would and I directed a scene in a tower.

Ford just lost interest in the venture. It was a flop.

He did save my neck.

I was riding sidesaddle, of course, as Queen Mary. Once when they were taking a shot of me at a full run, Jack yelled, "Kate, duck!" I did—and missed a branch of a tree which would have decapitated me.

We remained friends. He was an extraordinary fellow. The Irish are a tough lot. His record is incredible.

The last time I saw him, he was sick in bed—actually, he was dying.

Tough—loved his friends—hated his enemies—loved Ireland— loved the film business—loved his hits—adored his failures— perverse—stubborn—relentless—arrogant—and a great friend.

Oh—and a dangerous enemy.

Stage Door

Director—Gregory La Cava. Starring Ginger Rogers and me, and using all the good girls at RKO: Lucille Ball, Gail Patrick, Andrea Leeds, Eve Arden, Ann Miller.

My career was at a low ebb, and as we started to shoot *Stage Door*

LEFT: *Stage Door* with Constance Collier

BELOW: *Stage Door*, with Ginger Rogers

I began to observe that I was sort of listening in on scenes instead of dominating them. After about two weeks of this I went to Pandro Berman and said, "Gosh, Pandro, don't you think—"

He answered, "Listen, Kate, you'd be lucky to be playing the sixth part in a successful picture."

I decided to say something to La Cava: "This character, Gregory, I don't know who I am. Who am I, Gregory?"

"You're the human question mark."

"What's that supposed to mean?"

He looked at me seriously: "I'm damned if I know, Kate."

I listened. I said, "Thank you." And I departed. I gave up. And I shut up. I knew that it would be hopeless to say anything more to anyone. I knew that there was nothing as boring as an actor on the skids who is sorry for herself.

Shutting up and being jolly was the cleverest thing I ever did. La Cava got sorry for me playing the rich girl and handed me the whole last part of the movie.

I had no idea until much later that in the first preview Ginger Rogers was billed over me. I don't even think that Ginger knew. At this preview so many cards came back saying, The best Katharine Hepburn picture we've seen and she is great. I'm talking about preview cards which would be given to the audience as they were leaving the theatre to jot down their opinions. They returned me to my first position. Lucky me.

Bringing Up Baby

Then, in 1937, *Bringing Up Baby*.

Howard Hawks directing—Cary Grant, Charlie Ruggles, May Robson and the Leopard.

This script was a good one. Cary Grant was really wonderful in it. And I was good too. And the leopard was excellent.

Cary had always refused to work with the leopard. Didn't care for it at all. Once, to torture him, we dropped a stuffed leopard through the vent in the top of his dressing room. Wow! He was out of there like lightning.

Bringing Up Baby, with Howard Hawks and Cary Grant

Cary was so funny on this picture. He was fatter, and at this point his boiling energy was at its peak. We would laugh from morning to night. Hawks was fun too. He usually got to work late. Cary and I were always there early. Everyone contributed anything and everything they could think of to that script.

I must add that I didn't have brains enough to be scared, so I did a lot of scenes with the leopard just roaming around. Olga Celeste, the trainer, had a big whip. We were inside a cage—Olga and I and the leopard—no one else. The cage was for us alone. The camera and sound were picked up through holes in the fencing. The first scene I had was in a floor-length negligee, walking around. I was talking madly on the telephone with a long cord. The leopard followed me around pushing at my thigh, which they had covered with perfume. I would pat its head. The scene went very satisfactorily. Then I changed into a knee-length dress with tabs on the bottom of the skirt covering metal pieces to make the skirt swing prettily. But—a large *but*—one quick swirl and that leopard made a spring for my back, and Olga brought that whip down right on his head.

That was the end of my freedom with the leopard.

We went wildly over schedule. It was my last picture at RKO.

Oddly enough, this picture did not do too well on its first release. Now it is considered a big hit. But I think that my presence—"box-office poison"—was the trouble.

The Philadelphia Story—the play

Who should produce?

I thought that the Theatre Guild—Lawrence Langner, Terry Helburn—would be the best and that I owed them the favor.

Phil Barry said no, that they had botched his last script.

I felt strongly, and Phil finally agreed—the Guild.

I did not realize at the time that the Guild was in a terrible state. Like Barry. Like me. They had had some bad failures and were at a low ebb.

Anyway, we were set to proceed. The Guild didn't know about my career nor did Barry. I did not know about the Guild. But we were all three in a rather desperate state.

So—we proceeded. I wanted a very strong and conventional director. Bob Sinclair had just directed *The Women*. I wanted a director who did not think that I was sort of the "second coming." Someone who was very down-to-earth and wouldn't let me be—well—fancy.

We got Van Heflin for the Reporter, Shirley Booth for the Lady Reporter and I persuaded Joe Cotten to do C. K. Dexter Haven. He was Orson Welles's right hand—but I think that I convinced him it was time to go out for himself. Anne Baxter was to do the girl, aged

The Philadelphia Story,
the play

twelve. She was shifted to Lenore Lonergan, who was ten and more appropriate.

A great setup. Ready to go.

But where was the third act?

Call Phil. They said he was in Florida.

Luckily, Phil called me. Asked me how were things going?

Luckily (I say again), I did not say: Where the hell is the third act? I just said, "Oh, nothing much is going on up here. We're seeing actors and we have a good director and we're trying to take real care."

After a bit more conversation, we hung up.

Four days later the third act arrived.

Can you believe it? Later, Phil said to me that he had been so nervous that we would be ready first that he couldn't think. After our telephone conversation he relaxed and it all just came tumbling out. Lucky me—usually I am a bit push-push.

Incidentally, *The Philadelphia Story* was immediately full of the hit atmosphere. I myself would have played it on tour first for a year or so. But Barry and the Guild wanted to open in New York.

In a wild attempt to deceive myself, I ordered a room at the River Club for the night before the opening and did my best to pretend I was in Chicago and that nothing unusual was going to happen. So I was happily in Chicago and we opened the play at the Shubert Theatre.

Yes—a HIT.

One of my favorite happenings on this play was when Lawrence Langner came back one night and said to me, "Kate, I think that the young girl Lenore Lonergan is—well—she seems to be sort of copying you."

"Oh no, Lawrence. You're wrong. It's the other way—I'm copying her. Isn't she great?"

The Philadelphia Story—the movie

The movie of *The Philadelphia Story* was made by MGM in 1939–40. The play opened in 1938. I have described selling it to L. B. Mayer.

Mayer had said that I could have Jimmy Stewart. I got Cary Grant. He chose to play C. K. Dexter Haven—Jimmy Stewart was the Reporter. Ruth Hussey played the Lady Reporter, the part played in the theatre by Shirley Booth. The young sister was Virginia Weidler. The part of the brother was cut out. The script was written by Donald Ogden Stewart. George Cukor was to direct.

It was all done at MGM under the most luxurious circumstances. The clothes by Adrian—great sets—music, etc. The script by Don Stewart retained all the delirious humor and quality of the play. We had great fun doing it, as we always did on one of George's pictures. All sorts of people came to visit, including Noel Coward, who stayed and watched one of Jimmy Stewart's big scenes—and then gave Jimmy a big hug of praise, which thrilled Jimmy. Noel was always generous with his praise.

George was very helpful to both Jimmy and Cary. And of course he was always perfect for me. He was a wonderful director and this was his ideal material. It's such fun to do a really good comedy. We all got nominated and Jimmy won the award.

Woman of the Year

As I've already told you, this was an idea and outline written by Garson Kanin, his brother Mike Kanin and Ring Lardner, Jr. Garson showed me the seventy-eight-page outline and I called Joe Mankiewicz (in California), who had produced *The Philadelphia Story* at MGM. Would he care to read it? It was for Spencer Tracy and me. It was to be directed by George Stevens. Joe said he'd read it and would call me back. He read it. Liked it. And said that the studio would be interested. I said that I would come out to California.

I called my friend George Cukor, and he said that I could stay at his house. Garson and Ring and Mike were already in Los Angeles, at the Garden of Allah.

The boys—Ring and Mike—gave me a Ford car. It was waiting for me in my driveway. Thrilling to get a car and not have to pay for it.

TOP: *The Philadelphia Story*, the movie

BOTTOM: With Cukor

Woman of the Year

With Cukor, Mankiewicz
and Stevens

There was great argument later, about the end of the picture.

I had always thought Spencer Tracy a wonderful actor, but when Garson said wouldn't Spencer Tracy be great as the man, Garson said I answered, "Oh—I don't know. I wonder whether we would be good together. We're so different."

Garson also said that when he suggested to Spencer Tracy that he had a script which would be wonderful for Spencer Tracy and Katharine Hepburn, Spencer had said, "Oh, really—do you think that we would be good together? We're—so sort—of different."

I, of course, don't remember this at all. I remember only how perfect I thought Spence would be as anyone and how great we would be together. I think that Gar is probably right. And that I am so blinded by years of whatever you call it—that my memory was not trustworthy.

Another report about S.T.: "How can I do a picture with a woman who has dirt under her fingernails and who is of ambiguous sexuality and always wears pants?"

After this he saw *The Philadelphia Story* and changed his mind.

True or false—who knows?

Adam's Rib

Adam's Rib was a Garson Kanin–Ruth Gordon script. Perfect for S.T. and me—both lawyers. It was a big hit and was exciting because it introduced Judy Holliday to the movies. Judy had made a big hit in Garson's play *Born Yesterday*. Naturally, when Columbia bought the movie rights, Judy was hoping they would let her play it, but the head of Columbia, Harry Cohn, thought it should be a movie star. Judy was friendly with Spence, George Cukor, me and of course the Kanins. We all felt Judy must play the part. We, or actually Garson and I, went East to try to get Judy to play a tiny part in our movie, which would show Harry Cohn what she could do and how she could look. Believe it or not, Judy was very reluctant to play that small part. Thought it would set her back rather than forward. Garson and I struggled and we finally convinced her—makeup, clothes—a

Adam's Rib, with Judy Holliday

tiny scene but a great scene. And with my back always to the camera, her face always in view—big close-up.

Finally she agreed and of course it paid off. We sent the scene complete to Harry Cohn. He was thrilled—signed her. She was thrilled. Well, why not? She was unique—so talented.

I've just talked to Garson, and he says it was entirely my idea to have Judy do the part in *Adam's Rib*—I thought it would be the perfect test. Well, I was right, thank God.

The African Queen

In 1950 I was touring in *As You Like It*. We were playing Los Angeles. I was living on Summit Drive in Irene Mayer Selznick's house. Her butler, Farr—his wife, Ida, who was the maid. They were both angels. There was also Emily, the cook. She was a woman of

With Irene Mayer Selznick in Los Angeles

temperament and I spent a good half hour every day with her—talking and discussing meals. She was a really great cook. From soup to dessert—thrilling. I was lucky—I love to eat.

One day Sam Spiegel sent me the book by C. S. Forester. I read it. What a story! I was thrilled. We met—Huston and I. Sam Spiegel had just bought the book. They weren't sure whom they were going to have for the man. At first, John felt it should be an authentic cockney. But when they began to think of Bogie, there was no one who could compete with him in personality or looks. They had him be a Canadian. Can you imagine anyone else in that part? He was perfection.

I've already written a book about *The African Queen*. The book was really a book about John Huston—For and Against. He was an amazing character. He had flashes. And those flashes were brilliant—when

John Huston

he told me to base my character of Rosie on Eleanor Roosevelt when she visited the hospitals of the wounded soldiers, always with a smile on her face. He had felt that I was playing Rosie too seriously, and that since my mouth turned down anyway, it was making the scenes heavy. Since I (as Rosie) was the sister of a minister, my approach to everyone and everything had to be full of hope. A smile. It was indeed a FLASH of brilliance. In short, he had told me exactly how to play the part.

I had heard from my London connections—Michael Benthall and Bobby Helpmann—that the one person to do the clothes was a Doris Langley Moore. She had a Museum of Costume. John had written me about someone else but I told him about Doris—FLASH—he changed without any argument.

I met her. She was a charmer and had a lot of all sorts of petticoats and underwear. She had been brought up in Africa, and this was a very lucky thing for me that we had her. She said that the materials we used must be able to stand *sweaty* heat—and not muss too easily and not show dirt and not show whether they were wet or dry.

So our first meeting with her and Huston and me. He was fascinated by the underwear. I tried on every variety of split-pants, of chemise—and I was terrified that he was going to have me wear nothing but an envelope chemise in the picture.

I kept asking for a script—but none appeared. John flew to Africa with Peter Viertel, who was helping him with the script. I felt foreboding but Bogie, who had worked with John Huston before, said, "Don't worry. This is the way he does it."

"But wow!" I said.

"You'll see—it's worth it."

So I went along with Bogie.

Bogie won the award.

The people still go in droves. What more can you ask?

Summertime

Summertime—this was the picture done from *The Time of the Cuckoo*, a play by Arthur Laurents. They called me and said that David Lean was going to direct it. Would I be . . . They didn't need to finish that sentence. I certainly would be interested in anything that David Lean was going to direct.

So I said yes—and it was of course going to be done in Venice. And Constance Collier, my friend, and Phyllis Wilbourn, her secretary, were going to go with me. Spencer was going to do *The Mountain* in the French Alps, so everything was perfect. He was busy—I was busy.

We got to Venice—the Grand Hotel— The clothes to be bought there. I found a house on the same island as the studio—Murano. It had a tennis court and a pool and I thought that it would be perfect. We moved in. It was hopeless. Poor Constance and Phyllis were cut off from any life that they would have had in Venice proper. The beds all had the deep image of the former occupant. The stairway was steep, was narrow, and had a bannister of loose rope. As Constance had very poor sight and was a bit unsteady on her feet, this was terrifying. To be brief, it was impossible.

Constance and Phyllis knew everyone everywhere and were accustomed to a very social existence. When I moved them to this strange island, they had literally no life at all. It was just far enough away from Venice proper to be totally impractical. How I could have been dumb enough not to realize this, I don't know. Anyway, after twenty-four hours I came to and quickly found an apartment as great as this one was lousy.

The apartment was on the Grand Canal almost opposite the Gritti. It was beautifully furnished—two stories—three bedrooms—three baths. It was on the third and fourth floors and had a beautiful garden on the river and a great staff: cook, butler, maid. We had our own gondola. It was perfection.

David lived in the Gritti. He was busy working on the script. He threw out everything but the main plot of a desperate lonely secretary finally finding Rossano Brazzi and then leaving him to go

Summertime

With Constance Collier
and Laura Harding

back to the United States. It was the story of a secretary taking a vacation in Venice. Arthur Laurents's play became a movie written by David Lean and his pal the writer H. E. Bates. I don't remember who had the writing credit, but David was always very fussy about a script and removed everything that didn't interest *him*—so this movie is really David in Venice. Not necessarily knowing a great amount about the famous treasures, but a person reacting to the beauties and the atmosphere of this remarkable city on a three-week holiday and a love affair, and then leaving on the train.

It was told with great simplicity in the streets, in the Piazza San Marco. We would shoot in tiny streets—only a few feet wide. The sun would come and go in a matter of minutes. It was a very emotional part, and I tell you I had to be on my toes to give David enough of what he wanted practically on call. But it was thrilling. And the music he picked was perfect.

It was fascinating to work for David. He was very basic—he was simple—he was true. He told a story. It's a slice of life you understand. In all its detail. He photographed what he saw in his mind's eye. It was a most extraordinary gift. He seemed to me to simply absorb Venice. It was his. He had a real photographic gift. He thought in a descriptive way. His shots tell the story. He was capable of a sort of superconcentration. It made a very deep and definite impression on me, and he was one of the most interesting directors I ever worked with. He had been a cutter for years before he became a sort of co-director with Noel Coward on *Cavalcade*. He had to get exactly the performance he wanted out of each actor so that it would fit in with what he had in his mind's eye. Thus his pictures are all of a piece. He paints a picture and it is his.

Wasn't I lucky to work with him?

Nothing was too much trouble for David. Noel Willman worked for him in *Dr. Zhivago*. There was to be a shot of cavalry officers numbering about three hundred passing by a field. David was there staring at the field—just silently staring.

Finally he turned to the assistant: "It's dull—I think it should be a field of red poppies. We'll plant red poppies every foot or so through the field. Send the cavalry home. Call that fellow on the

With David Lean

corner past the hotel to . . ." It took them three days. It was a field of poppies. It was spectacular.

The search for the red goblets in *Summertime* was wild. He finally had a glassblower blow about six in slightly different shades of red to get exactly what he had in mind.

But when it was all over, one had the real deep satisfaction that one had done one's best. Perfection was always David's aim.

Long Day's Journey into Night

This was a great experience—Sidney Lumet directing—Ralph Richardson playing the lead—and my two sons Jason Robards and Dean Stockwell. It is a brilliantly written play, the character of the mother described with such sensitivity that it was an inspiration to do. We rehearsed it for three weeks at that big room down on Second Avenue, and learned the parts so that when we shot it in an old house on City Island, we could do long scenes. One could never be better than the part. O'Neill's knowledge of people, and his analysis of that couple, was really thrilling. I just had to think and to concentrate and to read the lines. I felt entirely supported by the words. What an experience! I'll never forget it.

When we finished the movie, we had a sort of party—very modest—food and a few musicians. After a bit Richardson came up to me—I was sitting talking to his wife, Mu Forbes. He asked me to dance.

"Oh, Ralph," I said, "I haven't danced for years."

"No no," said his wife, "dance with him."

So Ralph and I waltzed off together and danced around the room. When the music stopped, Ralph stopped, stepped only a slight step back from me, kept his hands on my shoulders and, with a soft voice of utter wonder and surprise, said, "I say—you're a very attractive woman!"

The Lion in Winter

Spencer died on the 10th of June in 1967. I had not worked much of any of the sixties. After he died, in California, Phyllis Wilbourn, now my secretary, and I had gone to Edgartown on Martha's Vineyard to visit the Kanins, Gar and Ruth. They were staying in Edgartown at a hotel. So did we. It was pretty, and we would drive out here and there to wonderful beaches and little towns.

One day a script was sent to me, *The Lion in Winter*, by James Goldman. I read it. I thought it was fascinating. Phyllis read it. She

Long Day's Journey into Night

agreed. I said yes I'd do it. Peter O'Toole was to be the King. He wanted a man named Anthony Harvey to direct it. He had been a very important cutter in London. It was to be produced by Joseph Levine. It was to be shot in France in the South. The costumes to be done in London by Maggie Furse.

Peter came to see me and showed me a short movie which Tony Harvey had made. *The Dutchman*. It was excellent and I said fine with me.

We rehearsed in London at the Haymarket with my three sons—Richard, Geoffrey, John—played by Tony Hopkins, John Castle, Nigel Terry. King of France, Timothy Dalton.

We lived in a very small hotel in the South of France and shot in the Abbey of Montmajour. Fontvieille was the name of the village. This was a thrilling location. It was a charming small hotel and they had very good food.

Nearby were several antique stores, all now well represented in my house in New York.

Peter lived in a different town. We had only a short ride to the location at Montmajour. This was a very interesting abbey—some of it in ruins—some we rebuilt—a pretty outside garden and several good big rooms. In the cellar some cells.

For my dressing room I established myself at the top of the Abbey and next to the garden. Everyone else was at a sort of entrance which was down the hill from me. I was lucky. It was hilly country.

We had great fun, as usual. Peter and I had the same makeup man. One day I was waiting and waiting for him. Finally I went down the hill to find him. He was doing Peter, who was not working until later.

"What the hell goes on?" I said. "He's supposed to be doing me. I'm in the next shot." I grabbed the makeup man and his box. I gave Peter a good swat on the head and we climbed back up the hill into my dressing room. When we were ready, we started the scene in the cellar and who should come in but Peter. His head was completely wrapped in bandages and he was walking with crutches and moaning. You can see we had fun.

There was a great shot of our boat coming down the Rhône River to land. The tide in the river was very high. We rehearsed the shot one afternoon, and by the next morning the pier where we expected to land was completely submerged. We shot down the river in a wild wind. I was in all my gorgeous robes.

I looked at one of my retinue, who was dressed in full armor, and said, "I hope that you have all that stuff unhooked. Otherwise when we turn over you will plummet to the bottom. I am myself totally able to step out of all this finery. I shall simply dive away and swim to shore naked." He was shocked. I don't blame him. It was exciting and the shot in the movie was great.

We moved to several places, including Tarascon, for final scenes. Then I left them to go to the very South of France to do *The Madwoman*

The Lion in Winter,
with Tony Harvey

Peter O'Toole

of Chaillot, with Bryan Forbes directing. Tony Harvey went to the hospital with hepatitis. He was sick but he got up and finished the picture. I must say he did a brilliant job. Such a talented man.

Rooster Cogburn

John Wayne is the hero of the thirties and forties and most of the fifties. Before the creeps came creeping in. Before, in the sixties, the male hero slid right down into the valley of the weak and the misunderstood. Before the women began dropping any pretense to virginity into the gutter. With a disregard for truth which is indeed pathetic. And unisex was born. The hair grew long and the pride grew short. And we were off to the anti-hero and -heroine.

John Wayne has survived all this. Even into the seventies. He is so tall a tree that the sun must shine on him whatever the tangle in the jungle below.

From head to toe he is all of a piece. Big head. Wide blue eyes. Sandy hair. Rugged skin—lined by living and fun and character. Not by just rotting away. A nose not too big, not too small. Good teeth. A face alive with humor. Good humor I should say, and a sharp wit. Dangerous when roused. His shoulders are broad—very. His chest massive—very. When I leaned against him (which I did as often as possible, I must confess—I am reduced to such innocent pleasures), thrilling. It was like leaning against a great tree. His hands so big. Mine, which are big too, seemed to disappear. Good legs. No seat. A real man's body.

And the base of this incredible creation. A pair of small sensitive feet. Carrying his huge frame as though it were a feather. Light of tread. Springy. Dancing. Pretty feet.

Very observing. Very aware. Listens. Concentrates. Witty slant. Ready to laugh. To be laughed at. To answer. To stick his neck out. Funny. Outrageous. Spoiled. Self-indulgent. Tough. Full of charm. Knows it. Uses it. Disregards it. With an alarming accuracy. Not much gets past him.

He was always on time. Always knew the scene. Always full of notions about what should be done. Tough on a director who had not done his homework. Considerate to his fellow actors. Very impatient with anyone who was inefficient. And did not bother to cover it up.

Politically he is a reactionary. He suffers from a point of view based entirely on his own experience. He was surrounded in his early years in the motion picture business by people like himself. Self-made. Hard-working. Independent. Of the style of man who blazed the trails across our country. Reached out into the unknown. People who were willing to live or die entirely on their own independent judgment. Jack Ford, the man who first brought Wayne into the movies, was cut from the same block of wood. Fiercely independent. They seem to have no patience and no understanding of the more timid and dependent type of person. Pull your own freight. This is their slogan. Sometimes I don't think that they realize that their own load was attached to a very powerful engine. They don't need or want protection. Total personal responsibility. They dish it out. They take it. Life has dealt Wayne some severe blows. He can take them. He has shown it. He doesn't lack self-discipline. He dares to walk by himself. Run. Dance. Skip. Walk. Crawl through life. He has done it all. Don't pity me, please.

And with all this he has a most gentle and respectful gratitude toward people who he feels have contributed very firmly to his success. His admirers. He is meticulous in answering fan mail. Realistic in allowing the press to come on the set. Uncomplicated in his reaction to praise and admiration. Delighted to be the recipient of this or that award—reward. A simple man. None of that complicated Self-Self-Self which seems to torment myself and others who shall be nameless when they are confronted with the Prize for good performance. I often wonder whether we behave so ungraciously because we really think that we should have been given a prize for every performance. And are therefore sort of sore to begin with. Well, as I began—he is a simple and decent man. Considerate to the people who rush him in a sort of wild enthusiasm. Simple in his enjoyment of his own success. Like Bogie. He really appreciates the praise heaped upon him. A wonderful childlike, naïve open spirit.

As an actor, he has an extraordinary gift. A unique naturalness. Developed by movie actors who just happen to become actors. Gary

Rooster Cogburn, with John Wayne

Cooper had it. An unselfconsciousness. An ability to think and feel. Seeming to woo the camera. A very subtle capacity to think and express and caress the camera—the audience. With no apparent effort. A secret between them. Through the years these real movie actors seem to develop a technique similar to that of a well-trained actor from the theatre. They seem to arrive at the same point from an entirely different beginning. One must unlearn—the other learns. A total reality of performance. So that the audience does not feel that they are watching. But feel a real part of what is going on. The acting does not appear acting. Wayne has a wonderful gift of natural speed. Of arrested motion. Of going suddenly off on a new tack. Try something totally unrehearsed with him. He takes the ball and runs and throws with a freedom and wit and gaiety which is great fun. As powerful as is his personality, so too is his acting capacity powerful. He is a very very good actor in the most highbrow sense of the word. You don't catch him at it.

When you buy a cotton shirt—you want to get a cotton shirt. Not nylon. It stays clean but it makes you sweat. Not drip-dry, which you don't have to press but you should. Just cotton. Good simple long-lasting cotton. No synthetics. That's what you get when you get John Wayne. That's what I got. And as you can see—I liked it.

"John Wayne is dead."
"Who? John Wayne? The hero?"
"Yes."
"John Wayne—dead, you mean. *Stagecoach. Rooster Cogburn.* The big man. The Duke."
"He's dead."
"That's terrible."
"Yes—terrible."
"But there's no one to take his place."
"No one."
"But could he?"
"Could he what?"
"Die?"

"You mean, isn't he one of those?"

"Those what?"

"Indestructibles."

"Yes . . . yes . . . I think so . . . up there somewhere."

On Golden Pond

This script was a playscript. I went to Wilmington, Delaware, to see it with Noel Willman. (He was the director of several plays I did; e.g., *A Matter of Gravity*.) It was played by two people about fifty, and they were very busy being old and slightly feeble. It was a good play. At the same time that I was trying to set it up as a movie, Jane Fonda found it too and thought it would be a perfect setup for her father, Henry Fonda, and herself as daughter and me as mother. I agreed. So she arranged it. Mark Rydell as director.

Squam Lake, New Hampshire, as location. Hank in one Mead house—me in the Mead mother's house. And the movie house another Mead house in a wood. And all right on the lake. They were all very nice houses. Being on the water, I could swim every day, which I did morning and night. It's a funny thing. As a child, I used to be dumped into a cold tub every morning. I still swim—winter, summer. At Fenwick I go across a snowy lawn, my poor feet freeze. But I go in. I dip. I swim a stroke—one stroke—then I rush out. Up the outside staircase.

Anyway, it was a great setup and also great fun to do. Jane and Hank were busy working out a rather complicated father-daughter relationship, and this was to be the solution. An ambitious father and an ambitious daughter find their solution with an ambitious friend. We all had a good time. The scenes were fun to do. Jane liked to have me watch her scenes with her dad. Why I never quite understood.

The house I lived in was in the most commanding location and often I would see Henry Fonda take his evening stroll along the base of my property—and I'd wonder what he was thinking about. He was a good painter. I never saw him go in his bathing suit—always just walking solemnly along. Fully dressed—not hurrying—not going

Cast of *On Golden Pond*

slowly—and a thousand miles away. He was an oddie. I never felt that I knew him at all. He wasn't given to a lot of talk and neither was I.

It is a very odd relationship acting with someone. You are of course thrown into a most intimate relationship with a person. Then the picture ends. You may never see the person again. But people— and especially ones writing articles or books—say, "What was he [or

she} like?" And I don't know. I don't really know them or anything
about them. I wonder if this is true of most actors. I know that my
father always advised an impersonal relationship with fellow workers.
I must say I followed his advice, but as I look back I wonder if I just
am like him. Not particularly given to easy friendships.

If you are a member of a big family, you always have someone at
hand for golf, tennis, walks, movies. You never have to "find company," so to speak.

I had given Hank Spencer's old hat at the beginning of the movie.
He was a big fan of Spencer's and I thought it would make him happy.
Later, at the end of the picture, he gave me a painting of three hats,
with Spencer's in the middle. It was charming and I was touched that
he had gone to such an effort. Then I found that the picture made
me sad—with Spencer gone and Hank gone. So I gave it to Ernest
Thompson, who had written *On Golden Pond*. It was his first big
success.

It was a very good study of the relationship of a husband and wife
who just really liked each other. Hank and I were the right age—we
were old—so we weren't busy acting old. It comes upon one unex-
pectedly. Suddenly you lose your spring. Your spring in the sense of
elasticity. Now—old—you don't spring up from a chair. You *get up*.
It is a very different act. Henry had lost a little more spring than I
had when we were doing the picture and we slid very easily into our
relationship. He was wonderful to play with—very true—very natural. He moved me deeply in the scene when he was beginning to
crumble. It really wasn't acting at all. I'm thrilled that he got the
award. I think it pleased him very much. He gave some wonderful
performances in his career.

His daughter was damned good too. Jane and I enjoyed our scenes
together. At one moment in the picture Jane had to do a back somersault into the water off a springboard. I would torture her by saying,
"If you can't do it, dear, I'll do it for you. It's one of my specialties."
You may be sure that she did it herself.

The picture was a success.

On stage at Stratford, Connecticut

Shakespeare

I like to get up early and work in the morning and afternoon. I like to sleep at night. But to build my career I would force myself to do a play. Night work. Then to keep it interesting I would take it on tour the minute the gross dropped below a certain figure.

Then Shakespeare reared his ugly head.

Somewhere along the line, end of the forties, I had become a close friend of Constance Collier. Constance was brought up on Shakespeare in England. I studied Shakespeare with her. We had great fun and I decided to do *As You Like It*. The Theatre Guild was interested, and my friend Michael Benthall—who at that time was head of the Old Vic in England—directed. It was a beautiful production designed by James Bailey, who was a friend of Benthall's. It played the Cort Theatre in New York and was virtually sold out for 148 performances. William Prince played Orlando and Ernest Thesiger, a brilliant actor, played Jaques. They thought I was O.K. Sort of half carps and half praise. Looking back on my notices which I had not read at the time, I have the impression that I was irritating to the critics. They liked me in *The Philadelphia Story*, but in Shakespeare—well—it was sort of "she has a nerve to be doing this." Well I don't know. I did study and work hard and Constance was a great help and it was exciting. At least I enjoyed it.

After New York we did a long tour of the United States. We did

The Merchant of Venice

The Taming of the Shrew

With John Houseman and
Alfred Drake

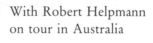

With Robert Helpmann
on tour in Australia

In Sydney, Australia

big business and they seemed to like it—audiences and critics. I learned a lot.

In 1952, I did *The Millionairess* with Michael Benthall directing again. We did ten weeks in London, took the summer off and then did another ten weeks in New York.

Later with the Old Vic, in 1955, I did *The Merchant of Venice*, *The Taming of the Shrew* and *Measure for Measure* with Robert Helpmann and directed by Michael Benthall. We toured Australia for six months: Sydney, Melbourne, Adelaide, Perth and Brisbane. It was fun and a great success.

Australia is a fascinating country. Wonderful climate—walking, swimming, wildflowers, many many flowers that are quite different from any that we've known. I saw everything that I could and would love to go back. Wonderful birds—wonderful animals.

I worked all these parts with Constance Collier. Phyllis Wilbourn was working for her at the time, and when Constance died, I was in Australia touring with the Old Vic. When I returned, Phyllis decided to come to me. I had not had a secretary who was also a sort of companion since Emily Perkins, who had decided to move to Maine. She was a really great cook and had always wanted to run a restaurant in Maine. So she did. She was very successful for about three years.

Then I did two summers at Stratford, Connecticut, with John Houseman and Jack Landau. In 1957 we did *The Merchant of Venice* (with Morris Carnovsky) and *Much Ado About Nothing* (with Alfred Drake). The second year (1960) I did *Twelfth Night* and *Antony and Cleopatra*.

I'm sorry that I never did *The Taming of the Shrew* in New York. It was a good production and I think that I had a really good basic idea there: that Kate was devoted to her father and had a hard time transferring her affection to Petruchio.

I thought I was good in *Antony and Cleopatra* too. Robert Ryan was Antony—and of course great-looking. What a play!

Anyway all these adventures were great fun and luckily the audience thought so too and came in droves—which is always reassuring. I was pleased with myself for reaching out.

Spencer

pencer Tracy is a star of real quality. He is an actor's star. He is a people's star. His quality is clear and direct. Ask a question—get an answer. No pause—no fancy thinking—a simple answer. He speaks. He listens. He is not wordy. He is not overemotional. He is simple and totally honest. He makes you believe what he is saying.

Take *Captains Courageous*—the Portuguese fisherman. This performance is to me one of the most shattering in his career. He wondered what he should do to make him stand out as a convincing character —an accent—what?

He finally got the studio to call a real Portuguese fisherman so that he could question him about this and that. The Portuguese expert came in. Sat down. Seemed a most cosmopolitan fellow. He smiled.

"Well," said Spence, "I have to sing a song about Little Fish as I sit in the evening singing to the sea. I've been wondering about this fellow's accent. Take, for instance, the word 'fish.' How would you pronounce it?"

"Fish? F-i-s-h—well, that is FISH, isn't it, Mr. Tracy? I mean . . ."

"Well," said Spence, "you wouldn't say 'feesh'?"

"Well, no. Fish is fish—'ish' not 'eesh,' Mr. Tracy."

So with a few other words. It was a hopeless conversation.

Spencer wound up calling it "feesh." It seemed to fit the moment. Curly dark hair and feesh. He added to the fisherman—who was the son, who was the grandson of the fisherman—who began on the sea—who ended stove in by the broken mast—who had been as much a part of the sea as the fish he was catching—and finally actually became the sea. It was his natural grave—not gone to earth—gone to the depths.

Then I saw *Fury*—the transformation of a good man into a monster. He became a fury locked in the body of a perfectly ordinary man. A body which was suddenly too small to contain him. He seemed to use himself, his body, as a container. A sort of box filled with the whole run of human emotions. His performance, an abstraction—a manifestation of character—is so remarkable that it is as total as birth or death, and needs no outer clothing—no accent—no makeup. The exterior was not applied, in other words. It became, automatically, the mirror of the passions whirling around inside him. So to us, the audience, his face would really be hampered by any makeup or applied comment. Spencer's face was his canvas—and he painted from the inside out—with magic.

One of the most fascinating examples of this unique quality was seen in *Dr. Jekyll and Mr. Hyde,* his biggest, his only real flop. Metro-Goldwyn-Mayer decided to do the picture. Spencer became involved. He was persuaded to don a large amount of makeup as Hyde. A wig—false teeth—all the usual fixings. When Jack Barrymore played it, he had even added an egglike extended head. Jack loved all this stuff. So did Fredric March. They both thought it was fun. It is fun. But is it?

No. Not for Spencer Tracy. That was not Tracy's style. He felt idiotic. He was so embarrassed by all this paraphernalia he used to drive down the lot in a limousine with the shades closed. Ingrid Bergman played the whore; she won an award, I think. This picture was one of the few for which Spence got bad notices.

Naturally, it's very embarrassing when you do a big picture with a famous part and you fail in the famous part. When I met Spence,

Portrait by Irving Penn

the subject was on his mind. Since I didn't know him, I was careful to see him in every picture of his that I could, and that included *Dr. Jekyll and Mr. Hyde*.

"Very interesting," I said.

"Oh no—no—nothing—rotten," he said. "I just can't do that sort of thing. It's like constructing a dummy and then trying to breathe life into it. I like to be the dummy myself, and then make people—force people—to believe that I'm whatever I want them to believe. Inside out—instead of outside in. No makeup.

"Well, it's too late now," he said. "But believe it or not, when they first mentioned *Jekyll and Hyde*, I was thrilled. I had always been fascinated by the story and saw it as a story of the two sides of a man. I felt Jekyll was a very respectable doctor—a fine member of society. He had proposed to a lovely girl and was about to marry her. But there was another side to the man. Every once in a while, Jekyll would go on a trip. Disappear. And either because of drink or dope or who knows what, he would become—or should I say turn into?—Mr. Hyde. Then in a town or neighborhood where he was totally unknown, he would perform incredible acts of cruelty and vulgarity. The emotional side of Jekyll was obviously extremely disturbed. The girl, as his fiancée, is a proper lady. But as his fantasy whore, the girl matched his Mr. Hyde. She would be capable of the lowest behavior.

"The two girls would be played by the same actress; the two men would be me."

Oddly enough, when he had this notion, I was the girl he had in mind. At this time we had never met. It still seems the most fascinating idea to me. Too bad he couldn't persuade them to do it his way. It would have been thrilling and very modern.

I wondered why he had happened to light upon this notion for *Jekyll and Hyde*. That notion—I couldn't get it out of my mind. Was there some very personal connotation?

The complication of our natures certainly seems to be infinite. A dose of this—a dose of that—stir it up—and out we come—most of us all tied up in ourselves.

The actor has an advantage here. The actor can escape into *creation*. The perfect actor—to my mind, S.T.—could stand in his own footsteps and change before your very eyes. With no utensils—with magic and the electricity of his thoughts he became someone else. He made you laugh—he terrified you—he made you cry. He convinced you that he was the man outside of himself. But that left him with himself, didn't it? Who was he?

I never really knew. He had locked the door to the inside room. I have no idea, even whether he himself had the key. I only suspected that inside that room was a powerful engine which ran twenty-four hours a day at full speed. It turned out some remarkable people— yes—all those different people.

But more about Spencer later. Don't be impatient. I wasn't.

IV

Memorial Day

Here is the circumstance:

Well, I had a dose of my own back. This was the Memorial Day weekend—not the 30th. Oh no—no more—the real Memorial Day is no more. Better Business ruled the roost. That's all gone. We celebrate all holidays on weekends. Now, the 30th that year was Friday, so it could have been convenient, but THEY wanted it on Monday. So May 24th, 25th, 26th—that was this Memorial Day weekend. And that was the one that did me in.

We set out the 23rd, spring 1986, midday, from New York— David Lean and Sandy, his first wife, my secretary, Phyllis, and I. It was to be a weekend of relaxation. They liked to stay up late. I was hoping that I could work around this and get to bed early. But they are sweet—simple and straight . . . and strong and savage; and he was the best movie director in the world. He knew how to make the soufflé. Roast the meat. And nothing—did you hear me?—I said nothing got in his way. He'll stand and look and stare. He won't be hurried. He won't budge until he can smell perfection. That's his aim—work or play: do it as well as it can possibly be done. Or don't do it.

Listen—I knew this—I'd made a picture with him in 1954— *Summertime*, in Venice. There was a day when he couldn't get the scene with Isa Miranda and he turned to me and said, "Kate, you try," and off he went ten feet and turned and stared.

With David Lean in Venice

"Isa!" I said. "Now, Isa, this is what he has to have—"
We got the scene.

Well—yes—we do share that quality. We don't give up. We say
we'll be there—we'll be there—we'll do it. You say you'll get to the
top of the hill—you do!

Now, let's get these plants out of the car luggage compartment.

Oh dear—I forgot to tell you. We were at Grove Nursery in
Clinton. John—he's the head fellow there—well, John quickly sensed
who was bossing the show. David.

"Now, Kate, don't you think that this would be a good idea,
quince? That touch of red. How many of these do you have, John?
Three? Yes, we'll have those."

Sandy came up with a lovely yellow broom: "Oh yes," said David.
"Oh yes," said Kate. "We'll have three of those."

"And how about these?"

"Oh, they're pretty . . . What are they?" (I was looking for the
label.)

"Oh, they are cotoneasters," said Sandy. She knows the names of
everything—Latin too. I know, but vague.

"Ah, yes," said David, "they have a pretty red berry in the fall.
I should think . . ." (He was talking to John.) "Let's see—six of
these—yes?"

"Lovely," I said. They really were charming.

Up came Sandy with an enchanting, very pert-looking pine—sort
of dwarf type.

"Oh, I like that. Do you have three of these, John?" He did.
They were ordered.

"Have you any wisteria?"

"No, gone. Sorry."

"Now I'll get the car and we can load them in here—yes?" David
and Sandy were off to another department. Tools. They were buying
a big fork and two small forks and a shovel for planting. By the time
I got to them with the car, they'd paid for everything.

I picked up a small cute-looking shovel. "I think . . ."

"It won't last," said David.

"Good size."

"It won't last," said David.

I bought it anyway. It broke almost immediately, on a weed.

Poor thinking, Kath—

I was being carried along, wasn't I? This was an unusual and, in
a way, a delightful position for me. And they seemed to be enjoying
it. Certainly I was—I'd been meaning to fix that driveway bank for
two years—just. Well, I hadn't done it. I didn't have the strength.
The weeds, the weeds, the weeds—and what plants to put in?

We got back to the house.

The Commander of the Troop addressed us: "Now, let's get these
plants into the shade. And let's get rid of those weeds."

The bank—it was medium steep. It had been planted a year and a half before with low-growing junipers. They were quite ugly and turned a sort of rust red in the fall. Not pleasing. The bank went down to big heavy stones which lined the edge of an inlet—tidal. We called it a swamp. Well, Dad called it a lagoon. But it looked more to me like a swamp. In a storm, especially one from the north, the water would rise up and this is why we had raised the road and made this bank. To act as a sort of dike to protect the house. An occasional Nantucket pine remained from the original planting before the bank was raised.

Aside from the junipers, there were weeds and terrible rag grass and sorrel and pampas grass. We started to dig. And we dug and we dug. Sandy with a fork, David with a fork, me with a spade. And we'd yank and pull, and together we would undermine the determined roots of the rag grass. Yank—bend—twist—pull—dig with shovel —pull with hands. Agony! My back, my hip, my fingers, my feet. Poor joints—where's the lubricant? David was resting a moment on the only chair.

His running comment: "It's absolutely no use unless you get the root. It will be back before you can turn around . . . Oh, you broke that one, Kate—too bad. It really pays to just dig down and get it. Slowly—don't be impatient."

David had been living in hotels and sitting at a typewriter for the last months. He was in worse shape than I was. Well—I suppose we're about the same age. He determined and patient. I determined and impatient. Sandy was a good thirty years younger than we were. We were all three trained by upbringing and nature to finish the task. Get it done. Get it done right.

At the end of the first day, we had done about forty feet of the bank. Load after load of weeds had been lugged to our dump. It was about a thousand feet away, slightly uphill. And the wheelbarrow was the heavy one—the big one. The one I liked was at Mundy's house—he's my nephew—Dick's son. Dick liked the light barrow. I don't blame him.

Pick it up—get it up after you dig it up—and lug it. Oh, I'm so tired—my back—my feet—my hands—my fingers. Forget all that. Just keep a-going, Kate.

In the garden at Fenwick

David continued: "Now, let's begin to get these plants placed. We're beginning to go into the second phase. The quince?"

"Shall I—?"

"No, Sandy will plant these—she's the expert. How about this, Kate? This touch of red . . ."

Sandy was working over the ground which we had freed of weeds. She was spading it all—and deep. David was placing the plants, studying the placement.

"I think that if we group the three yellow broom—a splash of yellow . . ."

"Kate, do you have any manure?"

"I'll get it." I went to the garage, got the forty-pound bag of manure—lifted it into the barrow. Oh lawks, I'm so tired—aren't they ever going to stop?

"That's great, dear. Now Sandy will open it."

"No, I'll . . ." I went into the house to get the kitchen scissors —I think I'm going to die . . . my back . . .

"That's fine, dear—just the corner—no, let Sandy do that, she knows just the amount. You see, this is the crucial step. Those things are all pot-bound and you have to soften all the edges of the hole and the bottom of the hole, then sort of loosen the edges of the root after you get it out of the pot. Of course, you have to be very careful not to worry the root and just bare the root and expose it—that's right —now turn it a bit more. That's fine. Oh—and when you put the manure in, mix it very carefully so you don't burn the roots by direct contact."

Fuck the roots! I thought; I'm going to die. What about my roots? These people are like a machine.

"There we are—now water—can we get water out to—?"

"I'll get the hose." I went around the house, getting all the hoses. They were attached to various taps around the house. "Come on now, girl—unscrew it! I'm so tired—oh, tough titty—you're tired, they're tired—the whole world's tired—unscrew it." I dragged the hoses around the house and fastened them all together. It was long enough. Now turn it on—not too fast—just . . .

"Turn it off—turn it off. I'll do it." David came to the water tap. "Now look, dear, just a drop—you don't want to drown it. Is that it, dear?" he called to Sandy.

"Right!" she answered.

"Look, dear, why don't you go in and rest? We can handle this . . ."

"No, I'm fine. I'll just get rid of this mess . . ."

Somewhere, sometime in the midst of this struggle, we stopped, cleaned up and went shopping—for more plants. We got two wisteria and three white broom and some ground cover called worm grass, and a tray of ivy. In a sort of desperation, I got a few annuals to fill in my flower bed at the front—Sweet William—a lovely cerise pink—a spirea—they would be easy to plant. And then I saw some very strong-looking plants—melons of some sort. I couldn't see which without my glasses. I picked out four.

"What are these?" asked David.

"Melons," I said.

"Melons?" said Sandy. "What kind?"

I had no idea. Cucumbers—squash—cantaloupe—watermelon? I just thought they looked big and strong and lively. And I'd never planted one. "Cantaloupe, I hope. I like cantaloupe."

"They need care," they said.

Oh well. And I could hear them thinking: Cantaloupe? Why is she buying cantaloupe—we haven't finished the bank. Why doesn't she stick to the point—careless! Trivial . . . impatient. Fine way to garden.

Were they thinking this, or was it my guilt? Back to the spade. We had got past the first pine tree. There was another twenty feet to go beyond it. And, of course, there were the weeds under the pine . . . By now I was numb. "You know what you are, Kate," I said to myself. My body was a mass of pain and despair. "You are the coolie laborer of this group. You are a dumb—uninformed—cretin. You want to stop. You don't care whether the plants live or die. Or where or how they are planted." The wind had begun to blow. From the north right into our faces. Well, thank God I'm under this pine—dig—pull—crouch. I looked up. A pine needle stuck in the eye—right in the eye. Oh God, I thought; I'm so tired I can't even blink.

"That looks lovely, dear. What a pretty shape that tree is."

It crossed my mind: Shit, I don't care what shape anything is—just my shape—and that's a bad shape.

"Thank you," I said. And I looked. It was a very pretty tree.

"Good—only twenty feet to go," David said.

He's onto me! He's cheering me on. Is he? Yes, I thought, twenty feet. If I live. Now, why don't you stop, Kath—just admit it. You're dead and go in and take a bath and lie down . . . No, I'm not going to do that. I'm too proud. I'm going to stay out here and struggle until they quit or until I die.

But my dear, they are not going to quit. They are going to get rid of the weeds, plant the plants—put in the ivy—two wisteria—the broom—water everything. It is never going to end and you are going to die—and they'll push your body out of the way and finish the job! Kath, Kath—how can you? They're your dear friends.

Another load for the wheelbarrow. Fill it. Take it to the dump. I was so tired I could hardly push the damned thing. Out of hearing, struggling to keep upright, I began to creep—just low-down, all-out gone. I'm beginning to die—I'm going to die . . .

Then I began to laugh. You poor old dolt—you just won't admit that you can't go on. That's your trouble . . .

I'm as good as you are! That's your problem. But you're up against two characters who are as irritating as you are. They'll keep going until they drop, and she's young enough to be your granddaughter. You've met your match! No matter—pull yourself together. Renewed, I returned with my empty wheelbarrow . . .

"Where are we going to put this one?"

I looked at one of the few remaining cotoneasters and the three new white broom. "I'll dig the holes."

"Look, dear, why don't you let Sandy do that—she knows exactly how to . . ."

"Well, you don't need to use my holes—I'll just . . ." Was I getting mean?

"Kate, you're getting impatient. You cannot be impatient if you're a good gardener. There's only one way to garden—the right way . . . Isn't that interesting, dear? You were never impatient when we were doing *Summertime*."

Yes yes, I thought, I'm impatient. Standing in this goddamned sun and the goddamned north wind and . . .

"Now, shall we put this one here or would they be better in a group? And . . ."

"How about this, David?" It was Sandy.

I'm impatient all right. I'm frantic. I'll go back to my hod-carrying cooliedom. I'll get all that rag grass—those long, pointed red-and-green things with roots ten miles long—and the sorrel. That's it! Get to the pine tree—it was the second pine—I'll dig three bloody holes for the white broom just to— Oh, I don't know why—just to give me a feeling of progress . . . Dig! . . . I'm with a big fork now. I'm doing a poor job, I know I'm doing a poor job. Here comes Sandy . . .

"Well now, I'll just turn some of this over. Give it a bit of ventilation."

David came along. "Yes, they look very pretty there. Come on, Sandy, let's get them in."

"How many more are there to put in?" I ventured from under a big pine branch. Oh Christ, it hit me in the eye again—a pine needle. My eyes are full of dirt and pine needles and stab holes from the needles. I'll be blind too.

Sandy was working on a pampas-grass root— It was one I'd given up on. "You'll never get to the end of that, Sandy! It's part of an underground system."

She broke it.

"You see . . ."

"Try again," said David. She did.

It broke.

"Once more," said David. She tried—it broke.

"No use," said David. "Let's plant the white. Get the job done. This wind is rather upsetting, isn't it?"

Hope? Is the end in sight? Oh progress . . .

They began the deliberate, careful process of preparing, softening, ventilating, getting the plant out of the pot, freeing the roots, getting the manure—a pause . . .

David: "This soil is all sand and rock. We need some topsoil." He looked at me.

"Let's see—yes, I'll get some—we have a pile of something."

"I'll come with you," said David. I took him to a pile. "No, this is manure, dear—or what is it?" God knows, I thought. I knew that I had some topsoil on top of a bunch of potted amaryllis and daffodils and narcissus.

"Over here."

"Oh yes, good."

I dove in, do I mean dived in, with my hands and loaded enough for the three holes into the barrow. We got back to the bank. Sandy was still hacking away. "You're just like me," I said. "You won't stop."

"I know," she said, "we're crazy. We have got to get to the trunk of this tree."

"Well, I'm sure you know the truth."

". . . Yes."

"Competition."

"Yes."

"I can work harder than you can."

"Yes, but my standards begin to soften."

"Tell me the truth."

"Soften, really. Oh, I hope not."

"Yes, I begin to work only on the surface. I leave a piece of root—looks done. I don't water enough—I make it."

David was staring at me in disbelief.

"But, Kate, you're dealing in fundamentals here, fool and trick life. Watering, for instance—you must do it thoroughly. Don't be fooled by the ground being wet on top. That is no good at all. It simply makes the roots turn up to take a drink instead of going deeper for the permanent drink. Better not to water at all—then the roots, if they have any gimp at all, will go deeper and deeper. Don't drown the plant—just give it a chance to absorb all it can. Roots are like us—they can't be forced—they must be made to work for their own future. But steadily . . . carefully . . . given a proper environment."

It was over. Now the job was done. It was night. I had had a bath and a swim and I was in bed. And I was thinking, You have now discovered the truth about yourself. Your parents gave you a great start. You were planted in good soil—fed—watered—carefully nurtured. And you were sent out into the world. And you were lucky. And apparently you have been successful. But have you accomplished all that you could have—given your beginning? No, you have been careless. You did not get to the essence of things. You can't do this and you can't do that, and you could have if you had concentrated and just stuck to it and got to the bottom of it. It's a bit late now, but profit by this—if you do it—do it. Get those weeds out. And plant carefully.

Well, that's the end of the story about refurbishing the south bank of the swamp.

I sent a copy to David and also to his property man. It delighted David.

A bit after this, I met the property man in New York. He was crazy about the piece. He said, "Here's another one about David and how, when he wants something, he always tries to get exactly what he wants:

"We were shooting a scene in Scotland—a big and important house. We were seeing car after car come up the driveway, then a beautiful white Rolls-Royce. They disgorged their passengers—they drove on.

" 'Now,' said David, 'I want you to be sure that when the white Rolls stops, the double 'R's on the center of the wheels are exactly upright.' "

"And were they?"

"Of course," he answered. "Perfection means perfection."

A year later: "Hello, are you two here again? The bank is sensational. Oh, it's—David, it's beautiful—the quince—the yellow broom—the white—the dwarf pine—and the ivy and worm grass— all just sensational. I think of you both every time I pass it—just great—lovely . . .

"The melons? What happened to them? Oh—you mean the melons. No, I never did find out what they were—they died."

Alec Guinness and Willie Rose

Willie Rose and His Maserati

William Rose wrote *Genevieve* and *The Ladykillers*, etc. He was a really talented and witty man. In 1966, Stanley Kramer was going to do his new script, *Guess Who's Coming to Dinner*.

It was to star Spencer and me. My niece Kathy Houghton was going to play the part of our daughter. Her name in the script was Joey. I didn't think it was a good name and I wanted Willie to change it.

Rose exploded. Called Kramer. Said that he was going back to Jersey—that Kramer should give Katharine Hepburn full writing credit, etc., etc.

Kramer called me. Told me to just plain shut up.

So I shut up. It was all idiotic.

Slowly as we shot the picture, Willie and I became friendly. He really was a very amusing man, about fifty, an American writer who had moved to England. He had a house—a lovely stone house on the island of Jersey—built in the late 1600s. (He lived there to avoid British taxes.) He and his wife had separated. Willie was on the set quite often; then for the sake of his visa he'd go to Canada, as his time in the United States was limited.

Spencer died a few weeks after making *Guess Who's Coming to Dinner*.

I was working on a Margery Sharp book, *Martha*, trying to get a script together. I was doing it with Irene Selznick as producer. I was to be the director. We had been working with a young writer, Jim Prideaux. After a while Irene decided that I would be better working alone. So we went on this way until we had a finished script. Then we planned to go to London to see if we could persuade Vanessa Redgrave's fat sister Lynn Redgrave to play the lead, which had to be played by a really fat girl.

When we got to London, we found that Lynn was no longer fat. She was very very thin. Well, fat young actresses are hard—in fact, almost impossible—to find. In the meantime I thought to myself, There's Willie Rose sitting over there. I wonder whether he'd be willing to take a look at the script. Irene said she'd come with me.

We got to Jersey. Willie was in a desperate state. He thought the script hopeless. Said so. Irene thought he was hopeless. She went back to London.

I was very worried about Willie, who was drinking much too much every day. I thought that he was desperately lonely. He kept talking about a Maserati—a car he wanted to pick up in Italy. He said one of the waiters in the restaurant where he had his dinner would pick it up for him.

I said, "How about us? Why don't we go over and get it?"

So we did.

And it was fun, and I thought that I could build a very funny movie script around the idea of an actress who falls for a young writer and then gets a better offer and ditches him.

Then years later her career is sagging and hoping to inspire him to write a script for her, she goes to visit him and they take the trip to pick up the car.

This is my version of our trip.

We were in London. The final papers for the car—the nice man at the Consulate. That was a lucky sign, wasn't it?

Just to refresh your memory, Willie—and to amuse myself—although naturally I am not suggesting that my memory could ever challenge yours.

Do you remember?

It was a rather wild day. We went with David Lowe, my English chauffeur, and Phyllis to the airport. For once I had sensible luggage. You had two rather large suitcases, as I recall. I had one Vuitton suitcase and two sort of duffel bags—also Vuitton. And of course my two huge handbags slung over my shoulder.

You were adorable, and I thought, What an enchanting creature. So handsome—masculine—naïve. What?

They announced over the loudspeaker that Milan was having a blizzard. That in all probability we would have to land either in Genoa or in Venice.

Oh Jesus, I thought. I didn't know Genoa but I did Venice. The trip from the airport—which was on the Lido—into Venice was ghastly. Then to find a garage where, with luck, one could rent a car. Hell. Oh dear.

"No no," said Willie. "We're landing in Milano. I have perfect confidence!"

You reached over and took my hand.

We got up and walked down the long corridor to board the plane.

It was going to be a gorgeous happy time, just the two of us.

I had really forced the trip.

I thought that he should pick up his own Maserati—then it would really be his. So few things that he cares anything about—but he does seem to get a boot out of cars. And this one will never be the same to him if one of the waiters picks it up.

Besides, if he doesn't get away from Jersey, he will never be able to get going again in his own trade. "That's what I'd like to have on my gravestone—WRITER," he had once said.

And now here we were in the airplane. Having a glass of champagne.

Willie never daunted. And me thinking what a brilliant and fascinating fellow—so strong and confident. Out in the world again. Great.

I really was trying to start out on this trip as a dependent female.

He is so bright that in the word game—or prognostications on almost any subject—I happily listened.

When I say listened, that is really true.

One of his great complaints was that I butted in on his most interesting monologues with some totally irrelevant comment and destroyed his train of thought.

Well, I shouldn't, I shouldn't actually say this, but *his* train of thought seemed to be the only train we ever took.

No—I mustn't talk or think that way about him. Look at him. He really is extraordinary-looking. He's asleep in the seat next to me or he's drawing a terrible and insulting caricature or he's asking me why I don't wear glasses because obviously I can't see. At your age you need glasses.

But it's all at this moment done lovingly and charmingly and humorously. Queer bird. Certainly he has an incredible brain. Smears me intellectually. This is a bit irritating at times, because I'm used to being considered rather bright. He makes me feel an ass most of the time. Only occasionally when I talk about him and his problems does he sometimes admit that I might now and then have an idea worth listening to.

We're over Milano. My God, the clouds are separating. We're landing. Willie, darling Willie, you're right. By gum, you have second sight—you're wonderful!

We're down. The porter took our bags.

There was indeed six inches of snow on the ground and still snowing. It was about twelve-thirty or one o'clock. My Italian, such as it was, took us to the Avis rental desk, very handy in the Milano airport. Also, the aerodrome was on the big autostrada to Modena where the Maserati factory was. I had sandwiches and a bottle of wine for our lunch, which I'd taken from our home in Elm Place. I had a map of the autostrada and an Italian *Blue Guide* for Northern Italy.

Off we went in our rented Fiat. I was to be the guide.

Which way? Right under the bridge, then left on the first turn —then right . . .

WILLIE

Look, don't tell me about the whole trip. Just here—what do I do? Which way do I turn now?

KATE

You turn left.

WILLIE

I thought you said right.

KATE

I did but I was wrong. You can't turn right. It's against the law. You turn left. In about a mile turn all the way around to the left, then past the aerodrome take first right. Go under bridge, then left onto—

WILLIE

Look, I'm not that bright and I can't see the map. I don't think that you can see the map either, without your glasses.

KATE

I told you I haven't got any glasses. I have twenty-twenty vision.

WILLIE

I know . . .

KATE

Left up here about five hundred feet.

WILLIE

Where?

KATE

There—there!

WILLIE

But that's exactly in the opposite direction.

KATE

I know. That's what we have to do. We go back past the airport, then . . .

WILLIE

Don't tell me a long story. I just hope you're right.

KATE

I am.

WILLIE

Yes, I hope so.

KATE

Have faith, my darling.

WILLIE

Wasn't that something the way those clouds parted and down
we came?

KATE

You're a genius.

WILLIE

You thought we were going to have to go to Venice.

KATE

I sure did. Thank God I was wrong.

WILLIE

You were wrong, all right.

KATE

Yup. Happy to be.

WILLIE

You're a pretty girl.

KATE

Thank you.

WILLIE

For which, the pretty or the girl?

KATE

Now watch it. Don't be unkind.

WILLIE

I don't understand why you're so self-conscious about your
age.

KATE

Well, I am, so shut up.

WILLIE

No, seriously. When you're a hundred and twenty-five I'll be
a hundred and fourteen. That's not such a serious difference.

KATE

I'll never know. Neither will you.

WILLIE

If we get together again, you can just say that your husband
has an irresistible attraction to the late late show.

KATE

Very funny!

WILLIE

Are you sore?

KATE

No, happy.

WILLIE

Hold my hand. May I play the radio?

KATE

Sure.

WILLIE

Light me a cigarette.

(I did)

KATE

Want some lunch?

WILLIE

Why didn't you ask me before the cigarette?

KATE

I'm stupid.

WILLIE

What?

KATE

I said I'm stupid.

WILLIE

Oh.

KATE

You're supposed to say, "Oh no."

WILLIE

How long will it take us to get there?

KATE

I'd say three hours.

WILLIE

Oh no, not possibly. You see, you can go as fast as you want
to on this road.

KATE

How do you know?

WILLIE

I've been here before.

KATE

Is that so?

WILLIE

In fact, several times. I like Italy.

KATE

Alone?

WILLIE

What do you mean, alone?

KATE

What I said. Were you traveling alone?

WILLIE

No, as a matter of fact, I was with—

KATE

Don't tell me.

WILLIE

Why not? There are things we have to face.

KATE

Oh—there are *things*, are there? Plural?

WILLIE

I hope that you're not comparing my poor wretched life with yours.

KATE

Willie.

WILLIE

What?

KATE

How about some wine and a sandwich?

WILLIE

O.K. While we're riding?

KATE

Yeah, sure. The wine's opened. I stole two glasses.

WILLIE

Thanks. Very nice. What's my choice?

KATE

Chicken. Beef.

WILLIE

Chicken.

KATE

Any good?

WILLIE

Great. You're pretty.

KATE

So are you.

WILLIE

I always thought I was nothing much to look at. Just another man.

KATE

No, really, irrespective of any feeling that I have for you,
you're handsome. You've got a great face. I like to look at it.

WILLIE

You're a nut—move over. No. Over here.

KATE

Isn't this paradise?

WILLIE

It certainly is.

(He turned up the radio)

Outskirts of a town—Modena—I think that this must be the
wrong road.

KATE

Well, let's turn around.

WILLIE

No—we'll go on a bit.

KATE

I think you're wasting your time. Look, ask that boy.

WILLIE

How the hell can I ask him?

KATE

Well, I will.

(We stopped)

Perdoni, scusi—Modena? Usine Maserati?

(The boy pointed back the way we'd come and spoke
in Italian)

KATE

Grazie.

WILLIE

Could you understand him?

KATE

No, not really. Anyway, turn around.

WILLIE

Look, let me drive the car, will you? I'll turn where it's safe
to turn.

(By now I'd found the city map of Modena. I located
the general location of the Maserati factory, which was
off the map)

KATE

Turn on the Via —there, there.

(We drove into a crowded town. We saw a cop)

Stop, a cop!

WILLIE

What's the use of stopping if you don't understand what he
says?

KATE

We'll understand enough.

WILLIE

You may. I won't understand a goddamned word.

KATE

Look, just stop. Why don't you? We have nothing to lose.

WILLIE

Nothing to lose but my sanity.

KATE

Stop! Don't get hysterical, son.

(We pulled up by the cop. It was a sort of small square
with terrific traffic)

Scusi, Usine Maserati?

(I handed him the map)

COP

Sì, Signora. Dritto, e al primo semaforo, girate a destra—Via Marghetta. E poi dritto al ponte e di nuovo a destra. La fabbrica è alla destra. Avete capito.

KATE

Sì, grazie tante. Go ahead . . .

WILLIE

(To the cop)

Thank you. *Merci—*

COP

Niente, Signore.

(We drove off)

WILLIE

What did he say?

KATE

Just go along straight . . .

WILLIE

What did he say?

KATE

Right at the first light—Via Marghetta . . .

WILLIE

Just tell me when we get there—I can't do everything—

KATE

Turn right.

WILLIE

Are you sure?

KATE

Turn right. Look at that church—fascinating . . .

(He gave me a long look)

God, what artists the Italians are.

(Willie looked)

Now, there's the bridge, turn right— Look, Willie—there it is through the gate. What's the man's name?

WILLIE

Signorelli.

(We went in the gate)

Three o'clock—not bad.

KATE

There's a man in that little office.

We drove through a gate and another gate. It looked deserted. Finally, we came into a yard with buildings on either side and a small porter's hut. I got out of the car and went in. Willie stayed in the car. It was a tiny room with a flattop desk and several telephones. It was all windows, so Willie could see us and we could see him. He got out of the Fiat and got his briefcase with his papers for the car.

KATE

Il Signor Signorelli per il Signor William Rose—un nuovo Maserati.

PORTER

Sì, Signora Rose. Un momento—

KATE

No— il non la Signora. Oh, non è importanto. Comprende?

(The porter did elaborate talking on the phone)

PORTER

Momento.

(Willie came into the hut with the papers)

Signore—momento—

(The porter left)

KATE

I wonder if there's a john around here?

WILLIE

Well, there certainly isn't one right here.

KATE

Don't you need to . . .

WILLIE

No.

KATE

You're a great traveling companion.

WILLIE

I just haven't got weak kidneys.

KATE

I'd hardly call four hours and a bottle of wine weak kidneys.

WILLIE

We'll ask Signorelli when he comes.

KATE

No, never mind. I'll solve my own problems. Just forget it.

WILLIE

Are you desperate?

KATE

No, not really. Just a thought.

(The porter came back, and with him was a Signore Retto)

SIGNORE RETTO

Signora—Signore Rose . . .

(We all shook hands)

Signore Signorelli is on the telephone. If you'll just come with me. We shall first look at your car, then we can take care of the papers. The test driver can show you how to run the car while Madame will be kind enough to wait for you? You will not get wet?

> KATE
>
> No—no—it's raining very little.

> WILLIE
>
> Are you all right, sweetie?

I tagged along after the two men across a courtyard and into the factory. This was about as big as a narrow but long soundstage.

> SIGNORE RETTO
>
> There is your car, Signore.

There it was—absolutely shattering—just the color of Château Lafite-Rothschild—a red wine which he liked very much.

This was his—the purchase of his life—the final gesture of his boyhood. His color—his own—bought by *his* money, which he had made himself.

His car . . . A moment in Willie's life . . .

> WILLIE
>
> I didn't order those wheels—I ordered wire wheels . . .

The test driver was standing, as was the man showing us around—and all the workmen in the vicinity, plus many of the work-men on the "line"—wondering how the Americans would react to their new car. Willie, being shy, didn't want to be effusive so he was being critical. We opened the luggage compartment. I sat in the car.

> WILLIE
>
> What about those wheels? They're so heavy-looking. How long would it take to change them?

KATE

I think . . .

Willie gave me a look.
The test driver was giving wild signs— Don't let Signore change the wheels.

TEST DRIVER

Va bene—è megliore.

KATE

Willie, he's trying to say . . . The man, he says the car drives more safely with those wheels—try them. If you don't like them, they can always send you the wire ones.

While all this was going on, I was sitting in the car and oh-ing and ah-ing . . .

Then we walked down one line and up the other, seeing a variety of their cars. Willie decided to keep the wheels.

In the meantime, several of the workmen had begun to suspect that I was who I am—and I was trying to play the gracious lady, so pleased with the car. Would I allow them to take a picture . . . Not my car—it's his car. And anyway I don't like . . . Very well, Signora . . .

We went out of the factory and up to the office. Signorelli had finished his call. By then they all knew who I was and were coming by to take a look from the door—mostly ladies—one very nice woman. I indicated "wash my hands." She took me to the john across the hall. That Willie—he'll go to the john now because I'll tell him where it is. But he's so stubborn he'd never ask for it.

I had conversations in Italian and signed endless autographs. Willie went out to test-run the car. The papers were finally done and we unloaded the Fiat, loaded the Maserati, and as dusk was rapidly falling, we set out for Firenze . . . I had the map and an enlarging glass and a searchlight.

KATE

He said turn left.

WILLIE

Right—left . . . Wiper—now, let's see . . . indicator—
lights—brakes off. It's quite stiff . . .

KATE

You mean hard to drive?

WILLIE

No—just stiff, really . . . Which way?

KATE

Straight—just straight—he said we couldn't miss it. Are you
pleased?

WILLIE

Well—it's a good color, isn't it?

KATE

Yeah—beautiful—

WILLIE

That red wine—

KATE

Yah.

WILLIE

The wheels make it look so heavy—

KATE

I like them.

WILLIE

Do you?

KATE

Yes—sits on the ground.

WILLIE

Well, I thought that the wire ones made it look so light—
and not so ostentatious.

KATE

Well, there's not much use trying to look unostentatious in
a car like this.

WILLIE

You mean you think it's showy—

KATE

No, not exactly.

WILLIE

Not exactly—you mean exactly.

KATE

Willie—I think that it is absolutely gorgeous and I can tell
you now—I'd like to order one for myself. It's comfortable
—it's . . .

WILLIE

Is this the highway?

KATE

Yes—turn—O.K. Now all the way to Florence.

WILLIE

You wouldn't be able to drive it. It's quite heavy. You
know—the shift—and the pedal. It's a man's car . . .

KATE

And you're a man, Willie.

WILLIE

So you really like it?

KATE

It and you.

WILLIE

You know when I ordered it, I felt an absolute—oh, I don't
know—I'd always thought it would be wonderful to—I sort
of imagined myself behind the wheel of— You know what I
mean . . .

KATE

Willie—you get to me.

WILLIE

You think I'm an ass, don't you?

KATE

I think you're adorable. You please me. The sight of you behind that wheel—

WILLIE

Are you glad you came with me?

KATE

I sure am.

WILLIE

How far is it?

KATE

Well, if we go into Firenze, which I think is better than Montecatini— Let's go there, then it's easy.

WILLIE

You're the boss.

KATE

God, what a terrible night. I never saw such rain. Doesn't it bother you?

WILLIE

Not really.

KATE

You're pretty cool.

WILLIE

Hold my hand.

KATE

Willie—it's fun, isn't it?

WILLIE

I don't know about fun . . . It's interesting.

KATE

Dive in, Willie. Dive in—what have you got to lose?

WILLIE

I can't swim . . .

KATE

I'll save you . . .

WILLIE

I wonder—

KATE

You'll save me—

WILLIE

More likely.

KATE

I'll admit that—more likely—if you'll get to work and write me a script.

WILLIE

Is that why you're here?

KATE

I don't think so. I just never could forget you.

WILLIE

Did you try?

KATE

You saw through me, Willie, to the wicked depths of my soul.

WILLIE

Do you have a soul?

KATE

By gum—you close that door, don't you.

WILLIE

I don't like to sit in a draft. I'm susceptible to chills.

KATE

Thanks.

WILLIE

Where are we going?

KATE

What do you mean?

WILLIE

Florence—what hotel?

KATE

As I remember, on that square—on the river there are two
—one rather quiet.

WILLIE

What is it called?

KATE

I'll recognize it when we get there . . .

WILLIE

You can't remember anything, can you?

KATE

I can remember you—

WILLIE

I wonder,—

(He pulled over to the side of the road)

I loved you with everything I had. I wasn't much of anything
then. But I did love you—painfully—

KATE

Maybe too painfully—

WILLIE

Don't be hard.

KATE

I'm not hard, Willie. I'm here, aren't I? I've been disappointed, haven't I?

WILLIE

Listen, sweetie, everyone is disappointed. Nothing that a good script wouldn't cure.

KATE

O.K.—I know what you mean. It's true. But only from moment to moment. I want something more secure.

(Willie started the car again and drove on)

WILLIE

For temporary relief only. If the pain continues, stop taking the medicine and consult your doctor.

(We drove on in silence)

KATE

The pain continues.

WILLIE

I'm not a doctor.

KATE

You're my doctor.

WILLIE

I wonder—I wonder if—

KATE

There's a sign. Firenze.

(He gave me a look. Didn't I care about how he was going to finish the sentence?)

WILLIE

Where do I turn?

KATE

I'll tell you— You were going to say—

WILLIE

I have no idea what I was going to say—and obviously you weren't the least interested, otherwise you couldn't have cut me off.

KATE

My golly, darling, I didn't cut you off—the sign—

WILLIE

The sign—what the hell do I care about the sign!

KATE

But it leads to Florence. It's where we're to spend the night . . .

WILLIE

Says who?

KATE

But Willie—we decided—

WILLIE

What do you mean—we? You—you decided—as usual . . .

KATE

Well, we can't just drive around in the rain all night.

WILLIE

Why not? We were about to talk about us. And what we can do about it . . . Is that so or not?

KATE

Well, yes—but—

WILLIE

Oh—just tell me what to do. All those pansies you've been going around with must have been delighted to be told exactly what to do—

KATE

Turn right.

We turned and drove in silence into Florence. I had the city map—and my light and magnifying glass.

WILLIE

Wouldn't it be easier if you wore glasses? I mean rather than handling so many—I mean I know you have twenty-twenty vision but . . .

KATE

No—I don't mind all this paraphernalia—and I couldn't read this map with regular glasses anyway—

WILLIE

How do you know?

KATE

I've tried . . .

WILLIE

Oh, then you have glasses?

KATE

Yes—I have . . . I just don't use them.

WILLIE

Maybe they're just too weak to be any good. Try mine—

KATE

No—I'm fine—thanks . . . Turn left—

WILLIE

Do you know where you're going?

KATE

Yes—down the river here and then we'll come to a sort of square and then there are two—here we are, turn—there are two hotels . . . That one's the one—the Grand.

WILLIE

It looks as though it's being rebuilt.

KATE

It's the best—and we won't hear it on the river side—and it's one night.

We drove to the other side where quite a number of cars were parked. We stopped. Immediately the doorman came over—opened the door.

WILLIE

What about the car for the night?

BOY

Garage?

WILLIE

Yes—can you drive it?

BOY

Signore! It is beautiful!

WILLIE

Thank you.

KATE

Open the back—take them all.

BOY

Sì, Signora.

The boy opened the back—lifted out all the bags. Another boy arrived—carried them in. The lobby was small. I went to the desk.

KATE

Do you have two rooms—two baths?

CLERK

Ah, Signora, we're very proud to have you here—

KATE

Thank you.

CLERK

Adjoining?

WILLIE

No.

    (She gave him a glance)

KATE

No—but not too far away from each other—very nice rooms.

    (Silent looks from the people at the desk)

CLERK

Passports?

    (We handed passports to him)

Thank you.

    (The clerk took a lot of keys. We got into an elevator.
    Stopped. Down two long corridors. And went into one
    room—tiny)

KATE

Too small.

CLERK

They are all small—a double?

KATE

Yes, a double is fine. Two doubles.

CLERK

I'll have to get other keys. *Perdoni* . . .

    (The clerk left. We sat down on a hall bench)

WILLIE

I wonder what they think when they look at those ages in the
passports. Ha-ha-ha-ha-ha. May I say something awful?

KATE

Why not?

WILLIE

Well, how about—"The Daughters of the American Revolution and the Boy Scouts of America have always been two of America's finest institutions."

KATE

Willie, how can you! Oh—God—how horrible! But you're funny. I do wonder what they think . . .

(The clerk returned with keys)

CLERK

Signore—Signora—

(He opened another door)

KATE

Ah, this is much better—fine.

WILLIE

Now another for me.

CLERK

Not adjoining but next door.

WILLIE

Thank you—I'll go in. Wash up a bit.

(Coming into the room)

Bang! Bang! Are you O.K.?

KATE

Come in. Yes, I'm fine. Look, here's an icebox—and champagne.

WILLIE

Give me.

KATE

You must be dead—all that rain and a new car.

WILLIE

In a way—

KATE

But you must be pleased—

WILLIE

Yes, I am.

KATE

It's so comfortable—extraordinary—

WILLIE

Cheers—

KATE

Cheers—

WILLIE

Well, we're doing pretty well—no fights—I'm very happy.
Are you?

KATE

Yes, I'm very happy.

WILLIE

Shall we eat downstairs?

KATE

I think the food will be better.

We went down to dinner. They put us in a sort of alcove. All
very nice. Then we took a walk along the Arno. Then back at the
hotel and outside my door:

WILLIE

Good night, sweetie.

KATE

(Calling down hall after him)

Shall I wash your socks and underpants?

WILLIE

Are you *kidding*?

It was a pretty room—nice bath. I washed my face. Put out all my little tokens: Spence—Mother—Dad. I looked at them for a long time. My people. To whom I had given. And who had given to me. And I wondered what I was doing here. What did I want? What did he want? I concluded that we were both absolutely desperate—belonging nowhere—dawn till dusk—and no one giving a rap.

I was better off than he was. I had the protection of good, good friends. He had a daughter whom he held at arm's length—as he held everyone—in a terror of being hurt.

There was a terrible pride somewhere in this man. He had been hurt and hurt badly. But when? He had been very well thought of always as a writer. Even before *Genevieve*.

But not as highly thought of as he felt he should be?

Or was it an overweening jealousy?

He was certainly incredibly jealous of his work—as if he were a novice. When I criticized the name Joey! What an experience that was.

I held him in as great esteem as it is possible to hold a man. I felt that if there was a man worthy of the name "writer," he was it. No tricks. Nothing cheap. A deep classic talent. But for some trivial reason I didn't like the name Joey. What kind of insecurity could so dominate a man that he could imagine that it meant any more than that? I meant exactly that—that I didn't like the name.

Of course it was the WE'LL THINK OF SOMETHING that did the damage—but God!

I felt like a mouse with a giant—but did this giant in his heart feel like a mouse?

No one with any brain feels like much of anything—most of the time. But somehow when one gets going in one's trade, one forgets one's self in relation to others. He must know that he has really and truly got what it takes He is just plain remarkable. And it is a curse that he doesn't get any joy from it—any confidence. What can be the reason?

I don't think that people with any sensitivity wander around feeling totally great about themselves. But wow! You wonder with him what to say. He's the only writer in the business against whom I have heard no criticism at all—none—he is universally admired.

And as a woman who has been trained to make people—children, parents, audiences, to say nothing of the opposite sex—feel good about themselves, it is a great challenge to meet someone like Willie.

If I were he—and could write as he can—I'd be the little Father of All the World. Of course, I am sure that he wonders if he can ever do it again. But everyone wonders that—surgeons, musicians—Alan Jay Lerner was talking about just that. He's a big fan of Willie's too. I think that being a writer must be an agony. And as you get older and better and fussier, it becomes harder.

Anyhow, I wish that I could give him a boost, but actually the only real thing to give him a boost is someone THERE—who loves HIM—so that he has a sort of cozy spot to be safe in. And then one day he'll begin. It's a happy problem really, because most people can never do anything—no matter what they do or don't do or try to do.

I had a wonderful sleep, although the waterfall outside the window made a terrible noise. We had agreed to leave about nine. I would call him, or vice versa. I ordered a big breakfast and studied my maps. The telephone:

KATE

Yes . . . Hello, Willie . . . Great . . . Fine . . . Did you?
. . . Nine o'clock—yup . . . I'll leave the door open . . .
Shall I tell them to get the car? . . . O.K.

I got dressed. I left a tip for the maid—packed—opened the door—put my bags there. Willie came by. We rang for a porter. Paid. He paid. The boy was loading the car. I walked right up and said:

KATE

No—this bag goes this way and this that. Then you put this here and—

(The boy and Willie stood like fools. Then we got into the car)

WILLIE

Which way?

KATE

We start out just the way we walked last night. Down there and to the left and then—when I say—to the left again, I would just love to drive by the Baptistery—the Ghiberti doors. Anyway, it is so thrilling and it's right on our way . . .

WILLIE

Oh.

KATE

Maybe we can park and take a look around.

WILLIE

No.

KATE

Well, we can drive around it.

WILLIE

All right. Look, we have to get this car on the boat. It has to be in St.-Malo on Friday. It was hell to get the ticket. It's impossible to go on another boat. Now, that is a fact and it's a long way.

KATE

O.K. But, Willie, this is only the second day. Tuesday. And it's not all that far.

WILLIE

It is exactly fifteen hundred kilometers and it is far—to me. I'm driving.

KATE

O.K.—O.K. Anyway, that street there—

(He looked at me)

We have to do that. The one last night along the river is one-way.

Arrivederci to the boy, whom Willie overtipped handsomely, and off we went. It was all very crowded.

KATE

Left here.

WILLIE

It's one-way.

KATE

Oh God—well, go ahead and go left on the next.

WILLIE

It would certainly help if I had a guide who could see. You look and look at those maps. I don't think you even know what country you're in and you send me the wrong way down a one-way street.

KATE

It doesn't say—or I mean indicate—which way the streets go . . . Left here—this is O.K.

WILLIE

Will this go where you want to go? I mean, so you can see what you want to see?

KATE

I hope so. You're sweet.

WILLIE

It's just—well, driving in a city.

KATE

Oh gosh—I know—I'd be frantic . . . Favor the right fork—

WILLIE

I wonder if it'll rain again.

KATE

I'm afraid it looks like it—

(We drove into the square)

Just go slowly around, maybe we can park. That's the Baptistery.

(I read)

WILLIE

Why don't you look at it? You can read about it afterward.

KATE

Those are the doors.

WILLIE

I can't look backwards.

KATE

This is the church. Park here.

(We drove in; were attacked in Italian)

WILLIE

Look—it's private. It's for buses or something.

(We drove out)

KATE

Go around the square again slowly as you are —again—

(I read)

WILLIE

Look, don't bother reading. I read all about it myself. It was built, etc., etc.

(He recited details of the Baptistery)

KATE

My golly—how in the hell did you happen to do that and, more amazing, how did you ever happen to remember it?

WILLIE

I concentrate.

KATE

Ketch.

WILLIE

Well, you don't, do you?

KATE

I don't know, Willie. Right fork. I think that I get excited or something and everything flies out of my head. I get an impression of colors and shapes and where things are. I can always retrace my steps.

WILLIE

So I've noticed.

KATE

Oh, you—but that was fascinating, wasn't it?

WILLIE

I was bowled over. Are you sure this is the right road?

We drove along quite easily out of Florence and onto the big highway toward Pisa. We passed Montecatini—then Lucca, which is a charming town—but we didn't see either because we were on the autostrada. Then we got to the coast. I thought that we should at least go to Pisa, which is a few miles south when you get to the coast, because it is most photogenic—have a look around and then hit our road north.

It very soon began to rain, then to pour. The trucks in long lines made it almost impossible to pass.

WILLIE

You're sure that this is the right road?

KATE

Yes—it's the only road.

WILLIE

I can't pass. It's too dangerous.

KATE

I'm sorry. I know we should obviously have gone back north from Modena.

WILLIE

Well, how could we know?

KATE

I've been on this road before. It was the same road. It comes back to me.

WILLIE

Oh—who with?

KATE

Good grief, who? I don't know.

(We drove along in silence)

Isn't that a great color, that house there?

WILLIE

Yes—it's great. Do you mean to tell me that you can't remember whom you were with when you were on this road before?

KATE

Well, it was probably Mother and Dad.

WILLIE

I don't believe that you have just said to me what you have just said to me.

KATE

What in the world can you find wrong in my traveling with Mother and Dad?

WILLIE

I think that you've thrown Ma and Pa to the dogs. You know damn well who you were traveling with.

KATE

Willie—you're just wrong . . .

WILLIE

That will be the day.

So we drove along with ups and downs. Past Genoa and then along the south coast of France. All those great spots.

The conversation was sometimes less delicious than it had been at the start. He was tired and yes, you're right, frankly so was I. We got to the last stop before the ferry.

KATE

That looks like a good spot for dinner.

WILLIE

Look—I'm dead. I don't want dinner, I just want—

KATE

You just want what?

WILLIE

I don't think that you really want to know.

KATE

Yes, I do.

WILLIE

Do you think that is wise of you? Someone might someday tell you the truth.

KATE

That's O.K.

WILLIE

You're sure?

KATE

Quite.

WILLIE

When I said I didn't want dinner, I meant it. I don't want dinner. I want to go to my room—alone—and just be quiet.

KATE

Well—what's so wrong with that? I'd be happy to do the same thing.

WILLIE

Oh—you would?

KATE

Yes.

WILLIE

Well, go ahead. Suit yourself. Don't let me stop you. That certainly is something you're great at—suiting yourself.

KATE

My God, Willie, what are you—!

WILLIE

Look—let me be, will you? I'm going to park the car here and I'm— What luggage do you want?

He stopped the car—gave me my luggage and went into the little hotel to get his room, which we had reserved. I waited a while, then got my key.

Well—life life. What now? Is traveling down this road a path to take? Well, order dinner. What a pig.

I had a delicious dinner, then a lovely sleep.

Knock! Knock!

Who the hell!

I opened the door.

WILLIE

Hello, sweetie! Don't you look pretty. Ready to go?

KATE

How are the Boy Scouts of America this morning?

With Phyllis, dressing for *The Corn Is Green*

The Corn Is Green

Well, that's that. The thing is virtually finished. I mean now they are cutting it. And since I am in the EAST and they are in the WEST, I will no doubt have little influence on it.

I'm back in Fenwick.

From my bed I see the sun rise. Between the inner and outer lighthouses. Across a field of marsh grass. Birds circling. A family of white egrets. Swans go honking by. Even an occasional osprey. I see the path of the rising sun gradually shift to the south as winter comes creeping in. I haven't seen the sun take its trip this year because I have been over in London struggling. But already it's coming up south of the inner light. Time is passing. Yes. Don't waste it.

As I said, I'm back. They've seen all the photographs. They. Brothers—sisters. Dick knows the play—*The Corn Is Green*. The rest are far off it. But they try. And there I am in my 1890 costumes. All dressed up, I thought. Looking a bit fat, I thought. And older than I remembered. Yes. Well, if you eat six ears of corn. We'd picked it up at the Viggiano Farm when we came in off Route 95.

Mrs. Viggiano said, "Now here is corn that is corn."

Tor, my nephew, ate six ears too. And a big helping of coffee ice cream. And a huge piece of zucchini cake. Great frosting. It was a nice welcome. Dick had cooked a huge ham. And a big macaroni-and-cheese. And a bowl of shaved carrots—sliced garden tomatoes—

crisp long romaine—Bibb lettuce leaves and fresh chopped parsley. You take what you want. I make the French dressing. Dick his own mayonnaise and garlic.

At dessert, Marion and El (sister and brother-in-law) appeared from their house with their grandson Jason. Had they been asked to dinner? Had they? Should we have waited? Anyhow, there was enough left and they pushed chairs in and ate. Well, here we all are.

My family. Dick—his son Tor. Bob—his wife, Sue. Marion— her husband, El. Peg—her husband, Tom. The whole gang. And we talked about me and showed the photographs.

"Oh, Katty, you look great."

"What's this? Oh, the boy? What boy is that? Oh—of course."

"The girl? What part does she play?"

They were trying but it was foreign territory. And soon the conversation shifted from me and Wales back to . . .

"Listen, let me tell you what happened just after you left."

But they were glad to see me. And I them. And I had a swim and got stung by a jellyfish. I was home.

"Look at that broken pane. Hasn't anyone mended that yet? Good grief! Where's the stop block that was on the floor? The door hits the corner of the table. Well, I'll go over to the hardware and get a pane and get a block and fix it."

At the hardware store: "Hello, Kathy. You back?"

"Yes. A pane twelve by eight. Fine."

"No. This putty is better. It's quite a job—Kathy. Be careful getting the glass out. It flies."

He was right. It is a frantic job. Took me three hours. Who said that carpenters were overpaid? Now what about that screen door that won't stay closed . . .

Oh. But I was telling you about *The Corn Is Green*. It was a funny time over there. I kept a diary at first. Then things got so terrible that I didn't dare write them down.

The possibility of doing Emlyn Williams's play came over the telephone when George Cukor called.

Ring. Ring.

"Kate. It's George. Alan Shayne—head of Warner's TV—has a dream. To do *The Corn Is Green* with you."

"Oh, George! Yes, George, I've read it. But oh dear— It's been done a hundred times. And what about all those illegitimate babies? Oh no. I should think no . . . Yes, sure I'll read it again but— You know they were going to do a musical about it. Changed the miners to black underprivileged. Awful. Well, I mean it didn't work at all . . . Yes, sure, I'll read it again . . . Yes, George. I know you made me what I am . . . No, I won't forget. You won't let me."

I got the play. I read it.

"Hello—George! I read it. Great. It's got power and it's got hope . . . Yes. And it's about something moving forward. Not falling backwards. About someone at the wheel of his own life instead of the present thinking: the me—the excuse dominated—my unhappy child-hood dominated—I am powerless moaning. The positive and delirious joy of really learning something. And using it. And moving on. The opening of the door of LIFE. Its tremendous opportunities for those capable of real work . . . Yes, George . . . Yes yes, I agree. It's a fine play. And funny. My, I laughed. And I cried and cried . . . Oh indeed—a wonderful part. Lovely for me. Such a relief. Alive—not half dead. And wondrous for the right boy. And that young girl. Outrageous and so funny. All good parts, aren't they? . . .

"No. Not California. Must be done in Wales . . . Oh yes, I agree. And a new boy. Right. Must be Welsh. Exteriors—Wales . . . No. Couldn't be faked. Like *The African Queen* being done in Africa. You pick up the indefinable when you go to the source. Something dif-ferent. Something that you can't just imagine. The air—the hills— the light—the mist—the soft soft water. The language. Very odd. Hard to catch. The sound. The drift sort of in and out of focus. The double 'L.' Put your tongue in the roof of your mouth. Keep it there. Now say 'L.' Or the double 'D.' That is pronounced as if it were 'TH.' No way to figure it out. You really have to be born there.

"And the people. Wide-eyed. Strong. No bunk. Independent. And a sense of humor. As for the miners. They really are a race apart. Is it the danger? The constant danger in their lives? Is that what keeps them so simple and direct?"

The decision was made. Cukor and I went to London. To find the cast. And to look for locations in Wales.

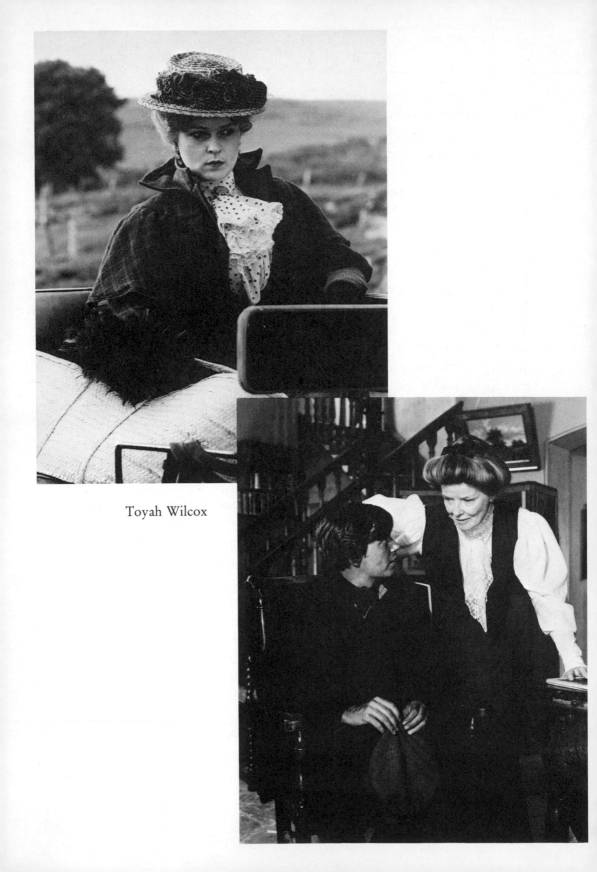

Toyah Wilcox

Ian Saynor

The first real chore was to find the boy—Morgan Evans. Without the right one we might as well not bother to do the picture. It is a most challenging part. He is called upon to grow from an ignorant boy of eighteen who is working in the mines—locked in by an almost total lack of education—to a young man capable of winning a scholarship to Trinity College, Oxford.

So we needed a tough fellow—with brains, energy—and, of course, someone capable of arousing the real interest of the audience. Warm and with a look in his eye.

They send you lists of suggestions. The well-known actors who are familiar to you—you can say yes or no too easily. But the unknown ones have to be seen. They—the casting experts—have to get in touch with all the agencies. They have to be aware of the schools, the colleges, little theatres, repertory theatres—and these are legion. Besides being aware of the new ones who have come to town.

We received the list of boys for the part of Morgan Evans. The first name on the list was Ian Saynor. Welsh. Had been in London for three weeks. Had had three years' experience in Wales. Playing in Welsh or English. Every sort of part.

That first day.

In the door came Ian Saynor. And we all nearly fainted. He had exactly the look. Close to six feet. Dark brown hair. Eyes wide apart and a lovely sort of greenish color. Good voice. A sort of dream-come-true of a boy, as far as we were concerned. He read the part for us. Wonder of wonders—he seemed really to be able to act. The first one to read. It was too good to be true.

Of course we couldn't settle for him then and there. That would have been too much. We went on searching. We tested three boys. Ian had no competition. I think that George Cukor would have settled for him that first day. He kept saying, "That's it. Why look further?"

I always have a tendency to wonder, What's around the corner? So poor Ian was dangled along for eight weeks. Then we tested him again. Finally, he was told that he had the part.

We got the girl too. A girl walked in by the name of Toyah Wilcox. Five feet tall. Tiny waist. Big bosom. Skin like the inside of a shell. Eyes . . .

Oh—did I tell you about the boy's teeth? They are TEETH. He

should pull them all out and sell them to the Arabs. Gorgeous! Anyway, Toyah's eyes are wide apart. And full of thoughts. Wicked thoughts. Suggesting so much. And so much fun too. Loves life and . . . well, she read the part with me. George and I howled.

Walking home from George's apartment, I have to say that a fleeting thought crossed my mind.

Incidentally, George lived at 95 Eaton Square. Rented apartment. Living room O.K. Not big. Not small. Dirty upholstered furniture. Two windows facing the square. Two bedrooms. One inside bathroom—small. One inside toilet and sink—small. Two windows in the bigger bedroom. Good closet space. The building was in the process of being redecorated. A mess. No carpets. Walls scraped. Noise constant. Elevator almost always in use carrying workmen and their junk. Three hundred pounds per week. That's approximately six hundred dollars. The expense in London   out of sight.

I was living in Eaton Square too. Down the way from George. Bobby Helpmann's flat, with a huge garden and full of charm. I was lucky. I always stayed there. Token free. I could walk or bike back and forth.

As I started to say—walking home from George's—a thought passed through my mind: What about those two young ones we've just interviewed? They are pretty attractive. Who's going to look at you, Kathy?

Oh, you're going to be wonderful, Kate. It's just your part.

I couldn't help thinking . . . I wonder what they said to Jack Barrymore when he decided to do *A Bill of Divorcement*? To Jane Cowl when she did *Art and Mrs. Bottle*? With those young girl parts— waiting to snatch glory. Young—beautiful—full of new potential.

Is it your turn now, Kathy? Oh hell, who cares? It's a great play. Yes. That's what you should be thinking. But are you thinking it, Kathy? Are you? Well—hell—I'm not an idiot . . .

But it's life, isn't it? You plow ahead and make a hit. And you plow on and someone passes you. Then someone passes him or her. Time levels.

The other parts were then cast. We had wanted Anna Massey for Miss Ronberry. She said yes. Patricia Hayes for Mrs. Watty. Artro

Morris, a Welshman, for Mr. Jones. And finally Bill Fraser was free to do the Squire. We were lucky to get each one of them. So much for the casting.

This was actually done over a period of weeks from the day we arrived. Carmen Dillon, who had done the sets for *Love Among the Ruins*, was in Wales looking for locations. She is a woman of the greatest good taste. Has knowledge and imagination in abundance. Unique she is. And is always out for perfection. George always had Carmen if possible.

Before we left the United States, we investigated the various key people—camera, sound, costumes. And the ones we wanted seemed to be interested in doing it. They were old friends of George's and of mine with whom we had worked before. And we were on top of the world.

The day we got to London, I knew that my first chore was to get going on the clothes. The period was 1890. The man we had was brilliant. And fun to boot. He greeted me with a gorgeous splash of flowers. And a note saying that he was away for the weekend, could not be reached by telephone. So Monday I called him.

"Hello. Well, isn't this exciting? The flowers were beautiful. You are sweet. And I'm so excited that you are doing it . . . Didn't I what? Didn't I get your letter? No. No letter. What was it about? . . . You're not what—? . . . You're not going to do us? You've accepted another job? What do you mean—what the hell do you mean? . . . You didn't think that we were going to go ahead? But why didn't you telephone? If you'd got a better offer, why didn't you simply call and say: 'Kate, I have a better offer.' My God! To just dump us—now—when we're about to—you have to be kidding. You've had months—I just don't believe . . .

"I see. You didn't think of the telephone . . . You don't know what to say? Well, I don't know what to say. Well, there's nothing I can say, is there? And nothing that you can say either. What a - - - -

"But we're friends. You can't just leave a friend stranded. I can't take it in. It would have been so easy just to call and say: 'Look, Kate, I've had a wonderful offer which I am dying to accept. Would you mind? You can get so-and-so. They're available. I've checked. And so-and-so could execute them . . . and . . .'

With Cukor

"Well, of course I would have been mighty disappointed. But I would have said YES. I would have had to. That's what friendship means. But just to dump us this way. At the last minute. You just have to be kidding . . . I'm appalled—struck dumb. People just don't behave this way . . ."

Well, they do. And he did. And we had no designer. And no one to execute the clothes.

Neil Hartley, our producer, who had worked a lot in England, set about finding someone else. He called David Walker, who had done *The Charge of the Light Brigade* for him and for Tony Richardson. Walker didn't want to take it on, but he could see that we were in a spot. And in a weak moment he said yes.

He had a terrible time. No fitters. He finally prevailed upon Jean Hunneysett to say that she would be responsible for my clothes and for Anna Massey's. That was great for us. But the others. There were three other 1890 productions being done in London. All the rental clothes had been picked over and were gone. To get anything made, especially men's clothes, was virtually impossible. We had been landed in a mess. Not enough time: to think—to discuss—to find materials—to learn each other's weaknesses. I really mean for him to learn my faults. The collars higher and higher. The draperies to hide the expanding here—the drooping there. For him to become familiar with—this THING that is known as me.

One of the funniest days. David Walker was to come to my apartment for a discussion of what general sort of look Miss Moffat was to have. What colors. What materials. To my slight horror and surprise, he arrived with Miss Hunneysett—the one who was to make the clothes. She seemed to be a very nice, efficient woman. She was to take my measurements. She opened a sort of bag and took out a very small corset. I gave the corset a quick look. About a twenty-inch waist, I thought. She took one look at me.

"Yes?"

She tried to cover her dismay.

"I always thought that you were very . . . I mean. You seem on the screen to have such a small . . ."

Well, of course she had been looking at the late late show full of me thirty or forty years ago. An eighteen-inch waistline. She speedily began to unlace the back of the corset but she didn't have enough lacing to expand it sufficiently to take care of the waistline which she now saw before her.

"We'll try it on . . . no . . . Actually, I think it would be better if I . . . Let's see . . . Well . . . Miss Hepburn . . . you see . . . I'm not really sure that you need a corset. I mean . . . I understand that you take your clothes off between each take . . . Yes . . . It might be impractical for you to . . . ."

David Walker chimed in to save Miss Hunneysett.

"You'll wear vests. We'll bone the vests. Much better than a corset."

"You'll wear vests."

"My rib cage—" I began.

"Yes," he said, "I know. I mean—I see what *you* mean. Prominent."

Well, one had to laugh. It was funny. By the end of the afternoon I felt like a product of Henry Moore. And you can't corset a Henry Moore.

Then I met the makeup expert. Ann Brodie. We put on a sort of trial makeup in my bathroom. It was rainy and dark. The lights were dim. My eyesight is O.K. I mean I can distinguish a man from a dog. But the fine points definitely elude me. I could feel her thinking: Well, this old girl has always used pancake and she's not about to want to change. And I've always thought that she looked the way she should. So why shift her? Keep her happy. Don't tamper with a good recipe.

I liked her. She was sweet. She surmounted trouble.

"No. You don't see that at all. If you hadn't mentioned that—I never would have noticed it."

Yes. She was sweet.

She suggested a man named Ray Gow as hairdresser. He turned out to be a hairdresser who could dress hair. And that's a rarity. When someone goes at your hair with a brush, you feel . . . Well, what is it? Either confidence or despair.

I explained: "Now if I try to curl my hair in Wales—it rains all the time, I understand. And we can't make George wait. He doesn't care for that at all. Doesn't understand hair problems.

"Oh no. No spray. Hair's too fine. This London water hard as nails. Yes, I've got a lot. Just poke it up. Fiddle it about. Watch those cowlicks."

He was great. He had the touch. And he knew about the misgivings of the actor.

"Oh yes. I see. A brush. No comb. Of course I can handle that. Spit on the loose ends. Push it about. Pray."

He saw a basket of my curlers lying on the dressing table. They were made of tightly rolled newspaper.

"Those your curlers—those things? I use those too."

"You do?"

"Yes."

"You're the first person I ever heard of who . . ."

"Oh, of course. Much the best. Absorbs the water. But you're better straight in this. Teacher. No nonsense. And the Welsh water is great. Soft. It will be perfect. You have lovely hair."

"Thank you."

As you can see, we hit it off. Bound by the newspaper curlers we never used.

David Walker, the designer now, had an assistant—Bob Ringwood. He was to take the responsibility when we went on location. And he did. And it was certainly a responsibility. Make it fit. Dye it. Do it now! Stretch it. Shrink it. Dirty it. Wash it. Age it. Pack it. Unpack it.

We had an understanding with a cameraman whom we had worked with, and he and his operator and second assistant had said that they would be available. They were top-notch people. Really first rate. The cameraman generally does the lighting. The operator rides the camera and follows the actors and frames the shot. The third man is responsible for holding it in focus. Very important and sensitive jobs. They therefore control how you look and what the audience sees. Naturally the director decides how the scene shall be played, but it is up to the operator to follow it and frame it with sensitivity. We were thrilled to be in such good hands.

Two weeks before we were to start, my dear old friend the cameraman called me on the telephone: "I can't do it."

"What . . . *what?*"

"We can't do it. We're all tired out. And my daughter is having her summer holiday. And my teeth . . . We're tired out."

"Well, my God! This is a hell of a time to . . . I'm tired out too. The whole world is tired out. So what? We don't start for two weeks—maybe three. You can rest . . ."

"I just . . . My daughter. She's . . . it's her last holiday at home . . ."

"Your daughter? You've known for months that . . . I just can't believe that you would throw us to the dogs . . . It's too late."

Then to Phyllis, who was standing next to the telephone: "His daughter's last holiday . . . I think I'm going mad. It may be my last movie!"

I went on: "But if you felt this way why didn't you telephone? So easy to get hold of either George or me. Weeks ago. When we had a chance of getting someone else to . . ."

"But my agent told you that . . ."

"No. That's not right. Your agent said that you were tired. That you were all tired. Naturally. And why not? You're lucky to be tired. You're busy. But she didn't say that you were going to dump us. How the hell can you even consider doing what you're suggesting? Just because you haven't signed a contract. I can't go on talking about it. No way. A thing like this can't happen. You're friends . . . You're . . . It's piggish and irresponsible and . . ."

I hung up. Why go on? I called him the next day and said in dead tones that I understood that he and the other two were not going to do it. Well, you can't force a man even if he has signed a contract. You can't. Too unpleasant. Too boring.

But can you imagine this? The second letdown. My good friends. What is happening to the world? You say yes. Then, too late, to say—No. And your supposed pal is left. With no one. And no way to get anyone. Luck! Come on, luck. Get busy.

London was busy as a beehive in the movie world. We tried. No. No. No. Then I sat and I thought. Teddy Scaife. He'd been a kid when he was the second unit cameraman on *The African Queen*. Jack Cardiff was our first. Scaife did quite a lot with Bogie and me when

In Wales, scouting locations

Cardiff had a recurrence of malaria. Then after that picture he'd done a lot of work with Huston. Nice man. Very much a cat who walks by himself. Independent. And bright and amusing. Try him. They did. Wonder of wonders, he said yes. And he got a splendid camera operator named Herb Smith. And the focus puller Tony Breeze.

Our sound situation was excellent. Peter Handford—one of the best in the business. Trevor Rutherford. Nick Flowers. Perfection is the thing that they insist upon. I like that.

During this period, Cukor and I had taken a trip to Wales to look at possible locations. We had stayed in a charming hotel in Llangollen. This is in the north of Wales. On the River Dee. We visited a number of farms about fifty miles west of there. Gorgeous country. Pouring rain. Mountains in the distance—Snowdon. Some of the farms seemed very primitive. The location we chose would have to be fairly free of telephone poles and such. We finally were taken to Carmen Dillon's choice. A village—Isybyty-Ifan—with a wide stream running through it. And a rather bleak look. And very close a farm—Hafod Ifan—which was owned by the National Trust and run by a family named Hughes. A stone house on the slope of a high hill. A group of long and beautiful stone barns. It was a farm where they raised cattle—Welsh Blacks. A very busy working farm.

Carmen told us how she could build on here and there and make the property fit our script. And how valuable would be its relation to the village. We saw it at the end of a long day in the pouring rain and our enthusiasm was a bit dim.

From there we had gone back to Llangollen. The Royal Hotel. Had dinner and a good sleep. Next morning we drove northeast to the town of Wrexham. Near it was the Bersham Colliery. We wanted the audience to realize that in 1890, ten- and eleven-year-old boys went into the mine to work a twelve-hour day. Mr. Owens, the manager, was away. Mr. Williams took us around. They had several buildings which were old enough for us to use.

At the end of our visit we all put on coveralls, gloves, hard hats, boots (I only needed a hat—my ordinary clothes were suitable, including my shoes). Then we got into an elevator. It was really an open cage with a second level. It could carry five on each level. One could not stand upright if one was over five-feet-six. Pitch dark. Thirteen hundred feet down. Fast and with a great roar and clatter. A rough-cut shaft. We stopped. We were in a tunnel. Dimly lit and with a narrow rail down the center. It was a sort of roundish, rough-hacked hole. Very uneven underfoot. The miners had to walk two miles through this tunnel to get to the spot where they were digging. Each one carried a lamp and a thing to detect escaping gas. (So did we.) And a gas mask. We only walked as far as a room where the men came to have a cup of tea. A few chairs. Darkish. And really only another hole in the ground. There was a constant draft of wind. Persistent and somehow exhausting. And one was covered with coal dust. And it was sort of cold. The reason that they used children was that some of the places where they dug were too small for a man.

As we were leaving to go back up, we heard a beautiful tenor voice start a song. Then others gradually joined in. Down so far under the earth. We were told that many of their songs were hymns. Can you wonder? It was, in a curious way, both moving and eerie. In times like this—under the earth—where each shovelful might release a destructive force of nature. Who is The Master? Only One? Sing a hymn. And it was so beautiful—the sound. Reaching through the shaft. Hard and dangerous work. Requiring a kind of daily courage. The miners looked and seemed quite different from other men. And they must be quite different. And yet full of laughter. That song. Such a contrast to the situation. And when we went back up, we saw that we were literally covered with coal dust.

So hard to get clean.

From there we drove south. Straight through Wales. The country is very much more gentle in the center and the south. We found nothing as suitable as the Hughes farm. We got to Cardiff, then drove straight east to London. A long day. But thrilling.

After Teddy Scaife, the cameraman, had said yes, we made one more trip to Wales. By then the Hughes farm had a pretty garden of flowers. A glasshouse. A lovely lawn. Paths with gravel instead of mud. Several new chimneys. And a few jut-outs, which were fake. It was much more civilized-looking. And since it was a pretty day— only misty and not pouring with rain—we thought it was lovely. I asked Mrs. Hughes if I could have my dressing table and clothes somewhere in her house. She said yes. That was lucky for me, as otherwise I would be put in a trailer. And the trailer would be put in a field. And every time you got out, you would be covered with mud. And the trailer would always wiggle slightly at every move you made. And as the days passed it would acquire a sort of discouraging look and smell. In the southwest guest room—second floor—bathroom nearby—I had a great setup. My blouses lying on the bed. My hats on the bedposts. My ribbons—scarves—gloves—veils—in a box cover on the bed. And still room on the bed for me to have a nice lie-down. The shoes under the bed. And the coats and skirts and vests on a rack just outside the door in the hall. And best of all—as it worked out—I could look out my window and see everything that was going on. In short—PARADISE.

At the coal mine in Wrexham

Not much more to tell, actually. When the shooting begins on a picture, it becomes a matter of health and weather and whether you have picked a good cast and crew. And whether, of course, the script makes any sense. And your own worth is also involved. Can you do it? I think most of the people involved in any art always secretly wonder whether they are really there because they're good or there because they're lucky. If they have time to think.

It's almost the same thing every day. The daily work. With me, it's up every day at five. Big breakfast. I get it myself. Fruit, eggs, bacon, chicken livers, toast, marmalade, coffee. On a tray. Carry it back to bed. Lovely the silence of the early hours. Do all my studying and thinking as I eat and drink. The sun rises. You seldom see it. But light comes. Misty. Slowly clearing. Light rains. Heavenly climate for a freckled skin. Then a cold bath or shower. A bike ride if I'm ready early—before the car gets there. Go to work around seven.

Phyllis and I had a little house at Capel Garmon. Near Betws-y-Coed. Pronounce the "W" as if it were "U." Three hundred years old the house. Lovely big fireplace in the living room. Three big blocks of slate. There are slate mines all over the place. We spiffed up the room with big spools of wool. They were very decorative. Red, blue, white, blue-and-white mix. About six inches high. Many thrilling woolen mills to visit. They make every sort of sweater, shirt, blanket, skirt, pants; coats, capes, caps, hats, bags. And you are always sorry that you have not bought more. Sheep abound.

Dinner on a tray in front of the fire. Pretty. First thing I do when I get home is to wash my hair. I've always tended to that myself. It saves repeated nuisance. I do it every night. I put it up wet. And it sort of dries before the fire while I'm eating. Seven or seven-fifteen, this is. Six days a week on location. Or I go to bed with it wet.

A man named George Potter was driving us. He was a wonder. Could do anything. Carpenter, electrician, plumber. And he had a joy of living which was a delight. The countryside around Capel Garmon and our location was heavenly. Hills, valleys, skies, flowers, fields, stone farmhouses, barns—narrow roads lined with pink-purple foxgloves. Sheep roaming the hillsides—every possible view. The mountains appearing and disappearing in the mist—in the distance. Each working day we took a different road home. Believe me when I say that it was intoxicating. The air—pure and so invigorating. The water soft. Sheer heaven. Lifted the soul. The beauty of life. The wonder.

Can you imagine a movie company—say, roughly, sixty people —moving into and around your remote farmhouse for three and a half weeks? Six days a week? The leading lady—me—moving into the second floor front? People keeping warm in your living room. Rain and mud tracked in. A group who arrived at 7 a.m. and left at 7 p.m.

The Hughes family consisted of Mr. and Mrs. Hughes—a very pregnant daughter; her son of about two, who spoke only Welsh. Her husband, who helped Mr. Hughes with the farm. Six sheepdogs. The family were never riled. Always fun. Bringing out coffee. Tea. Wonderful currant cake. Now, this currant cake is really a sensation. Here's the recipe:

1 lb. or 3¼ cups self-rising flour	1 cup granulated sugar
¾ lb. margarine	2 eggs mixed with a little milk
1¾ cups black currants	1 tablespoon brown sugar

Rub margarine into flour. Add dry ingredients. Add eggs and milk. Mix. Place in cake tin lined with greased wax paper. Sprinkle top of cake with brown sugar. Place in top of oven at 400 degrees for 15 minutes. Reduce heat to 325 degrees and bake for another 1¾ hours.

Every Sunday we would go out for long drives and long walks in the mountains. Or to the sea. Picnics. Or to Bodnant Gardens. If you like real air and every color of green, Wales is the place to go.

Doing the scenes was the usual combination of agony and joy. And the eternal question: are you really as good as you can possibly be? At the beginning of the picture I ride a bike through the hills on my way to the house, which has been left me by my uncle. We'd go up to the top of a steep hill to shoot me on the 1890 bicycle (stiff, and it weighed a ton) riding down the hill. Then because of the position of the sun, they would shift and decide to shoot me riding up the hill. For me this was almost impossible. They had a twenty-four-year-old lady athlete who was an excellent double for me do one of these shots.

I was humiliated. Nearly had a stroke. But I just could not pump up that hill. Infuriating failure. I have always been able to do my own stuff. But my legs just could not push hard enough to keep that bike from a drunken wobble. They thought that I was silly to be so

Riding the bicycle

mad that she could and I couldn't. Yes. I suppose so. But there it is. I still am mad. Damned old legs. Anyway, they didn't use the shot of her. I scared them off it. Said it would be bad cess to the whole thing.

Heard a funny thing the other day. Someone asked someone who was about my age: "How are you?"

Answer: "Fine. If you don't ask for details."

That's about it. Isn't it?

When we got back to London, we worked a five-day week. That's lovely, isn't it? The setup at Lee Brothers Studio was very pleasant. They are a new studio run by Lee Electrics. They built me a dressing room. Great. Windows that open. Spacious. Bath. Shower. And all the rest of the comforts. All white. And right off the stage on which our set was.

We worked hard and fast. The scenes were long and very concentrated. The set was perfection. The crew really interested because it is a true and fascinating story of Morgan Evans, a young man who takes the giant step from ignorance to knowledge. He opens the door on his life. Helped by a teacher—me—Miss Moffat—who knows that he can do it if he can keep working. It's funny and exciting and just rouses you up. Because you suddenly realize what a tremendous opportunity it is just to be alive. The potential. If you can keep a-goin'—you actually can do it. So just keep a-goin'—you can win. It's when you stop that you're done.

V

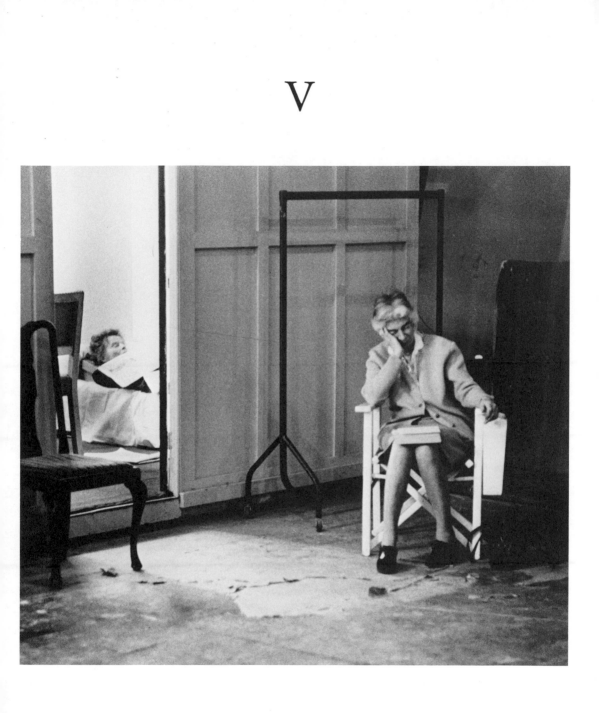

Phyllis

Phyllis Wilbourn is my right hand. She came to me in the middle fifties. Her employer, Constance Collier, had died. She had worked for Constance for twenty-odd years. She has worked for me since then. We're both in our eighties. She a few more than I.

She is a totally selfless person—(well, I have to say to you what just came into my mind)—working for a totally selfish person.

She can do everything, which through the years has been wildly handy for me. She is a very good cook. She can talk to anyone—from the President to the doorman. She never takes a vacation. She backs me up. And she is—what should I say?—she is *there* to help me—to keep me company—to let me be alone—to do things for other people which I should be doing for other people.

Well—what the hell—make it brief. She's unique. She's an angel.

Brief Encounter

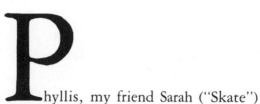hyllis, my friend Sarah ("Skate")
Forbes and I were packing up the car to go to New York. It was
Monday morning. It was a pretty day, warmish like the rest of this
winter's days. We left about ten-thirty, stopped for gas, stopped at
the post office and then got going on Route 95. Suddenly I saw in
the distance a woman stopped and she seemed to be putting a tire
back in the luggage compartment. I pulled up, got out. So did Skate.
Phyllis didn't get out because she was buried in flowers and groceries
in the backseat. Skate and I were in front.

"Are you in trouble?" I asked.

"I have a flat tire and I don't know how to change it," she said.

"Have you got a jack?"

She went to look. She was a sort of neither-here-nor-there woman,
about thirty-five or so, frowsy hair, sort of helpless-looking. I'd
changed tires before from time to time, had a sort of hazy idea of
what to do. And anyway I'm handy. And I knew that no one would
stop for her. Skate helped her look. I was studying the bumper—
brain whirling—bumper jack—bumper jack—axle jack—no no—
that's your childhood, that axle jack business.

They came with the main section of a jack.

"Yes—now, it has a bottom . . . it has a handle . . ." I said.

Skate found the bottom. Fine. They went back—I fitted the

bottom on and went again to the bumper—it was the right front that was flat. I put the jack about where I thought it should go to balance well. Jesus, I thought, the bloody car will slip off. How to . . . . I slid my hand along the bumper. It's so thick, I thought.

Skate came up with the handle.

I said, "Yes, that's right. I wish I knew how the hell the jack hooks to the bumper to really hold on to it. There should be directions . . ."

"Oh, there are directions," said the woman.

Skate went back—she found them. She called, "Yes . . . there's a hole . . ."

I lay down on the road. Oh yes, a hole—I've got it, here it is. Good. Everything fitted. The handle fitted. I found the gadget which makes it go up and down. Wiggled it around. I pumped away. Then suddenly, thinking, I asked, "Is the brake on?"

"Yes," the woman answered. I continued pumping, and up went the car.

Lovely, I thought.

Now, just a little higher so that we can get the wheel off. O.K.—fine—there, the wheel turns easily. Then I took the handle out of the jack and pried off the plate that covers the lugs which screw on the tire.

Now, good, there we are, that's off. Now we unscrew these . . .

I turned the handle around to unscrew them—tried to. Now let me see—clockwise—counterclockwise—either way wouldn't budge. And in any event every time I tried to use force, the bloody wheel turned. Yes, you're a fool. You jacked it up too high.

The girls tried to hold the tire from turning—impossible. I went to the jack, changed the position of the up-down gadget, then put the handle back in. I don't know why—I pumped but the thing didn't go down. Well, I thought, loath to admit my stupidity, I can get it off the jack if I can change the tire in its present position by just starting the motor and backing up. I went back to the unscrewing —I was losing my cool.

"Look, are we doing the right thing? Which way do you unscrew a nut?" I thought about it. This way—that way. "Look, go to my toilet case, Skate, and get a bottle and see which way it undoes."

Skate did this. Counterclockwise.

"Now hold the tire from turning." I made a last wild and desperate effort to turn the screw. They tried to hold the tire. We all failed. No hope.

"We need help."

I stepped to the highway side of the car and held up my hand. Skate and the woman did the same. Man after man after man passed—without even a hesitation. A truck passed. He was going very fast. Woman's lib, I thought. We asked for this!

In the distance another truck . . .

This time I went to the center of the slow lane and held up both hands. The truck driver braked—pulled up about two hundred feet ahead—got out—a young, slim black man. I went to meet him.

"A flat tire—we can't unscrew the screws—I can't lower the jack."

"Fine, fine," he said. "Brakes are on . . ."

"Yes, sir," I said.

He lowered the jack. He had a different rhythm and he was very sure of what he was doing.

"How did you—?"

"Well, you just flip this, Ma'am, then up—or down [gesturing]."

"Yes," I said, thinking: Well, I flipped. Maybe I just lost my nerve.

And anyway, down went the tire and off came the lugs. Then he jacked her up again and on went the good tire so that the tire spun free. On went the screws again and, holding them with the handle wrench, he spun the tire to wind one up. Great, thrilling—a ballet. So lovely—to change a tire, to know what you're doing. Head down, enjoying it.

"You know, Miss, you look just like—sound like . . ."

"I am," I said, leaning over, watching.

Spin spin—he didn't hear me.

"You . . . like Katharine Hepburn."

"Yes, I am."

"You what?"

"I am . . ."

He let out a howl, then looked at me. And another howl. "No . . . no, I don't believe . . ."

"I am . . ."

Another howl and a laugh and a whistle. "I'm just not about to believe that."

"I'll prove it. Skate, get a letter out of that batch of mail in the front seat of our car."

We showed the letter to him—name typed clearly, a bill. He was reluctantly convinced, but no, he couldn't believe it and his symphony of "oh"s and "ah"s and "no"s and "whee"s and "whee"s continued as he threw the flat in the back.

"I'll prove it. Give me your name. I'll send you my picture."

He did—Robert Chatman. An address in Jersey.

We all shook hands. He started for his truck, turned back.

"Goodbye," I said. "So grateful!"

He shouted to the winds, "I can't imagine . . . I don't believe it. I was empty and I was just sleeping along and what—the one and only Katharine Hepburn!"

I went back to the girls.

"I don't believe it," I muttered. "We struggle and try—we fail. Desperately we try to flag someone down—we fail. Then just as we were about to give up, a big trailer truck just rolling along—and he stopped—the one and only—gentleman."

Can we still use that word?

Voice

There is seldom a way to explain what are the things that hurt one deeply. They are usually quite foolish. Some little hope or pride—like my singing, for instance—or the size of my eyes.

When I was a kid, I always hoped that someone would say, "What beautiful eyes you have." The wolf said that to Grandma, but no one ever said it to me.

Or: "What a pretty voice. I heard you singing and . . ." Well, singing is another thing.

Marcia Davenport, Russell Davenport's wife, saw the movie of *The Little Minister*, and she said, "Was that your voice, singing through the woods?"

"Yes—yes, Marcia, it was." That was 1935 or '36.

"Well, I think that you should do something about it."

"Oh," I said. "I'm not very musical. I mean, I studied. I studied the violin once. For two years with a sweet man. Monsieur Beauchemin. I was ten or twelve, I suppose. I . . . I . . . well, I just wasn't any good. I imagined that I would be, but I just dwindled away, gave it up. Just couldn't do it."

"No, I don't mean that you should take up the violin again. I mean singing. Have you ever studied voice?"

"Oh yes—I mean talking." I've struggled with that with Frances

The Millionairess, with Robert Helpmann

Robinson-Duff. You'll remember she had a system of blowing at a lighted candle to force the air to come from the diaphragm. Anyway, I felt her diaphragm—but I couldn't make mine do it. We'd sit there blowing away. I did this for years. I'm not complaining. She gave me the greatest gift any teacher can give. She gave me her interest; she stimulated my imagination and she gave me confidence. But blow I couldn't. And I lost my voice when I played. For years.

The worst times, *The Warrior's Husband*—then about twenty years later, *The Millionairess* by George Bernard Shaw. Both parts where I was using a lot of shouting. It was new to me when it happened in *The Warrior's Husband*, 1932. I was using a low pitch, trying to be masculine. Finally it got so bad that it was nip and tuck whether I'd begin to miss performances. Dad sent me to a throat man in Hartford,

Dr. William Dwyer. He told Dad that I would never be able to have a career, that my vocal cords were covered with nodules and that I was in a serious mess.

"Just don't tell her that," said Dad. "Don't say a word." Bill Dwyer didn't.

Well, the play was coming to an end and I was on my way to Hollywood and my nodules calmed down.

The Lake wasn't that sort of strain. There I nearly lost my mind but not my voice. *Jane Eyre*—*The Philadelphia Story*—*Without Love*—*As You Like It*— no trouble. Then *The Millionairess*. I pitched that louder and wilder than I could sustain and I began to have trouble. We'd opened in London. After about six weeks or so I began to get hoarse, then worse and worse. At the end, I never talked at all offstage. Just wrote notes.

We closed to take it to America. We had the summer off. Several months. Then in the fall, two dress rehearsals with audience. My voice immediately went. Two performances!

Lawrence Langner said, "We'll postpone the opening."

"Oh bunk," I said in despair. "What's the point? I'll either die or I won't die. I've had a whole summer off. What's the point of kidding ourselves? Keep a-going, going. The question is, when comes 'gone'?"

We opened. We'd been a smash in London. Our advance in New York was almost sold out for ten weeks and that was all we were playing. I struggled through that opening—half-strangled. It was difficult. The notices were O.K. Naturally, with such a limited range vocally my performance hadn't the thrill and abandon required. No ring. So the play suffered and I certainly suffered. No zing. And it was a story about a woman of great zing.

What to do—what to do.

I went to a theatrical doctor. They are the only ones who realize that you absolutely have to go on no matter what, if you're an actor, or die onstage. "Well, Miss Hepburn, you're all wound up, aren't you? Why don't you just take a little drink and relax . . ."

"My God . . . take a drink! I can't take a drink . . . my God! My mind would go. Don't you know anyone—any teacher—

someone—some help—I've got a whole company . . . I've got to keep going. There must be something . . . someone . . ."

"Well, there's a man named Alfred Dixon. Why don't you . . ."

By this time I was spending the weekends up at Columbia Presbyterian hospital, contemplating jumping out the window—anything—anything—"I can't . . ."

"What have you got to lose?" said Bobby.

"Well, send for him."

Bobby Helpmann, Sir Robert, was the Egyptian Doctor in *The Millionairess* and he was my friend. Bobby came in the door of my hospital room. With him came a man—not tall, not short—inclined to be hefty. Fat, really. Big head—eyes far apart—big face. Sitting in bed, in despair, I thought, Well, he's not going to save my life . . .

"I'm Alfred Dixon . . ."

"Yes—so—what do you teach in a case like this? What can you do?" I was antagonistic, hopeless.

He tried to explain what he thought had caused my extreme hoarseness, and his method of voice projection. Something about dogs and panting. Good grief, I thought. Desperate, that's what I am— I'm desperate and you're talking about panting dogs. I want to die. I want to dive out that window and die. He's a big, pompous ass and I just wish he'd leave me to suffer.

I could hardly bother to listen. I was defeated. "Thank you, I'll think it over."

He left. Bobby stayed for a bit. But as I couldn't talk, he too left. And I sat there staring at space. Tomorrow another week would begin . . . agony . . .

I left the hospital to go back to my house. I was really low. Down—down . . . What to do? Monday. Six days to Sunday. Then I began to think. Don't be a hysterical ass. Try it. I called Alfred Dixon.

"I'd like to see you. Now—if possible."

"O.K.—1 p.m."

"No, I'll come to you." Make the effort. Go to him. His atmosphere.

I went to Thirty-sixth Street. Shabby building, I thought defen-

Alfred Dixon

sively, a bit grubby. The pupil before me left. I went in. Immediately he started with a group of exercises. The central idea of the whole thing was to get off the vagus nerve, which—when one is excited, scared, as actors are most of the time—makes one tighten up one's neck and throat and stop the natural flow of air from the diaphragm through a relaxed passage. My tendency had apparently always been to grab with my throat. Right off, I understood what he was talking about. I'm sure Duff and that bloody candle were the same idea in essence, but at that point in life I didn't get the message. I suppose I was too occupied with my own adorable self. Now, just about to drown, I could feel that somehow it made sense. And it relaxed me. I stayed an hour. I felt better. Now I'm sure that I didn't actually— I mean—I wasn't actually any better as far as my enraged vocal cords were concerned. But my mental attitude had changed. Instead of cowering, waiting for disaster, I was trying to find a path—a hole—

a ray—a way out. I was going forward, not floating. I was swimming. Against the tide, but swimming.

Every day I went to him. I understood more and more. And although I did not get better, I did not get worse. And I began to realize that if I could do it this way, I would not get worse. I could control it. Not it—me. And I maintained my status quo—just. I had a positive attitude. I kept afloat. And . . .

But I must go back. I was telling you about Marcia Davenport and singing.

So she said, "Why don't you study a bit? Your voice is pleasant."

You can imagine how pleased I was at that.

What should I do?

"Well, I think that I might be able to get Sam Chotzinoff to take you as a pupil."

He was a very important music critic and he was married to Pauline Heifetz. I used to go there once or twice a week. It was a world of which I was totally ignorant. Toscanini used to have dinner there. Toscanini! The Chotzinoff children—two boys—would peek at me as I was singing and sometimes would solemnly compliment me. "You sang well today, Miss Hepburn." Then I would walk out of the brownstone—he lived west of the Park in the Sixties—feeling musical. But of course it didn't last, because I wasn't—I mean, I wasn't musical. I sang a song in *Without Love*, the Philip Barry play turned into the Donald Ogden Stewart movie of the same name—"Parlez-moi d'Amour"—not bad—but not good enough. Oh dear—why can't I be a singer! I can see myself just letting go and the most glorious sounds come out. But only in my imagination. Why . . . why . . . a block—I think it—I can't do it. Tennis the same. Painting the same. Why, oh why! Not enough talent, that's the problem. But so hard to swallow that.

You're just not good enough, my dear.

Who said that?

I said that: I'm your common sense.

Time passed, I forgot. Well, what next? I did *Coco*. I worked and worked. I studied with Sue Seton. Daily. I learned and it helped me too with talking. Sue Seton had studied with Madame Sembrich.

Added to Dixon, the whole concept of that sound coming up from way down below by the diaphragm and traveling through that relaxed tunnel—well, not tunnel—shaft really, then into my head. "Head tones," said Sue. "Feel the vibrations?" Yes yes. Head, not throat. Bypass the throat. Forget the throat. The chest bones, top of skull. That I could do.

And I knew, I mean I felt in my bones when to start and in my skin how to follow the orchestra. I'd hardly to watch Bobby Dolan, the conductor. And they all would tell me how great I was. But . . . well, I'm just not a fool. Oh, I could tear them apart—I mean the audience—in my heart and soul. But that little peanut sound— that's you, Kath—that just *is* you. You're going to tear them apart with that . . . are you?

If I could describe to you the terror—the sinking inadequacy— the blank horror which I felt every night before I went on. Like playing tennis without a racquet. Or, say, with a racquet with no strings—impotence—and pretense—Katie sings— Well, to me it was a great example of Katie *doesn't* sing. And this in spite of the devoted help of Sue Seton and then exercise in my dressing room with Lynn Masters, who was an assistant of Dixon, who was now dead.

Now this to me was a dreadful fact. I was back there in my hole waiting to go out into the ring. They were out there sitting— waiting—and they'd paid a big price for those tickets and they had a right to the best and here I was about to go forth—armed with a squeak. A mouse posing as a lion.

I got my face on—fixed my hair—the shoes—the costume—the hat—then I sat, heart pounding . . . Relax—relax—they don't expect you to be Callas . . .

No no, you don't get it—*I* expect *me* to be Callas—otherwise why am I here?

I prayed—I wept—I did my exercises—I prayed—someone help me—and out I went. Please, God . . .

And do you know what? Love came across the footlights. And in waves and hugs . . .

That's all right, Katie—so you can't sing but we get it—we hear you—we feel—we know you. And so together we worked it out. And

I got a little better—enough better so that I didn't die. And I continued working with Sue Seton. And Coco was a great character and Lynn Masters came every night for weeks to warm me up. And I relied on what I could do, and so I went on and then on tour. It was fun.

What did I say?

Now to get back to the beginning of this talking about how things can get your goat.

Well, I got a letter from a man named Ben Bagley. Spring, 1979. He said how about doing a record of some Cole Porter songs.

I called my friend Sue Seton.

"Can I come and talk to you?"

"Yes—come."

"When?"

"Now."

I went.

Sue and I met every day trying to work ourselves—or I should say myself—up to giving an audition for Ben Bagley and a man named Arthur Siegel, who would play for me. Actually, he *is* a very good performer himself, plays and sings.

Now I should be able to sing Cole's "Thank You So Much, Mrs. Lowsborough—Goodby." This really is in my line, so to speak. There were two other Cole Porter songs—"The Queen of Terre Haute" and "A Woman's Career." I thought they were not as good for me. Not as obvious. Especially since the latter required real singing. Somehow as I stood there at Sue's piano, I thought I really did sound a bit better—or was it that I felt a bit better?—or was it that Sue, who is an adorable and sensitive creature, was able to convince me that I was a bit better? I mean there was some actual sound there. Wasn't there? Was there?

Finally came the day that they were to come to hear me.

How many times has this happened—these, shall I call them, auditions? That's what they were . . . are. And I suppose I give them so that my employer will see—hear—for himself and never be able to blame me.

The first was—and I hope this is correct—oh, 1965 or so—Ray

Stark, Howard Dietz and someone else. They wanted me to do a musical of *Mrs. 'Arris Goes to Paris*. This was at my house. I had been studying with Ruby Ward. Someone told me she had worked with Ethel Merman. So . . . isn't she great, Ethel Merman? Now, why the hell can't I do that—just why? But—well, they seemed pleased that I could sing on key. I don't remember what I sang—and nothing happened anyway. The show was never done.

Next time it was Alan Jay Lerner, 1969 or 1970. He played the piano and I sang "Nearer My God to Thee." I'm good on hymns. He said, "Yes, O.K. Now I have a script on Coco Chanel and . . ."

"Listen, Alan. That may be good enough for you but—I tell you what I'd like to do. I'd like to work with someone—you must know someone who could . . ."

"Yes, I do," he said. "Roger Edens."

"Who is he?"

"He's just the best—Judy Garland . . ."

"Would he—?"

"Yes . . . yes, I think he would."

I started working on a few songs with Roger. Roger was an extraordinary man. He helped people who could do it to make the song interesting, fascinating—whatever. He was a sophisticated friend of Alan's. He was a realist. We worked on "Miss Otis Regrets," "Thank You So Much, Mrs. Lowsborough—Goodby," "I've Grown Accustomed to Her Face."

I struggled. Roger was not easy to please. Now, I was quite aware that to him I was not even one step up from a DUD. Sometimes that cold look in his eye froze my soul. And by the same token, if I by some wild chance pleased him, I drove home full of joy.

We worked every day for an hour or more. One day Roger said, "Well, we will have our audition. We'll ask George Cukor; Shirley Burden and his wife, Flobelle Fairbanks; Gar Kanin and Ruth Gordon to come to dinner. We will have a musical evening. And if you live through that, we'll do the same for Alan."

"Yes," I said.

The evening arrived. I was of course in a panic. I told Roger that we should get the musical evening over with first, then have the

Coco

dinner. So we did. He played, I sang. And all those sweet people, very good friends, were most kind. And Roger smiled. And I think he thought that with my extreme limitations as far as talent went, I had done as well as could be expected. Then, of course, we did it for Alan. He was by nature a positive enthusiast. So he did his positive enthusiast act. And we decided that I should take the chance—or was it that Alan and Freddie Brisson should take the chance . . . I should do *Coco*.

Then this last audition—for Ben Bagley, with Arthur Siegel at the piano. I was in my usual state of panic. And they were two darling people who were impressed with Katharine Hepburn. That means, "Can she get away with it? Well, why not? Yes—it's not bad at all."

I learned something early on playing tennis at the Beverly Hills Hotel with Harvey Snodgrass.

"Oh God, Harvey. Those people watching—I can't bear it."

"Don't worry, Kate, they won't stay. You just cannot, unless you are totally insane—you just cannot watch a rotten tennis player for long." There are no two ways about it. He was right. In those days, I was young and playing mediocre tennis. Now I'm old and with a fake hip and playing mediocre tennis. Well, I'm more interesting now because I'm still trying.

So with singing. I can't sing but I can do words. Can't I? Anyway, I'm better off than I am with tennis.

So their attitude: "It's not bad at all—is it?" This just isn't my attitude—all this negative approval—this "adequate" business. I'm not after that.

Anyway, I did the record for them. The three Cole Porter songs. Oh dear, that—what is it that's not there—that just makes it not quite—certainly not arresting to listen to?

It's like painting. It is thrilling to do. And you finish it and it looks devastating and you hang it on the wall. Then gradually you realize that you just can't keep looking at it. And finally you take it down and hang it in another room—one which you don't go into so often. And if anyone says, "Those lilies, who painted that?" Thrilled, you say, "I did." But you know in your heart.

The record looked pretty in its holder or whatever you call it. I

STEREO
PE 1371

BEN BAGLEY'S
COLE
PORTER
REVISITED
VOL. IV

Katharine Hepburn

in alphabetical order

Blossom Dearie
Helen Gallagher
Dolores Gray
Patrice Munsel
Arthur Siegel

Vocal & Musical
Arrangements by
Dennis Deal

BEN BAGLEY'S
CONTEMPORARY
BROADWAY
REVISITED

STEREO
PS 1381

Katharine Hepburn

in alphabetical order

Alan Arkin
Kaye Ballard
Helen Gallagher
Anthony Perkins
John Reardon
Margaret Whiting

Vocal & Musical
Arrangements by
Dennis Deal

Cast & Material
Assembled &
Directed by
Ben Bagley

took it to Fenwick—to the big round kitchen table with the Tiffany lamp hanging over it. I put the record on the table knowing that Dick couldn't help seeing it there. Dick—my brother—he's musical.

Well, I have to tell you that the record just sat there—Friday—Saturday— Finally, on Sunday—I . . .

"Aren't you going to play the record?"

Dick: "What record?"

"That one—on the table."

"Oh—Cole Porter. I can't stand Cole Porter." Oh cruelty! Oh wounds of life! Crushed . . . I went out of the kitchen. What a goddamned bastard—how mean can you get . . . I wanted to— In fact, I . . .

His friend Virginia Harrington—who is the meaning of the word kindness—had been in the kitchen during our conversation. And all of a sudden I heard—the record. It was being played in the study. Phyllis was in there too. No, not Dick. He was still in the kitchen. How could he be such a pig? My songs and he wouldn't . . . I stood in the hall and listened.

And then *I* listened hard, and the truth came to me. Why are you so upset, Katharine? You are so upset because you can hear— and it just isn't—that's it.

It just isn't.

If you thought it was good, you wouldn't give a rap what Dick did or didn't do. But you know. And then you thought some more. And he won't listen to it because he just didn't dare. What could he say . . .

"Oh, K—not again!"

So, as I said—the little things that upset one. And I laughed— at myself really, because I did know that my misery was really caused by the fact that I myself knew that again I had done it but NOT done it. Ah, life . . .

Well, next time.

Or should I say—next life.

Eyes

AT THE DOCTOR'S OFFICE

es . . . Yes. I understand that.
The skin is shrinking. Yes. It's pulling the eye down.

"It's not—what did you say?—senile ectropia. Yes . . . I see.
But it is ectropia. Yes . . . I mean the . . . well, the lower lid is
drooping . . . I mean pulling down . . . out . . . Yes, exposing the
mucosa.

"No. They don't tear. Well, they do . . . when I walk in the
wind . . . or cold. Yes, tear.

"Yes, they look red and they itch.

"Exposed, yes . . . I understand that. Yes, dry.

"Well, it does make one nervous. You know, itching is . . . well,
yes, sir, it makes one nervous, naturally. Now, I understand that
. . . Yes, I've been told that before. You would take part of the upper
lid—the upper part . . . and use that to lengthen the skin from lower
lid to the chin.

"Yes, I understand it would be a different color. Yes, only for a
while. Makeup. Yes, but I don't use makeup in ordinary life . . .

"Well, we all have to change some habits, don't we? Yes—I
suppose we—

"Oh . . . You would prefer to use the back of the ear. I see. The
skin is tougher . . . stronger. Yes, I understand perfectly.

"Thank you . . . yes."

Phyllis and I got back to the car.

DRIVING HOME

You see, what I don't understand is why they can't just give it a yank at the side. Take a tuck. God. It's creepy . . . A white patch under each eye. I'll look like that raccoon peeking out of our garbage can. And what is going to make the eyelid stay against the eye? Haven't you noticed some of those old men who have drooped eyes? Senile ectropia. Well, they have plenty of skin and the lid droops anyway. I wish I had more faith . . . Creepy . . . Eyes.

CONFERENCE

"How do you do. Thank you, Doctor.

"Sit right here. Yes . . . fine. Oh, it's just a gradual deterioration, I suppose you'd say. I come from a red-rimmed, red-eye-rimmed family. You know, freckled, red-haired. Sties when I was a kid. Then shilazians. Then a staph infection from the Venice canals . . . No, I swam in one. Well, I was supposed to back into one making a picture . . . I did. Eyes wide opened. Mouth wide opened too. I never thought of eyewash. Took a bath, of course . . . thought of everything. But not eyes. All the other openings . . . not the eyes. Next morning they were bright red. No, not the lids . . . the whites were red.

"Well, I just wondered whether you couldn't take a sort of . . . well, tuck . . . and turn here at the side . . . I mean, the lower lid is sort of dead tissue . . . and maybe . . .

"You don't agree. I see . . . you mean you think the only possibility is the flap. I mean, putting the upper lid under the eye. I mean, part of it. Or putting the back of the ear under the eye. Well, yes . . . I see . . . I mean, at my age I could be, shall we say, usable for maybe a few more years and I would prefer to enjoy them not looking like a raccoon. Yes. You think perhaps it's worth the try . . . Oh, well, yes. That's a ray of hope. A Dr. Mustarde in Scotland."

"Listen, Phyllis, let's go to Scotland. You and me. See what he says. We might at least try."

SCOTLAND

"Well—here we are—Scotland plus two hours to Glasgow. He said he could do it and we could spend several days in a hotel. Of course, the papers will say that I'm having a face-lift if they get hold of it. Well, we might just get away with it. Worth trying . . . Let's go."

OVER THE MAP

So here we are. Glasgow.

He lives here. The airport hotel is here. Turnbury Lodge is here. As far as I know, the operating clinic is actually *in* Glasgow. I'll take a chance and call him. He got such a brief look at me . . .

ON THE PHONE

"Hello . . . Yes. Dr.—I mean, Mr. Mustarde, please . . . Oh, it is . . . Yes, it is . . . How do you do, sir. We're just getting into Glasgow and I see by the map that you live nearby . . . I mean, we could stop and you could take another look at me . . . Fine . . . Yes, I know where that is . . . Ask for Sister Charles . . . Yes, fine . . . Oh, two hours, about, don't you know? . . . Fine."

CLINIC PARKING LOT

"You think it may help? No, I understand. It won't last. Well, who knows. Maybe it will last . . . Hope springs eternal. You operate on the baby at eight. My goodness—what a tragedy. Only half an eye.

"Oh, you mean you take the half lower lid . . . and add it to the half upper to make one upper . . . then what? Make a new lower . . . then a glass eye.

"Well, mine is a sort of nothing at all, isn't it? I mean, I have the eye . . . Oh yes. And I can see . . . you bet. I'm certainly aware that I have had very good use of all my faculties. It really is just a question of maintenance. I mean, I'd like to sell myself as an object as long as it's practical. I mean, I'm in a business where I sell myself. And if I have bright red lower eyelids, it makes it a bit difficult to be . . . I mean, they itch too. And I think about them . . . I mean, worry about . . . Well, anyway, I think that it is worth trying. If you think it might work . . . Right . . . See you tomorrow at eleven."

AT THE HOTEL

"Come on, in we go. David [my English chauffeur], you take the bags in. And all the food.

"What about this . . . not bad at all. We shouldn't have judged by the lobby. I'll take this one. It has a tub. I've got to wash my hair. May not be able to for several days . . . weeks."

They didn't have a regular dinner, only sandwiches, but that was fine; the sandwiches were good and we of course had bits and pieces with us. The window opened, we could hear the planes. But it wasn't bad. And they had electric coffeepots, hot-water pots, tea, coffee, sugar, milk and a roll and butter sitting there waiting for the morning. Attractive.

We got to the clinic early. Mustarde had run into a longer operation than he had expected trying to make an eye for the little girl baby. I must say it sat there as a glowing example to me of "Don't moan, you've had two eyes for quite a while."

I went for a bit of a walk, then we were called in. I went upstairs. A very nice small private clinic. They took me into the nurses' locker room where I took off my gabardine trousers, so as not to crease them, and of course my shoes and my shirt. And they gave me a gown and told me to bind up my hair and to put a cap on. I did this, then walked down the hall to the operating room. Very nice.

I lay down on the table. Was covered up—hands under a sheet and bound down, since obviously he didn't want me reaching out, as he said, ". . . to help me do the operation. This won't hurt—much."

I was stabbed just to the left of my left eye with a needle which seemed to go straight through my skull. Wow!

The anesthetic.

"Yes."

"Now you tell me—can you feel this?"

"Well, yes—no—I think—no."

"Now I'm going to begin."

"Yes."

I could hear the knife go through the skin. It was weird. And quite revolting. Then I could feel the blood trickle down my cheek. And he—or I guess one of the nurses—daubed it up. He was obviously having a bit of a problem with a bleeder, but I of course could only follow it by what they daubed. So he finished that eye. The right one was not as bad but also had to be done.

Stab!

"Oh."

Then suddenly it was done and I was finished.

"Get up?" I asked.

"Yes, slowly—sit for a moment."

"I'm fine . . ."

"Oh yes, you'll be fine."

I got off the table, wandered about . . . "Yes, I'm fine. I'll drive right down to Turnbury Lodge and go to bed."

"Well, it's a lovely trip down the coast road."

"Fine, we'll go by the coast."

"I'll call you and see how you feel."

"Fine. Thank you."

I went back to the locker, put on my shoes, pants, shirt and went back to the car and got into the front seat with David. Off we went.

It was a very hot day. The sun was pounding in through the windshield. I am very sensitive to the sun. My skin, my eyes—in fact, the skin shrinkage and resultant eye droop had been caused by the California sun when I played tennis. I certainly never lay or sat in the sun if I could possibly avoid it—but tennis—that was a must. And in those days no sunscreen. And anyway, I'd sweat so that anything on my face would drip off in no time.

We got to the coast. Driving west then southwest. The sun relentless.

We stopped to take a few pictures and I said to Phyllis, "I'll get in back. The sun is too much for me."

She got in front and on we went.

I should explain that my big dark glasses covered the cuts, which were not bandaged. I had five or six stitches at the corner of the eye and slanting down. He had cut out a piece of the lower lid and twisted it in to try to make it lie closer to the eyeball.

We got to Turnbury Lodge. It was a typical sort of late-Victorian-Edwardian golfing hotel. On the top of a hill looking over the golf course and the Irish Sea. A winding drive going up to it. Then you circled the hotel. Three stories high. Big porches. Then on the first floor (it would be our second) where our rooms were, two rooms, two baths. Not adjoining, with small balconies. Very expensive. We circled the hotel and there was the front door. Two wings, a large circle of neglected flowers and of cars parked. Not too many. We parked. Not too far from the door. I wanted to get in without being seen. The rooms had been taken in Phyllis's name.

"Now, look here [me talking], go to the hotel—to the desk—get the keys—find out where the elevator is—come back—get me—no luggage. David can do that later."

They headed for the door. I was left in the backseat.

My God, it's hot, I thought. Hotter here than on the road. I'm dripping wet. I put my hand up, took off my dark glasses and lightly put my hand on my cheek—took it down. It was covered with blood. Good grief. That can't be happening. I put the hand back. More blood. Well, what in hell—it's burst open. Where—the paper towels—yes—unrolled a few squares—folded them up—good grief—how am I going to get into the hotel—good grief—here they come. Oh lawks, there's a porter with them . . .

"Yes . . . David, tell the porter later for the luggage—move him around back of the car. Phyllis, wait—my wound must have opened—I'm bleeding. Do you know how to get to our rooms? O.K., lead."

I followed.

"Turn left . . ."

"Yes."

It was quite dark. No one was around.

"Where's the elevator?"

"Across here."

"Right."

We got to the elevator door. No elevator. "Where's the button?"

"I can't see . . ."

(Phyllis has glaucoma. She can't see in the sudden dark. I couldn't see because my eye was full of blood.)

"Feel . . . I only have one hand."

Desperately we felt all over the wall. Finally . . .

"Here's the button."

Then the elevator.

"Close the door."

We went up. The door opened. There were people coming down the hall.

"What number?"

"Rooms 430 and 431."

"Get out the keys."

"Here."

"No, you, you fool . . ."

The people passed. We went down the hall.

"Here—430."

The keys were huge. Poor Phyllis, she struggled—Oh God.

Finally—the door opened.

"O.K., this is fine. Close the door. Ring for some ice. Ice, you fool—for my eye. Clot the blood. Ring. Telephone. I'll take my junk off and lie on the bathroom floor—it's tile. Easy to clean if we spill the blood."

I went into the bathroom—took off my trousers. Left on my cotton turtle and underpants and shoes. Got out the bath towels— lay down on the floor and pressed a towel to my eyes. Pouring blood. The door opened.

"What's that?"

"The ice."

"Give it—call the doctor."

"Where?"

"Well, where? How the hell do I know? His house—his office. Get David."

"I'm here, Miss Hepburn."

"Look, David, take off your shoes and socks and your pants— and get into the tub and try to get the blood out of the stuff I throw in there. Just run in cold water and then stamp on the rags. And, Phyllis, look, if you can't get him, get the clinic. Maybe there's a doctor there who can tell us what to do. The numbers are in my purse, in my book."

Well, Phyllis called this—called that. Couldn't find the doctor. So she called the clinic. Got a doctor . . .

"I've got a doctor."

"Let me talk."

I went into the bedroom—pretty nice view. Took the phone.

"I seem to be hemorrhaging. I can't see where the blood is coming from because I can't put on my glasses."

"You sound a bit frantic, Miss Wilbourn [he thought I was]. Why don't you take a little whiskey . . ."

"*Whiskey?*"

"Yes, a bit of whiskey. Then sit up in bed and it will stop . . ."

"SIT UP—me?"

"Yes, were you lying down?"

"Yes."

"That was wrong. Keep your head up."

"Yes . . ."

"Are you O.K. now?"

"Yes, I am."

"Mr. Mustarde will call you. I'll locate him."

"Thank you—thank you very much."

"Whiskey . . ."

"Whiskey?"

"Yes, both of us—ice—soda—it's stopping. I'm a wreck."

Happy New Year

hat's that? What did you say?
Have a good day— Oh yes, Happy New Year. Yes, of course. How
stupid of me. You too. Happy New Year."

(There is the sound of a door closing and the room is dark.)

Did they say Happy New Year? Well, maybe. I suppose that's
one way of putting it.

I'm lying here in bed in the Hartford Hospital. Phyllis is lying
twelve feet from me. We're in a two-bed room on the sixth floor
of a building—part of the Hartford Hospital complex. It is about
10 p.m. and our 3–11 p.m. shift has just said good night. Lin
Remington—her name. Yes, she came New Year's Eve night. I told
her to go home early—in time for the great midnight moment. Just
damned nice of her to come at all. I agree.

Oh, they've taken great care of us, our whole crew. Lin and
Gail—Bernice—Sue—Kathy—Diane and Marsha and Rhada really
put themselves out. Rhada even came Christmas Eve night. So generous. Because the others, they all have kids and it's the Christmas–
New Year's holiday. What? What are we doing here?

Oh, didn't you hear? I ran into a telephone pole. Yes, got across
the causeway from Fenwick to Saybrook Point. Went about, oh say,
fifty yards—then either looked up or down or away or who knows
what I did. We ran head-on into a telephone pole—right square bang
head-on.

Can you believe it? I can't. I really am—or is it was?—a good driver. Could something have gone wrong with the steering? How in hell did it happen? Did my mind go blank?

Anyway, it wasn't blank after the bump.

Crash!

Yup, there it is—the telephone pole growing right up out of my radiator. Yup, there it is.

Phyllis, looking up at me, but not seeing—from the front seat next to me, and most of her on the floor between the glove compartment and the seat.

I seem to be sitting upright. Blood flowing out of my nose. My right leg—foot—still on the accelerator. Well—in a manner of speaking. Something not quite right about that right foot and ankle. Not really headed in the right direction and not feeling quite right and very mucky—bloody. Well, now what to do?

"Come on, Phyllis. Wake up. Wake up. You're not dead, are you?"

Better blow the horn. Get someone.

Bing—*bing bing—bing bing bing. Bing*— Hey— Someone— *Bing bing bing!*

"Come on, Phyllis. Open your eyes." Lawks. This bloody nose. Aah, the Kleenex box. That's better. Must have hit my nose.

"Come on, dear—aah—here they come."

Cops galore.

"Right here, Officer. No I'm O.K.—I mean I'm—well— Look, call my brother Dick, will you? Tell him to come to Hull's Marina, that I've had an accident. Call Hartford—my brother Dr. Robert Hepburn. Tell him I've had an accident. That we'll get to the Hartford Hospital. Get us a double room and six nurses— Come on, Phyllis. That's right. Open your eyes.

"What? Yes, I've got a license somewhere. My brother Dick will be right here.

"No no, we didn't skid. I would have been aware of a skid. No. I just think I must have been dumb enough to look away or well— up, well, whatever. That telephone pole— Yes, that one growing out of the radiator. That telephone pole walked right into me. Can you imagine? Aah, good Phyllis, that's better! An accident, dear—wake up. I drove into a telephone pole. We're going to—wait a minute.

"What's he doing—that cop—taking pictures?

"Hey, you. Don't you take my picture. Aah, here's Dick. Oh and here are some ambulances. Two of them. Yes, Officer. I think I have a badly broken ankle—just—

"Just relax, Phyllis—they're trying to get you onto a stretcher.

"Hartford Hospital. Oh, we have to go to the clinic on Route 156 first. O.K. Just scoop up my foot. Slide it onto the—

"That's fine. O.K. Off we go.

"Get all the junk out of the car, Dick. My purses—my license is in one of them. They wanted—goodbye."

We were separated. Inside two ambulances—one for Phyllis, one for me. We went to the clinic near Riggio's. Then after a pause, we were put into two other ambulances and went to the Hartford Hospital.

We were rushed into Emergency.

"We'll have to take your clothes off, Miss Hepburn."

"I see—fine."

Then I heard: "Here, give those scissors to me. We'll cut the trousers—"

"What? What's that?" I said, "Wait! For God's sake—don't cut them off—they're English slacks. Cost two hundred and seventy-five dollars— Take off the boots, then the pants will come off easily.

"Does it hurt, did you ask? I think it must, don't you? But I really don't feel a thing. It just looks—well, a bit—"

So anyway, we each make our own trips to the operating room. Mine was a very, very messy compound fracture, with lots of pulverized bones perforating the skin. And Phyllis, a broken left wrist—a chip off a neck vertebra—a broken right elbow—and two cracked ribs.

So they glued us together, and what was missing they made out of wires and plates, and then delivered us to our room.

I understand they put five different casts on my right ankle before they were satisfied with the X-ray. Dr. Pasternak, helped by Dr. Butterfield—Dr. Beebe. Dr. Stevens was giving the anesthetic.

What's that smell? Terrible. Rancid. Oh yes, my hair. Oh dear. I woke up with a huge cast on my right leg—foot to crotch.

Phyllis with a cast on her left arm, elbow to wrist, a contraption on her right elbow—and a neck brace, which had to be on all the time—one for lying down, a stronger one for walking around. She could walk—yes.

So my life began. I could hardly lift the cast on my right leg. It was heavy—and, of course, it was the fake right hip which had to maneuver the heavy cast. I should tell you here that Dr. Neer called. Dr. Neer, of New York Columbia Presbyterian, who seven weeks before had operated on my right shoulder for the second time! Yes—

a rotator cuff. (The first operation was in June, 1980. I had loused it up by doing the movie *On Golden Pond*.) Four weeks after this first operation, Dr. Neer had told me that I would ruin that operation if I worked before twelve or fifteen weeks. Now, what could I do? They were all waiting. Henry Fonda—Jane—Mark Rydell, the director— Billy Williams, cameraman—the set—the living quarters—they had to start immediately. Otherwise an impending general strike in the movie business would stop them and they'd have to wait a whole year for another summer. So I said yes. Let's go.

Well, the doctor was right. I ruined the shoulder—the first time. I certainly didn't want to jeopardize the second operation.

"O.K., Dr. Neer. I understand. That's right, sir."

No crutches—no weight-bearing . . .

How to manage: the ankle in the heavy cast was not supposed to touch the floor. The right hip, being fake, had to be carefully watched for possible strain. The left leg and foot had to do all the carrying.

For instance, bed to wheelchair: lug the injured leg in its cast off the bed. The nurse keeps the foot off the floor. I put my left foot down and hop around on the left leg so that I can put my rear end neatly into the seat of the wheelchair. The nurse lets down the foot-rest and puts the bad foot on it. Off we go to the john. Through the door.

"Watch it! *Narrow door! Watch your hands—watch your elbows!*"

Anchor the wheelchair. Lift the bad leg off the footrest. The nurse takes the foot to keep it off the floor. I put down my left foot. On the tile floor I can turn myself around by moving toe to heel, a sliding progress toe down, heel forward—heel down, toe forward. So I progress to wherever and then sit. Then get up and toe-heel, toe-heel sidewise to the wheelchair. Back into the bedroom. Sit in my chair until lunch—then until dinner. Then bed again. Raise the foot of the bed, lower the head of the bed. Sleep. And—the nurses take turns tickling my toes, which stick out of the end of the cast. Soothing— to sleep to sleep.

Yes, that's about it—I mean, that's the story. Now it's New Year's. All that was almost four weeks ago. We couldn't get anyone for the three-to-eleven shift. Not surprising New Year's night. We were planning to go home to my sister Marion's house in West Hart-ford on New Year's Day.

I woke up early that morning and was being wheeled through the bathroom door by the 7 a.m. shift. My hair was so dirty. Cleanliness is next to Godliness, I thought, but what can I do? Then I looked up. There above the john was a thing, a sort of hose with an end— a spray.

"Gail, what's that thing—that hose and spray?"

"That's for washing out the bedpans."

"And are those hot and cold taps?"

"Yes—hot and cold."

"I could wash my hair?"

"Where?"

"Over the toilet. I could lean over the toilet. You could use the hose. See what I mean? My good leg around the john. See? My head over the john. Sit in the wheelchair pushed right up to the toilet. Put my bad leg into the shower, hook the cast on the edge so it won't slip off. And my head over the john. Come on, let's go. Get my soap. Let's go. It will work.

"Here we go—action—right leg out of the way. Right. You take the hose. Give me the soap. Right. O.K. Soak my head. More water—hot—better. O.K.—off. Now the soap. Good—enough. I'll rub. Oh, it feels so great. O.K., O.K.—now, Gail, here—here— scratch. Spray. Good—good—now a towel. Turn off the water— done.

"It's done. Wrap it up."

It's a first. Can you imagine! What a triumph! Clean hair! Wow! And on New Year's morning. What a sign— Happy New Year. Yes, indeed, what the hell. Happy New Year!

VI

Love

ow I'm going to tell you about Spencer.

You may think you've waited a long time. But let's face it, so did I. I was thirty-three.

It seems to me I discovered what "I love you" really means. It means I put you and your interests and your comfort ahead of my own interests and my own comfort because I love you.

What does this mean?

I love you. What does this mean?

Think.

We use this expression very carelessly.

LOVE has nothing to do with what you are expecting to get— only with what you are expecting to give—which is everything.

What you will receive in return varies. But it really has no connection with what you give. You give because you love and you cannot help giving. If you are very lucky, you may be loved back. That is delicious but it does not necessarily happen.

It really implies total devotion. And total is all-encompassing— the good of you, the bad of you. I am aware that I must include the bad.

I loved Spencer Tracy. He and his interests and his demands came first.

This was not easy for me because I was definitely a *me me me* person.

It was a unique feeling that I had for S.T. I would have done anything for him. My feelings—how can you describe them?—the door between us was always open. There were no reservations of any kind.

He didn't like this or that. I changed this and that. They might be qualities which I personally valued. It did not matter. I changed them.

Food—we ate what he liked.

We did what he liked.

We lived a life which he liked.

This gave me great pleasure. The thought that this was pleasing him.

Certainly I had not felt this way with my other beaux. I was looking for them to please me. It is a very different relationship. It's like a wonderful cocktail party. But it ain't love.

Luddy loved me—in my sense of the word. He did everything he possibly could to make me happy.

Luddy took care of me and gave me confidence.

I took care of Spencer and gave him confidence.

I shared the two best types of relationships.

I loved Dad and Mother. They always had the last word with me. If they wanted it—I did it. And happily—also they loved me—and I felt this and it made me very happy.

There is an enormous difference between love and like. Usually we use the word "love" when we really mean like. I think that very few people ever mean *love*. I think that like is a much easier relationship. It is based on sense. A blind spot—love.

What was it about him that fascinated me? Well, that is not a difficult question to answer. He had the most wonderful sense of humor. He was funny. He was Irish to the fingertips. He could laugh and he could create laughter. He had a funny way of looking at things—at some things, I should say.

There was a group—Spencer Tracy, James Cagney, Pat O'Brien, Frank Morgan, Frank McHugh. They had a weekly meeting on Thursdays. It was called Irish night. It was at Romanoff's. Sometimes at Chasen's. And *finally* it was at my house when I lived in the Boyer house. I used to go to bed—or clear out and go to another house to sleep. I had a wonderful cook—a great projection room. I'd order the food—get the movie—and there was Irish night. I think it sort of came to an end. Well, we all do just that, don't we? I know that finally I moved out of the Boyer house and down to Spence's tiny house, which we rented from George Cukor. Spence wasn't all that well and it was better to have me there. And there were no more Irish nights.

People have asked me what was it about Spence that made me stay with him for nearly thirty years. And this is somehow impossible for me to answer. I honestly don't know. I can only say that I could never have left him. He was there—I was his. I wanted him to be happy—safe—comfortable. I liked to wait on him—listen to him— feed him—talk to him—work for him. I tried not to disturb him— irritate him—bother him—worry him, nag him. I struggled to change all the qualities which I felt he didn't like. Some of them which I thought were my best I thought he found irksome. I removed them, squelched them as far as I was able.

When he was sort of toward the end of his life—his last six or seven years—I virtually quit work just to be *there* so that he wouldn't worry or be lonely. I was happy to do this. I painted—I wrote—I was peaceful and hoping that he would live forever.

What was it? I found him—totally—totally—total! I really liked him—deep down—and I wanted him to be happy. I don't think that he was very happy. I don't mean that he did anything or said anything which would indicate that he was. How can I say—well, who is happy?—I am happy. I have a happy nature—I like the rain—I like the sun—the heat—the cold—the mountains, the sea—the flowers, the— Well, I like life and I've been so lucky. Why shouldn't I be happy?

I don't lock doors. I don't hold grudges. Really the only thing I'm not mad about is wind. I find it disturbing. I mean wind in the heavens.

Spence didn't like cold—he didn't like too much heat—he— well, he liked comfort. I think that states it.

He was a great actor— Simple. He could just do it. Never overdone. Just perfection. There was no complication. The performance was unguarded. He could make you laugh. He could make you cry. He could listen.

Someone once asked me why I said that Spencer Tracy was like a baked potato. I think it is because I think that he was very basic as an actor. He was there skins and all—in his performances. He was cooked and ready to eat. The only person to whom he could be compared is Laurette Taylor.

Now I must add that the baked potato description only refers to the incredible perfection of their performances. In his *life*, Spencer was as far from a baked potato as possible. He was as complicated as a human being could be.

I've just had a thought. He did not—he *could not* protect himself.

How can I explain what I mean? I think most of us have a sort of shell of self-protection. We can hide behind it even when we are acting. Whatever the circumstance, we can protect ourselves. Spence couldn't. He had no shell.

Maybe that is why at his most vulnerable age he liked to drink —and he drank too much at times. He had a strong character. He could stop. And then sometimes he wouldn't have a drink for a long time—a year or two or three. And then—but he'd stop, and finally he didn't do it anymore. He didn't allow himself to get into situations which tormented him.

We made nine pictures together.
Woman of the Year
Keeper of the Flame
Without Love
The Sea of Grass
State of the Union
Adam's Rib
Pat and Mike
The Desk Set
Guess Who's Coming to Dinner
Never rehearsed together at home. Almost never used to discuss the script. It was curious. I always loved to work on the script. Not Spence. He'd read something. Say yes or no. And that was it.

With Susie, Spencer's daughter

Someone asked me when I fell for Spencer. I can't remember. It was right away. We started our first picture together and I knew right away that I found him irresistible. Just exactly that, irresistible.

His father died before I knew Spencer. I never met his mother. I don't know much about either of them. His father was a heavy drinker. I do not think that he was very close to either of them. Certainly not like my relationship with my parents. He had his brother Carroll, who took care of all the business end of Spencer's career. But they were not really—well, they were entirely different in personality. Carroll was married to a woman whom he had known back home in Wisconsin—Dorothy. I now have a good friend in Spence's daughter Susie. She is quite like him but with an easier nature.

Someone asked me what about Spence and Mother and Dad. Well of course they met. He went to Hartford several times and to Fenwick. But they were never close. I think that they liked him—but Spence felt a bit uncomfortable with them. After all, he was a married man.

I don't think that Dad and Mother were bothered too much by this. But there it was as far as Spence went—and he felt uncomfortable—unrelaxed. So we seldom were together when I went home.

I have no idea how Spence felt about me. I can only say I think that if he hadn't liked me he wouldn't have hung around. As simple as that. He wouldn't talk about it and I didn't talk about it. We just passed twenty-seven years together in what was to me absolute bliss.

It is called LOVE.

Leaving the California House

Dear little house—I'm deserting you. This is almost my last look. Corners—lights—shadows. Good days and bad days. Here's where I lived—this was mine. It was yours but it was so many years mine. Nights—days—conversations. You sat in the rocker, Spencer. Remember when I got that old horsehair rocker? It was in a window in an old wreck of a shop in Olvera Street. Just a naked frame. I mean, no stuffing—just springs in a frame and the round bars on which it rocked. You were nervous— you liked to rock. Fanny Brice's Mr. Schwartz could rebuild it— black horsehair buttoned in. The chair had such a pretty shape. The top of the back slightly scooped and the ends of the arms a bit up— pretty angle too. Hopeful and light for a stuffed one. I must have that chair. A Chinese owned it. It had belonged to his grandfather. He said no—not selling. But I went back so often. I told him how you needed it to sit in and to rock in. So he finally let me have it. For quite a lot. He didn't lose. Nor did I. Nor did you. That was your seat in your corner. The oak gateleg was your table—big enough. Good lamp—basket base—lots of bulbs—lots of light. All the books you liked the best. And the encyclopedia and the Oxford dictionary and the radio and the TV control, and on the left the telephone table and a footstool. Two telephones. You were comfortable. I hope you could see the fire. We had one almost every night. Summer—winter.

There was a red upholstered chair that I sat in. I moved it about according to the occasion. Not too heavy. It seems heavier now. It wasn't then.

The room was made of planks of wormy chestnut. The ceiling high rather than low, going up to a square a yard wide, which might have been a skylight but wasn't. There was the desk at one end—in front under a glass roof. French windows on either side. The desk was one of my creations. You had lived in a terrible little apartment on South Beverly Drive down an alley off the actual drive. Trying to make it attractive was really not possible. In desperation we had Erik Bolin—French furniture maker—make some wooden valances for the curtains. When you moved, I took those for the top of the desk— laid them on top of two three-drawer chests two and a half feet wide, which were at either end, that the carpenter made for me—cut out a center section of the lower valance for leg space. It was a great success—$40. Lots of room. Slots between the valance top—good for telephone books. Then I designed a mantel of the chestnut, which was put above a rather too small fireplace in a chimney of brick painted white, which was about ten feet wide. The uprights were at either end of the wide chimney with a cut six inches from the top, which made the shelf. The mantel to rest upon about four inches. Chestnut against white chimney—attractive. Made the fireplace look bigger.

Dad had found a pretty corner cupboard in Cromwell, Connect- icut. It was pine—stood in the corner left of the fireplace. It will come back to Fenwick now with me. My African chair was next to the cupboard. There was a big white carpet-type rug and on top of it a heavenly Navajo rug—pink red on white, some black, some French blue, about ten by twelve. Old—remarkable—I got it in Seattle when I was playing in *A Matter of Gravity*. You never saw that rug, did you—no. Opposite the desk at the far end of the room, which was all windows. Long—high—sliding. Looking onto the patio—no view—a bit of a glare, actually. I had a pretty wood-and-woven screenlike thing made. You remember that. You could sit in your rocker—a lovely light—made the patio mysterious.

Strange to be going. I couldn't bear to leave the house after you died. I kept it—even the books on the oak table. I sit in your chair now. The books have never been moved. Silly, I suppose. I was trying to keep you there. Now we're both going. I've had an offer on the old Thunderbird. I wanted to keep it but it is just too impractical. Whitney (George's dog), a yellow Labrador retriever, has torn the leather to pieces. And it has not been properly cared for. Dear old Bird. Fun to drive—not so much now. Beginning to wonder whether it will just have a cardiac arrest. But it's yours—I mean mine. I had to buy it back from Louise when you died.

I'm sitting in your bedroom writing all this. You liked to have everything shut in—or was it shut out? I never close the windows. They slide back—the big glass ones into the patio. If you want to, you can close the white shutters—I don't. Your bed is in the same spot. Next to the bathroom door. Looking into the room and out at the bit of the sky. The bit above that old messy shapeless banana tree, which stands there year after year on the upper level growing huge leaves that rot and break and turn brown and are generally ugly. I notice them because I've moved into your bedroom and I eat breakfast in bed very early and look right out across the patio at that silly tree. Doesn't even grow bananas. It's still there—so shapeless. Albert, the head gardener, won't trim it back. He loves those dead leaves.

Sometimes—often, really—I think of you in this bed—turning turning turning. Do you remember at the end—well, we didn't know that it was nearing the end but it was—I would put a quilt and my pillow down on the floor. Sometimes even the living-room sofa cushions. You would have taken your sleeping pills. The lights were out—my head was practically out one of those big glass doors that went into the patio. I'd pull the blind back to get a bit of air. You didn't give a damn about the air. You just wanted to be all safe and closed in. We'd talk a bit. Your problem was—can't get to sleep. So I did most of the talk. I guess really that I bored you. But I don't guess you cared. There I was. I was certainly yours. And you knew that you had someone you could depend on. But you would toss. And you would turn and turn and turn and sigh. What is it? What was it? What . . . what. Never at peace. And you should have lived to be an old man. And you were only sixty-seven. Tortured by some sort of guilt. Some terrible misery. Was it that you couldn't stand yourself? There was never an actor like you. You and Laurette. That's what I always said—thought. And you were both Irish. And both in misery with life. And both hunting for a sort of oblivion. Of drink —of laughter—of something. Your acting was the easiest thing, wasn't it? You could just do it. All those nerve ends longing to be occupied. Acting took up the slack.

It was weird at first, wasn't it? Right off, I was living up in Edgar Bergen's house. Bob McKnight, my old friend, had been spending the summer with me. Why in the world don't I marry him? I know him . . . I like him . . . we both like tennis. We've known each other since I was fifteen. I invited him to spend the summer. We— you and I—were going to do *Woman of the Year* with George Stevens. I'd just met you. You thought I had dirty nails. I think that you imagined that I was a lesbian. But not for long. Did you. Very early forties—'41, I think. Mike Kanin and Ring Lardner were involved through Garson. They had never done anything spectacular. I'd sent Metro a seventy-eight-page outline of the story of a sports editor— you—and a political commentator à la Dorothy Thompson—me. I said that the price was $250,000 for the whole lot: me, $125,000, half; and the script, half.

But that was just before they bought the thing. Before the house—before us.

I'm on the plane now. It's raining. It's November 21, 1978. The furniture was to be put on the truck today. But I didn't want it to be loaded in the pouring rain. And I mean pouring.

It was a strange thing packing up that house. Now it's done. Bit by bit by bit, one removes one's self. After almost thirty years. One's friends come in—Susie and Susan. (That's Spence's daughter and her friend.) They took a few little tokens. That crystal egg with your birth sign. Kathy Houghton, my niece, gave you that. You're April 5th. They took some art books—*The Old Man and the Sea* first edition, signed by Hemingway: "Spencer from Papa." And that wonderful Christmas card from General Montgomery signed to you. He is seated at a table. Opposite him is Winston Churchill in his big hat—like a Stetson—cowboy. They were in a tent together having a drink. Very relaxed. Susie loved it. She'll have it framed. I told her that great story about how you were crossing on the *Queen Mary*. Remember? You were invited to the Captain's quarters for a drink. Montgomery was there.

"Spencer Tracy?" he said. "Is that right?"

"Yes," you said, "that's right."

"And where do you come from?" he asked (no recognition in his eyes).

"Oh—California, I suppose you'd say," you replied, vouchsafing no more.

"Where in California?"

"Well, Los Angeles—suburbs, really."

"Pretty state."

"Yes . . ."

"Were you born there?"

"No—very few seem to be born in California."

"How long have you . . ."

"Oh—a number of years—no—yes indeed."

"Do you have some business there?"

"You might call it that—yes."

"Some business specifically connected with California?"

"Not really. Well, yes I suppose one might say that it is especially connected with—and yet . . ."

"Yet what?"

"Oh nothing, really . . ."

He was determined that you were going to admit to him that you were a movie actor. And you were equally determined that you were never going to tell him. Obviously he was doing a Mrs. Pat Campbell in pretending that he did not know that Spencer Tracy was a movie actor and was yourself . . . I can just hear you telling me that I've loused up that story.

And I gave Susie the framed and bejeweled-sparkle painting which Kramer gave you one Christmas. And those figurines—the orchestra, silver and brass—also from Kramer—eight figures. Remember? We'd just finished *Guess Who's Coming to Dinner*. I found the card. He gave them to both of us: "May your music go on and on." But he really meant just you. So I thought Susie should have them. I kept the card.

And the Toulouse-Lautrec pencil sketches of the horses and men—gold frame. I gave it to you one Christmas. Bill Self got the boat off the mantelpiece. And he bought a little table from your bedroom. The only other thing I sold was the oak gateleg next to your rocker. Alan Shayne bought that. He wanted those two big chairs—either side of the fireplace. But Betty Bacall wanted those, so I had no choice as I had had them copied from a pair she had. She's got a country house now and her original two are in town. How uncomfortable they are—but very good-looking. We're taking the rest with us—old letters—old wires. If they had to do with your career, I gave them to Susie. All the sad ones about when you died I kept.

All the things that happened in that little house—that night you died. You'd gone to sleep. When I thought that you were settled, I'd crept out of your room. Always the same thing. You had the buzzer right next to you and then the cord—two miles long. I used to take the bell with me if I went anywhere inside—outside—so that I'd always hear it ring if you wanted me. That night you didn't ring. It was about 3 a.m. You had wanted a cup of hot tea. Remember how we always kept the kettle on a very low boil? No, you didn't ring. But I heard you walk down the hall. And then heard you go into the kitchen. I got up. Put on my slippers and went to the kitchen door. Just as I was about to give it a push, there was a sound of a cup smashing to the floor—then clump—a loud clump. It was you falling to the floor. I was through the door. Yes—it was you. You were—just—dead. As if everything had stopped. Suddenly stopped. All at once. The End . . .

Yes—the engine has stopped. Three o'clock in the morning. June 10, 1967. Just stopped—BANG! The box broke. The container had just become too small for all that—what would you call it?—all that wild stuff whirling around inside. Peace at last. Oh yes I hope.

I crouched down and took you up in my arms—dead. No life—no pulse—dead. Spence is dead. He is not alive anymore. He doesn't inhabit his body anymore. He is gone. His eyes are closed. It is tea spilled all over him. He never knew what happened . . .

Dear dear friend—gone. Oh, lucky one. That's the way to exit. Just out the door and—gone.

I sat. Oh yes—lucky. That's good, Spence. Good. Well done. You hated wondering and not feeling well. But you weren't really sick. No agonies or pains or helplessness. You were independent—gone. And never coming back.

What to do—what to do. Oh dear. Gone.

Call Phyllis. She was living up on the hill—1300 Tower Grove Drive. Jack Barrymore's birdhouse. We had it as a sort of studio. She slept there. Our house in the trees. Skylights—high ceilings—windows—sun—God's light. We grew orchids. And I painted. Badly. Fun, though. And people came to tea—but that was long ago. It had a lovely view.

I called Phyllis. "Spence's dead."

"I'll come . . ."

You dead. I put you on a rug. You were too heavy for me to carry. I say "I"—I mean then I called Willie and Ida Gheczy, who lived next door. She was our housekeeper. Willie was George Cukor's assistant gardener. George rented Spence the house—so our gardener too. They came and helped get Spence back to bed. And I drew up the covers and lit the candles. He looked so happy to be done with living, which for all his accomplishments had been a frightful burden to him. So quiet. He who had turned and turned in that bed. No one able to help him really. One builds one's own jail. I never knew him, I think. And he is the only one who ever knew me—who was onto me. I think I was a comfort to him. I hope. Dear Friend.

What should I do now. Call the family? Call Stanley Kramer? Move out—no—yes—then call. Phyllis came. We moved all my stuff—clothes, personal stuff—out into my car. Then I thought—God—God—Kath—what are you doing—you've lived with the man for almost thirty years. This is your home. Isn't it? It is part of you. These walls—this roof—this spot on the earth. I carried everything back into the house. You can't deny your life of thirty years.

Now what? I had called the doctor. "Yes—he is dead—coronary. The best death. Yes, he's very lucky."

"Let's call Howard Strickling, head of publicity at MGM. He will know what to do and how to handle the press."

We got Howard. He would come, right off. Then George Cukor.

"Get dressed, George. Come down. Spence is dead."

"I'll get dressed."

I called the family—his wife, Louise; his children Susie and John. And his brother Carroll and Carroll's wife, Dorothy. Spence is dead.

They began to arrive. Cunningham & Walsh, the undertakers, were called by Carroll.

The family came in.

"He's in there."

"We have coffee and a bit of breakfast—eggs? Bacon? Toast? Fruit? Anything you . . ."

"Please eat . . ."

"Yes, of course, take it in with Spence."

"Please . . ." This was Louise.

She went down the hall with her cup of coffee. Well, she was in a peculiar spot—no doubt about that. She could never bear to admit failure. Now he was dead. And he would never come back. She had dreamed—hoped—imagined that he would. But now all those hopes had died with him. This strange woman—me—had obviously been with him when he died. And he is mine—oh—oh—oh . . .

And now the undertakers were there. "What suit? Oh, the old gray pants and the brown tweed—the old one—everything is ready. They've taken them out there . . ."

"But he's my husband—I should pick out the . . ."

"Oh, Louise—what difference does it make?"

And suddenly he was gone and they were going and Dorothy was asking for the keys to the house.

And Phyllis was saying: "What did you say, Dorothy? The keys to this house—our house?" And Dorothy shut up—silenced by English elegance and indignation.

Susie had been a bit faint and walked in the patio with Phyllis. Johnny had been given two pills and was sort of confused by the whole event of death and in this strange house and with these strange people, for he was deaf and life was complicated. There was so much that he missed.

The doctor left too. No more to do. Then George. Then Howard Strickling. He'd talked to the press. And it was 6 a.m.

All that happened in this little house. Our little house. So strange to be packing it up. Worse—or no, not worse but I wonder—I never saw Dad and Mother's house after I packed it up. Couldn't bear to even go past it at 201 Bloomfield Avenue. They were so much a part of it. And now this house. All the many years spent here. And when you died I kept it because it was all that was left of you. For a long time it was exactly as you had it. Then it slowly changed. I began to throw away your medicines and this and that. I kept—I mean I had kept for years the pajamas and the red flannel pajama coat which you died in. It hung on the old oak chair in the bedroom when I was in residence. You left the house in it when they took you to the undertakers. You were there for several days having a sort of—not wake—but viewing or whatever they call it. I would go down after everyone had gone and sit a bit. Meaningless, really. But all that was left of what we know. And in my heart of hearts I had to be glad. You—that lovely wild spirit full of laughter—yet so sad—were you sad? What was it—what? Was it John being deaf and you feeling responsible? Was it that you felt that you should have remained married? Well, you were still married to Louise. I think that this is what she wanted. She just could not settle for the fact that her marriage had been a failure. I don't believe that she realized that it is almost never another way when a child is born who is handicapped. The wife devotes her real center of energy to the child. And the husband somehow wanders off. Driven by an inability to face the reality that a child of his could be anything but perfect. And the wife is in no state to realize what is going on in the husband's mind. The misery, the excitements to drown the misery—the drink to forget the excitements. And in the end—you're really the victim of a situation which was an uncertainty. You couldn't leave her if she didn't want to be left. She'd done all the work with Johnny. What to do? What to do? I must say that I couldn't figure out what I would have done if I'd been in your spot. So nothing—you did nothing. And time passed. I didn't fight for marriage. And we seemed to have a happier and happier time in spite of the fact that you had physical problems. We led a tiny little life. But it was very satisfactory. I felt very necessary to you and I really did enjoy that immensely. At a time when most ladies of my age were falling apart because they were no longer desirable—either personally or career-wise—I was wanted every hour of the day and night. You worried that I had sort of dumped my career. I was totally protected from wondering how I would have done professionally because I was not on the market, so to speak. Free—I felt—of that damned—Myself.

Looking back—well, I suppose that now I am influenced by Susie and the fact that I know her now. How we met was a funny and a very moving thing. I used to play tennis every day with Alex Olmedo at the Beverly Hills Hotel. One day I went in with Dog Lobo. He was Spencer's and my dog. He was about three years old—part police—part coyote—half the size of a police—smooth coat and one ear up, one ear down. Half his tail was gone. He was a mutt with the warm humor of a mutt—bright—handsome head elegantly marked—big eyes full of joy. He was my friend and went everywhere with me. He had a snooty manner and his nose turned slightly up. Fun. Anyway, you can see I liked him a lot.

So—we went through the gate into the tennis court. All of a sudden, almost following us, came a girl—blushing madly—the blush spreading over her face—up her neck—but she was determined.

"It's Lobo, isn't it?"

"Yes," I said. "Yes, it's Lobo." Who—who? Could it be? Yes it is, I thought, Susie—it's Susie. Spence's daughter.

"He looks fine."

"Yes, he's fine, Susie."

Suddenly we were at a loss for words—silence.

Then I: "Look, Susie, if you would like to get to know me, that can be very easily arranged. You know where I live and you know the telephone number. Any time . . ."

So she called. And we became friends. Just like that . . .

It really was she who has made me wonder whether I did the right thing in never straightening out the relationship—so that I could get to know Susie and Johnny with Spence. It certainly would have been more simple. And actually it might have removed Spence's sense of guilt. It would have been honest.

After Spence died—a few days later—I called Louise and said,

"You know, Louise, you and I can be friends. You knew him at the beginning, I at the end—or we can just pretend that— I might be a help with the kids."

"Well, yes," she said. "But you see, I thought you were only a rumor . . ."

After nearly thirty years? A rumor? What could be the answer to that? It was a deep and fundamental wound—deeply set—never to be budged. Almost thirty years Spence and I had known each other —through good and bad times. Some rumor. And by never admitting that I existed—she remained—the wife—and she sent out Christmas cards. Spence—the guilty one. She—the sufferer. And I—well now, I was brought up in a very unconventional atmosphere. And I had not broken up their marriage. That happened long before I arrived on the scene. And as I said before, I could never make up my mind which would pain Spence the least. So I never mentioned it except to say, "I'm fine. And don't leave me any money—money makes trouble and I have enough to see me through." And in California I did not go out in public with him. And no one ever got a picture of us together—socially—privately, that is. And actually—as time passed—the media let us alone. The respect earned by time. So the surface was smooth.

I think now that I took the easy road. It is better to straighten things out. Then everyone—and in this case Susie and Johnny— would have been able to know their father with me. It would have been better. But it would have had to be pushed by Louise—the loser in the situation. Yet it would, I believe, have been ennobling to her. And supremely honest. And it would have made it easy for him to do—what would in this case have been the direct and simple thing for him to do. Then he could have had the best of both worlds. And if he had felt that it was her idea, his guilt would have been removed.

Oh yes—but if she'd done that she would have had to have been a saint. Well, yes. But what's wrong with being a saint? Too much to ask, I agree. Louise was in a hopeless situation.

And as for me—I was complacent. I didn't push for action. I just left it up to him. And he was paralyzed.

I must say it taught me a lesson—one must figure out how much

you care about this or that. Then put up a fight. Or don't. Do you
love someone? If you love someone, and the person gives every evidence
of wishing to part and you know really that it is finished—let the
person go! Do yourself a favor. Be noble. It has a better lasting effect
than hanging on and constantly reminding yourself and the other that
your life together has been a disaster. And it is honest. And it is
going forward. The status quo in a bad marriage is not a productive
state. The new relationship may open many doors beneficial to everyone concerned. That solidified failure is so sterile.

"Hello!"

"Good morning."

"Good night."

"How is Johnny?"

"How is Susie?"

"How are you . . ."

Hollow. And endless until death. Sad. A mistake sitting right on
your lap for life.

Well, that's the way it was. And it's not going to change. Spence
is dead. Louise drifted off. And now she's gone too. I'm sure that it
was all a great burden to her also. Traveling down a road which really
didn't exist.

The morning of the funeral. Well, actually the last night of the
rosary or whatever they call it when you lie on view at the undertakers.
I went down after everyone had left. I went in.

"I'm sorry, Miss Hepburn, the coffin is closed. Mrs. Carroll Tracy
told me to close it. I . . . shall I . . ."

"No—no—leave it . . . it doesn't really matter, does it. I just
had a few little tokens—but it doesn't matter. Leave it. I'll stay just
a minute."

I would have liked to have seen his face once more—but what
was the difference—yesterday—today—tomorrow . . . He was
gone—Dad was gone—Mother was gone. Their story is told. And I
am still here and in my mind they are so solid a part of me. They
are me. I've been lucky, haven't I? I walk for all three. Sad the coffin
is locked. I wonder if they found my little painting of flowers I put
under his feet. I don't think so. And it doesn't matter—things. Never

fight about things. That's what Dad and Mother said. Things don't matter. And they don't and he's now safe from harm.

The next day was the funeral at a Catholic church, in Hollywood, down Santa Monica Boulevard. Phyllis and I, of course, didn't plan to go—too conspicuous.

Well, I got to thinking about Spence's last trip through the town and I said to Phyllis, "Let's go down to Cunningham & Walsh and see the old boy take off."

We went. We peeked. No one was there, just the hearse. So we drove up into the driveway.

"Is anyone coming?"

"No."

"May we help?"

"Why not?"

So we helped lift Spence into his spot in the wagon. Closed the door and off they went and off we went after them. His cortège. Down Melrose, then left on Vermont; then we could see the church. They went on toward it. We stopped. Goodbye, friend—here's where we leave you . . .

And we turned and went back home.

Dear Spence

ho ever thought that I'd be writing you a letter. You died on the 10th of June in 1967. My golly, Spence, that's twenty-four years ago. That's a long time. Are you happy finally? Is it a nice long rest you're having? Making up for all your tossing and turning in life. You know, I never believed you when you said you just couldn't get to sleep. I thought, Oh—come on—you sleep—if you didn't sleep you'd be dead. You'd be so worn out. Then remember that night when—oh, I don't know, you felt so disturbed. And I said, Well, go on in—go to bed. And I'll lie on the floor and talk you to sleep. I'll just talk and talk and you'll be so bored, you're bound to drift off.

Well, I went in and got an old pillow and Lobo the dog. I lay there watching you and stroking Old Dog. I was talking about you and the movie we'd just finished—*Guess Who's Coming to Dinner*—and my studio and your new tweed coat and the garden and all the nice sleep-making topics and cooking and dull gossip, but you never stopped tossing—to the right, to the left—shove the pillows—pull the covers—on and on and on. Finally—really finally—not just then—you quieted down. I waited a while—and then I crept out.

You told me the truth, didn't you? You really could not sleep.

And I used to wonder then—why? I still wonder. You took the

pills. They were quite strong. I suppose you have to say that otherwise you would never have slept at all. Living wasn't easy for you, was it?

What did you like to do? You loved sailing, especially in stormy weather. You loved polo. But then Will Rogers was killed in that airplane accident. And you never played polo again—never again. Tennis, golf, no, not really. You'd bat a few balls. Fair you were. I don't think that you ever even swang a golf club. Is "swang" a word? Swimming? Well, you didn't like cold water. And walking? No, that didn't suit you. That was one of those things where you could think at the same time—of this, of that, of what, Spence? What was it? Was it some specific life thing like Johnny being deaf, or being a Catholic and you felt a bad Catholic? No comfort, no comfort. I remember Father Ciklic telling you that you concentrated on all the bad and none of the good which your religion offered. It must have been something very fundamental and very ever-present.

And the incredible fact. There you were—really the greatest movie actor. I say this because I believe it and also I have heard many people of standing in our business say it. From Olivier to Lee Strasberg to David Lean. You name it. You could do it. And you could do it with that glorious simplicity and directness: you could just do it. You couldn't enter your own life, but you could become someone else. You were a killer—a priest—a fisherman—a sportswriter—a judge —a newspaperman. You were *it* in an instant.

You hardly had to study. You learned the lines in no time. What a relief! You could be someone else for a while. You weren't you— you were safe. You loved to laugh, didn't you? You never missed those individual comics: Jimmy Durante, Phil Silvers, Fanny Brice, Frank McHugh, Mickey Rooney, Jack Benny, Burns and Allen, Smith and Dale, and your favorite, Bert Williams. Funny stories: you could tell them—and brilliantly. You could laugh at yourself. You enjoyed very very much the friendship and admiration of people like the Kanins, Frank Sinatra, Bogie and Betty, George Cukor, Vic Fleming, Stanley Kramer, the Kennedys, Harry Truman, Lew Douglas. You were fun with them, you had fun with them, you felt safe with them.

But then back to life's trials. Oh hell, take a drink—no-yes-maybe. Then stop taking the drink. You were great at that, Spence. You could just stop. How I respected you for that. Very unusual.

Well, you said on this subject: never safe until you're seven feet underground. But why the escape hatch? Why was it always opened—to get away from the remarkable you?

What was it, Spence? I meant to ask you. Did you know what it was?

What did you say? I can't hear you . . .

Climbing the Ladder
—with Help

Yes, I was lucky I had people. Well, yes—Mother and Dad—and then Luddy came along. Oh, Luddy—what would I—could I—have done without you? Eddie Knopf—my first job. He looked at me and took a chance. Yes, come on in—join us. That was in Baltimore in 1928. Wow! Then he moved to New York. Again he took a chance—gave me a leading part—then he fired me. But I'd been seen. Yes—by Arthur Hopkins. He had a nice part in a little play. It was a showy bit. It closed in two days but he gave me another job, understudying Hope Williams in *Holiday*. And Luddy again and my friend Alice Palache—"You're great, Kate—you're just . . ." What would I have done without that backing?

Laura Harding—what strength she gave me. She sophisticated me. I thought *she* was wonderful and she convinced me that *I* was.

Phyllis Wilbourn—*always* there twenty-four hours a day, seven days a week. Forever.

George Cukor. So many pictures!

So through sixty-odd years the group has grown. My backers—my saviors. They gave me courage. This is what you have to have to come out on top.

My dear friend Laura Fratti—she taught me how to fake playing the piano in film and on the stage. That makes her a genius.

I'm sure I'll miss many of my pushers—the steadies who were there every day—pushing me, listening to me—protecting me—driving me. Charles Newhill, forty-three years—L. C. Fisher, and now Jimmy Davis.

And Norah—the thought—the unquestioning—the food—the infinite care—the love. "Here it is, Miss Hepburn."

And Sharon Powers—listen—without you—total chaos.

Tony Harvey. Friend—real friend.

David Eichler—*my* Philadelphia Story.

Scott Berg—my chief critic.

And, of course, Cynthia McFadden—my buddy who remembers my life better than I do.

Freya Manston—my agent—I should say my slave driver—who really got me going on this book.

And again Mother and Dad and Peg and Bob and Dick and Marion and Kathy Houghton.

And now—Sonny Mehta, head of Knopf.

Memories—all there—Oh thank you.

Yes, lucky!

PHOTOGRAPHIC CREDITS

A NOTE ON THE TYPE

The text of this book was set in a film version of Garamond No. 3,
a modern rendering of the type first cut by Claude Garamond (1510–1561).
Garamond was a pupil of Geoffroy Troy and is believed to have based his
letters on Venetian models, although he introduced a number of important differences,
and it is to him we owe the letter which we know as old style.
He gave to his letters a certain elegance and a feeling of movement that won
for their creator an immediate reputation and the patronage
of Francis I of France.

Composed by PennSet, Inc., Bloomsburg, Pennsylvania
Printed and bound by Arcata Halliday Lithographers, Inc., West Hanover, Massachusetts
Designed by Dorothy Schmiderer Baker